Studies in Jewish Culture and Society

A SERIES OF THE
CENTER FOR JUDAIC STUDIES
UNIVERSITY OF PENNSYLVANIA

CONTRIBUTORS

ANTHONY GRAFTON is Dodge Professor of History, Princeton University

MARTHA HIMMELFARB is Associate Professor of Religion, Princeton University

ELLIOTT HOROWITZ is Senior Lecturer in Jewish History, Bar Ilan University

MOSHE IDEL is Max Cooper Professor of Jewish Thought, Hebrew University

SARA JAPHET is Professor of Bible, Hebrew University

GIDEON LIBSON is Professor of Comparative Law, Hebrew University Law School

DAVID N. MYERS is Associate Professor of History and Director of the Center for Jewish Studies, University of California, Los Angeles

DEREK J. PENSLAR is Associate Professor of History, Indiana University

DAVID B. RUDERMAN is Joseph Meyerhoff Professor of Modern Jewish History and Director of the Center for Judaic Studies, University of Pennsylvania

ISRAEL JACOB YUVAL is Senior Lecturer in Jewish History, Hebrew University

EDITED BY DAVID N. MYERS
AND DAVID B. RUDERMAN

_____

*The Jewish Past Revisited:
Reflections on Modern Jewish
Historians*

Yale University Press/New Haven & London

Designed by Nancy Ovedovitz and set in Galliard type by Keystone
Typesetting, Inc. Printed in the United States of America.

Library of Congress Cataloging-in-Publication Data
The Jewish past revisited : reflections on modern Jewish historians
/ edited by David N. Myers and David B. Ruderman.
p.   cm. — (Studies in Jewish culture and society)
Includes bibliographical references and index.
ISBN 0-300-07216-3 (cloth : alk. paper)
1. Jewish historians — Biography.   2. Jews — History —
Philosophy.   3. Jews — Historiography.   4. Judaism —
Historiography.   I. Myers, David N.   II. Ruderman,
David B.   III. Series.
DS115.7.J48   1998
909'.04924'0072 — DC21   97-36811

A catalogue record for this book is available from the British
Library.

The paper in this book meets the guidelines for permanence and
durability of the Committee on Production Guidelines for Book
Longevity of the Council on Library Resources.

10   9   8   7   6   5   4   3   2   1

For Martin D. Gruss

Contents

Preface

It is most gratifying to inaugurate a new series in Jewish studies. This book, along with those that will follow it, constitutes a part of the written record of a broad conversation between Jewish studies and the Humanities that has taken place at the University of Pennsylvania's Center for Judaic Studies for the past several years. The Center, established in 1993, built upon the proud legacies of Dropsie College (founded in 1907) and the Annenberg Research Institute (founded in 1987) to create the only advanced institute for post-doctoral learning exclusively devoted to Judaic Studies. Through a careful selection of themes and participants from around the world the Center has created an environment of focused interdisciplinary study and intense socialization among widely diverse groups of scholars both within Jewish studies and in related fields. The weekly formal seminars together with the numerous informal conversations that take place throughout the year culminate in a major colloquium bringing together some of the best thinking of members of the fellowship as well as other invited guest speakers. The volume before you represents a part of such an annual undertaking.

Visions of the Jewish Past Revisited emerged from the annual theme of the Center in 1994–95 on the dialectical relationship between the writing of history and Jewish collective memory. The group consisted of scholars of Jewish history, literature, and thought ranging from the biblical period until the present. It also met with a wide array of scholars outside Jewish studies who considered the subject from other comparative perspectives. In reflecting on some of our "professional ancestors," as Anthony Grafton has called them, the contributors to this volume hoped not only to situate them in their historical contexts but to consider their understanding of the past in relation to our own. The rich essays of this volume reveal to what extent the historical narratives of a past generation and this one are contingent on relevant cultural concerns and perspectives. In this respect, Jewish historiography is no different from other historiographies; within its novel reconstructions and revisionism are embedded both the uncertainty and existential dilemmas facing contemporary Jewish life in particular and the human condition in general.

It is my expectation that future volumes of the University of Pennsylvania Studies in Jewish Civilization will appear on an annual basis. A volume on 'Learning, Literacy, and the Transmission of Jewish Culture', the Center's theme for 1995–96, is presently being edited for publication. Another volume on 'Divergent Centers: American and Israeli Cultures in the Twentieth Century', the theme for 1996–97, will soon follow.

What remains is the pleasant task of thanking those individuals directly involved in this collective enterprise. They include my co-editor David Myers as well as the other contributors to this volume; David Goldenberg, editor of the *Jewish Quarterly Review* published by the Center, who generously offered his wisdom and manifold editorial talents in preparing the book for publication; Rena Potok, who carefully and diligently copyedited the entire volume; Charles Grench, the editor-in-chief of Yale University Press, for his continual commitment to Judaic scholarship; and finally all the scholars who served as fellows at the Center in 1994–95 and created the remarkable ambiance that inspired the formation of this work.

In dedicating this volume to Martin Gruss, we acknowledge the vision of a man who intuitively understood and enthusiastically endorsed the profound value of the dialogue between Jewish civilization and world culture which the Center of Judaic Studies embodies. He not only established the annual Gruss colloquium in Jewish studies, but insisted that the oral "Torah" of the Center be permanently recorded as a written one. I am hopeful he will be pleased by the results that follow.

David B. Ruderman

Director, Center for Judaic Studies

University of Pennsylvania

Introduction

DAVID N. MYERS

In his famous book, *The Idea of History,* the English philosopher of history R. G. Collingwood offered a revealing criticism of the late-19th-century German thinker Heinrich Rickert. According to Collingwood, Rickert failed to grasp an essential truth of history:

> The peculiarity of historical thought is the way in which the historian's mind, as the mind of the present day, apprehends the process by which this mind has itself come into existence through the mental development of the past.[1]

Rickert's infatuation with the individual historical datum, isolated and frozen in the past, suppressed the impulse to examine his own intellectual origins. To avoid this trap, Collingwood suggested, historians must analyze—or historicize—their own line of inquiry and acknowledge that facts do not constitute "a dead past but a living past, a heritage of past thoughts which by the work of his historical consciousness the historian makes his own."[2] Failure to do so risks self-delusion about one's own existence as an historical being. In a similar vein, Collingwood's countryman, Sir Herbert Butterfield, implored historians to study the history of their predecessors in order to situate themselves "within the long, unceasing stream of history."[3]

For Butterfield, this act of self-contextualization was a major stimulus to recording the history of historiography. And yet, historians have not always or universally regarded the study of scholarly predecessors as a noble or worthwhile pursuit. The unreflexive impulse of historians is particularly evident in the case of Jewish scholars, about whom no comprehensive history was written until 1993.[4] Thus, the rather rich tradition of modern Jewish scholarship, extending back at least to the early decades of the 19th century, offers almost no parallels to 20th-century histories of historiography written by Fueter, Gooch, Barnes, Breisach, or Blanke, among others.[5] Anecdotally, I can report that my first awkward forays into the history of Jewish historiography, as a graduate student, were met with disdain by more than a few scholars in the field. It was not deemed suitable by them to study historiography at the beginning of one's career. Such work, if undertaken at all, was best left to the twilight years, after one had earned the right, through a series of rigorous monographs, to meditate more expansively upon the discipline of history.

The veil of inauthenticity that cloaks the study of Jewish historiography relates, I think, to the unwillingness of Jewish scholars to relent on the steadfast claim to objectivity that has accompanied their efforts from the advent of *Wissenschaft des Judentums*. While Jewish scholars have frequently directed polemic volleys at their predecessors, they have rarely sought to contextualize their own work through systematic analysis of the social context and intellectual direction of earlier generations. To do so would be to acknowledge extra-"scientific" considerations in the production of historiographical work, thereby undermining the validity of the scholar's quest for truth. The price of such acknowledgment is often perceived to be too high. For researchers of Jewish history are not merely scholars; they tend to be Jews, and as such, members of a group that has struggled to define its identity in the midst of powerful social pressures and in the absence of satisfactory categories of group identification. The rather desperate adherence of Jewish scholars to the ideal of objective scholarship, and concomitant obtuseness to their own biases, reflected a decided lack of security over their own societal position. As a result, *Wissenschaft* came to serve as "an existential and epistemological anchor," a source of stability and validation in often turbulent and uncertain milieux.[6]

The hyper-scientism of Jewish historical scholars has not gone unnoticed. A distinguished line of Jewish thinkers from Samson Raphael Hirsch and Samuel David Luzzatto in the mid-19th century to Franz Rosenzweig and later Baruch Kurzweil in the 20th has called attention to the defects and delusions of Jewish historians. Noticeably, few of these critics were historians. Indeed, Jewish historians rarely trained a critical gaze on themselves or their intellectual roots — at least until quite recently. They were, to paraphrase the words of Norman Hampson, too busy teaching, writing, and being Jews "to worry very much about the nature of what they are trying to do."[7]

A landmark departure from the tradition of opacity among Jewish historians was Yosef Hayim Yerushalmi's *Zakhor: Jewish History and Jewish Memory*. Published some fifteen years ago, Yerushalmi's brilliant reflections inaugurated a new era of introspection into the history and practices of Jewish historians. With sweeping erudition, Yerushalmi cast a doleful eye on the enterprise of modern Jewish historiography, noting its instinct to strip the cloak of sanctity off traditionally remembered events or figures. In sharp contrast to the holistic force of pre-modern collective memory, historiography had become "the faith of fallen Jews."[8] Several years after Yerushalmi's retrospective was published, his great teacher Salo Baron brought out a slim volume, *The Contemporary Relevance of History,* which analyzed the historiographical currents against and out of which his own scholarship emerged. Without making reference to Yerushalmi, Baron offered a defense of modern historical research, lauding its "methodological pluralism" and advancing the belief that history could still "serve as a sort of new historical *midrash* and help answer some of the most perplexing questions of the present and the future."[9] To bring matters full circle, Baron himself became the subject several years later of a full-length biography by Robert Liberles.[10] These developments are emblematic of a wider and overdue interest in historiography emerging among Jewish scholars over the past decade and

a half, and reflected in the work of Jacob Bernays, David Biale, Shmuel
Ettinger, Shmuel Feiner, Amos Funkenstein, Michael Meyer, Reuven Mi-
chael, Amnon Raz-Krakotzkin, Arielle Rein, Ismar Schorsch, and Perrine
Simon-Nahum.

The introspective turn of Jewish historians is not merely the product of an
inner resolve to redress the neglect of previous generations. At the risk of
affirming the banal, it must be noted that like Jewish history, Jewish historians do not operate in a vacuum. They are exposed to the same intellectual
currents that induce periodic meditations on, and even crises of, historicism. Contemporary students of Jewish history, for instance, inhabit the
same postmodern world as other historians, a world in which fixed meaning—literary, historical, or otherwise—is assumed *not* to exist. The pervasive skepticism of the postmodern moment has undoubtedly disrupted received wisdoms regarding the very possibility of historical veracity. But it
has also mandated that historians adopt a new critical self-awareness as they
go about selecting subjects, sifting through evidence, and producing historical narratives.

It is out of this moment that the current volume takes shape. The essays
collected here represent a unique collaboration by students of Jewish history
intent on examining old scholarly truths and practices. More than half are
the product of a group of scholars fortunate enough to have spent the 1994–
95 academic year as fellows at the University of Pennsylvania's Center for
Judaic Studies. In the extraordinarily congenial environs of the Center, the
fellows engaged in constant and stimulating debate on the shaping and
reshaping of Jewish historical narrative. The fellows' deliberations culmi-
nated in an end-of-year conference in May 1995 to which a number of other
distinguished scholars were fortuitously invited.

Based on that conference, the papers in this collection offer a series of
sustained insights into the work of Jewish historians whose work extends
across the Jewish past—from antiquity to the modern period, and from the
land of Israel to Italy. They are not intended as a complete catalogue of all of
the great figures and themes of modern Jewish historiography, but rather
focus largely on important 20th-century Jewish historians. Hence, there is
no essay-length discussion of the founding figures of 19th-century *Wissen-*

schaft des Judentums, a topic that has developed its own small coterie of experts.[11] Nor does any of the essays engage the three grand narrators of Jewish history in the modern age: Heinrich Graetz, Simon Dubnow, and Salo Baron. Each of these three has already received significant, though by no means exhaustive, biographical attention.[12] And yet, with the exception of Gershom Scholem (surely one of the most intriguing of 20th-century Jewish scholars), the remaining figures discussed in this volume have largely escaped careful analysis and scrutiny. It is thus the mission of the volume to fill a considerable gap in the modern writing of Jewish history.

The task of revisiting one's predecessors is a most complicated one, not least because it invariably activates deep anxieties of influence. As Anthony Grafton avers in his richly textured essay on Jacob Bernays and Joseph Scaliger, "historians of scholarship set out to identify and study their betters." In doing so, they are condemned "to struggle with more Oedipal demons" than they can handle.[13] Grafton's essay hints at a powerful mimetic impulse in the history of scholarship; the historian's treatment of an earlier scholar tends to follow the latter's interest, priorities, and strengths. What results is a "heroic portrait of a past master, robed in purple" rather than a critical uncovering of "a past physiognomy, warts, period features and all."[14] On this reading, the history of scholarship approximates the *shalshelet ha-kabbalah,* or scholarly genealogy, that surfaces frequently in medieval Jewish literature.[15] Grafton relates that Bernays "saw himself as one link in a chain of tradition — and held that anyone who hoped to join that chain must do so by finding a connection, as Bernays did, to earlier links."[16] Grafton acts on Bernays' charge in a particularly intimate way — by linking himself to the chain of tradition which Bernays represents.[17] Indeed, he undertakes the same kind of scholarly excavation of Bernays that Bernays undertook of Scaliger. Grafton thereby exemplifies what Hans-Georg Gadamer calls the fusion of horizons, a site where present interpreter meets past scholar or, in Grafton's works, where historians come to terms with their historiographical betters.[18]

While Grafton uncovers — and himself manifests — a reverential impulse in the history of scholarship, he is hardly uncritical of either the 19th-century Bernays or the 16th-century Scaliger. Indeed, by analyzing the glaring omissions Bernays made in writing about Scaliger, Grafton exposes the points at which Bernays demonstrably departs from his predecessors. At the same time, he signals his own desire for critical distance from Bernays. Grafton is not content merely to replicate the tendencies of his predecessor, for to do so would be to deny his own need for intellectual autonomy. In general, the historian's quest for both autonomy and self-understanding requires an awareness of the breaks and ruptures, as well as continuities, in historical consciousness. Concomitantly, this quest entails an exercise in self-contextualization vis-à-vis one's precursors — as part of the essential act of exorcising one's "Oedipal demons."

Inspired by Grafton's example, the essays before us move between the reverential and critical poles, constantly seeking to arrive at a meaningful fusion of horizons. It is precisely this balancing act that lends the volume its distinctiveness and authority. But its importance extends, like all good histories of historiography, beyond the nuanced readings of the essay writers. The volume also attests to an historical moment, or series of moments, significant on their own terms.

One such moment gives impetus to the cluster of papers addressing the formation and development of Israeli historical scholarship. While none of the authors professes to be a "New Historian" intent on upending established truths and foundation myths of Israeli history, each is clearly informed by a critical perspective toward the historiographical past that grew out of broader political, cultural, and generational transformations in Israeli society. Thus, Moshe Idel continues the mission begun in his *Kabbalah: New Perspectives* (1988) by challenging the schema for the history of Jewish mysticism set out by the legendary Gershom Scholem. In fact, Idel's task is even broader: to revise Scholem's sweeping view of Jewish history based on the dynamic and subversive force of mysticism. Idel begins to unravel an alternative view of Jewish history attuned not to dramatic rupture, but to the preservative force of stasis. An essential catalyst toward this new view is his critique of the historical method of Scholem and his "school" of disciples. Idel argues that Scholem's "historico-critical school" lacks a sensitivity to the structural parallels and continuities that run throughout Jewish intellectual and cultural history, and so possesses no instinctive feel for a phenomenological approach to Jewish mysticism. Idel's corrective directly confronts two pillars of the Scholemian system: first, that there was an ancient

Jewish mystical tradition that predated and/or was uninfluenced by the sudden intrusion of Gnosticism; and second, that intense messianic concern was not a direct outgrowth of the expulsion of the Jews from Spain, but, rather, has a pedigree in the history of Kabbalah that long precedes the Spanish expulsion in 1492. The effect of Idel's challenge is to highlight, perhaps in exaggerated fashion, the *immanent* features of Jewish history, those that resist or are unmoved by "external" events and which explain the survival of the Jews throughout history.

In this regard Idel embraces, paradoxically, the immanentist position for which Scholem and his Jerusalem colleagues were often accused. This point emerges periodically in Israel Jacob Yuval's study of the intriguing career of Scholem's friend and fellow German Jew, Yitzhak Fritz Baer. After decades of distinguished scholarly work in medieval Jewish history, Baer turned his attention in the late 1940s to the Second Temple Period. Yuval begins his inquiry by participating in the mimetic work of the historian of scholarship, suggested by Anthony Grafton; that is, he notes Baer's appreciation of Christian influences on medieval Ashkenazic Jewish culture, and thereby locates an eminent precursor for his own important and controversial work in medieval Ashkenazic history. And yet, Yuval's short piece has a more important task: it demonstrates that Baer's shift in scholarly emphasis to Second Temple history was motivated by the desire to find a pre-Christian Judaism; this desire, Yuval implies, was impelled both by the historical trauma of the Holocaust, and by the impulse to find ancient roots for the new Jewish state. Ultimately, Baer's journey throughout the Second Temple period was to lead him to "an authentic Judaism, free of Christian influence, and yet European."[19] In this regard, Yuval suggests that Baer pushed in the direction of a more immanent explanation for Jewish history. At the same time, he observes that Baer's search for pre-Christian roots led him to "the encounter between Judea and Greece in Antiquity" out of which an authentic Judaism emerged. The tension between the immanentist and externalist explanations, as well as the failure of Baer's model of a pre-Christian Judaism to sink deep roots in Israeli historical consciousness, may well have resulted from Baer's own European roots. As Yuval concludes, Baer's philosophy of history was most "suited to the biography of a German immigrant who had settled in Jerusalem."[20]

The suggestion that Baer and his fellow first-generation colleagues at the Hebrew University in Jerusalem did not fully remake themselves — or, for that matter, Jewish historical scholarship — stands at the center of my own contribution to the volume.[21] Despite frequent programmatic declarations of innovation, the "Jerusalem scholars," as I call them, transported deeply entrenched institutional and conceptual models from their European homes. Not only were the disciplinary priorities of the Hebrew University's Institute of Jewish Studies similar to those of European rabbinical seminaries, the Jerusalem scholars also remained beholden to the mesmerizing ethos and language of *Wissenschaft,* which so captivated 19th-century Jewish scholars. Moreover, they departed from "orthodox" Zionist ideology in locating historical value in, rather than negating, the Diaspora past. In focusing on both the continuities and changes represented by this generation of Jewish scholars, I argue that they were possessed of a dynamic, unresolved, and hybrid identity. Just as they swung between the cultural universes of Europe and Palestine, so too the Jerusalem scholars moved between the competing demands of collective memory and critical history.

My own efforts to rethink the historical contours of the "Jerusalem school" are situated in a distinct moment in which new approaches to the Jewish and Israeli past seem to abound. In Derek Penslar's lucid paper, the author sheds new light on that moment through a systematic review of Zionist historiography over the past three decades. Eschewing the tendency to label all historical service rendered by scholars committed to Zionism as "Zionist historiography," he offers instead a careful analysis of academic scholarship on Zionism and the history of the land of Israel / Palestine from the 1960s.[22] Underlying Penslar's treatment is the conclusion that much of what passes for New Israeli History in the 1980s and 1990s (for example, the work of Benny Morris, Avi Shlaim, and Zeev Sternhell) was anticipated by scholars in prior decades. Here again, despite fervent claims to intellectual innovation, old arguments were replicated in whole or part (suggestions, for example, that Israeli "statist" ideology, or *mamlakhtiyut,* was born before 1948, or that Labor Zionism did not maintain a steadfast commitment to socialism). Whereas the "new historians" have been both celebrated and condemned for their novelty, Penslar's important work of historiographical contextualization provides a much needed and nuanced framework in which to evaluate their work.

If Israeli historiography forms a distinct subtext throughout the volume, perhaps even more pervasive is the theme of the dynamic nature of Jewish cultural interaction. Thus, David Ruderman offers a re-assessment of Cecil Roth, the delightful and oft-dismissed historian of Italian Jewry (among other subjects). Ruderman's paper is, in essence, a super-commentary, offering an extended gloss on the stinging criticism of Roth by the contemporary scholar Robert Bonfil, and challenging Bonfil's characterization of Roth as a base apologist for the idea of a Jewish Italian Renaissance. Contrary to Bonfil's claims, Cecil Roth was not intent on portraying Italian Jewish life as "a carousel of servile imitation."[23] Rather, Roth provides a "perfectly balance argument that Italy was never immune from hostilities and anti-Jewish agitation."[24] Moreover, Roth was dedicated to demonstrating that Italian Jewry stuck a creative balance between its own religious and cultural heritage and the surrounding environment. In concluding his discussion, Ruderman seeks to mediate between the competing perspectives of Bonfil and Roth, but ultimately identifies himself more with the latter. It is Roth's passion for describing "those dimensions of Jewish culture closely related to general civilization" that Ruderman finds so valuable. This should not come as a total surprise. Both Roth and Ruderman are Diaspora Jewish scholars, wedded to the image of the cosmopolitan and interactive Jewish culture whose boundaries are constantly and creatively redrawn. Such a perspective stands in contrast to the image of Diaspora Jewish life that emerges from Robert Bonfil's work — or, for that matter, from the work of Yitzhak Baer, Bonfil's predecessor in Jerusalem. For the two Israeli scholars, Diaspora history is fraught with elemental dangers, ranging between the poles of persecution and self-negation. In this respect, they both embody a deep skepticism toward the Diaspora that forms one pillar of the Zionist historiographical enterprise.

The historiographical optimism of Cecil Roth — so tellingly contrasted to Bonfil — is matched by a fellow Englishman, Israel Abrahams, whom Elliott Horowitz treats in his paper.[25] Like Roth, Abrahams has been regularly dismissed as an engaging, but shallow, historical popularizer whose narrative favored florid description over penetrating analysis. Horowitz adds nuance to this conventional image by situating Abrahams within the historical context of late Victorian England. He argues that Abrahams absorbed the Victorian nostalgia for the "lost paradise" of the Middle Ages, particularly in the widely disseminated *Jewish Life in the Middle Ages*. Comparing the medieval Jew favorably to the later "ghetto" Jew, Abrahams sought to expose "the genuine pleasures which had been made possible by the more robust popular culture" of the Middle Ages.[26] In this respect, Abrahams preceded his countryman, Cecil Roth, in incorporating popular culture into the narrative account of the Jewish past; likewise, Abrahams preceded Roth in holding "that the vitality of Judaism was enhanced by exposure to and interaction with outside cultures."[27] Horowitz's "recovery" of Abrahams thus calls attention to a frequently neglected "tradition" of Jewish historical writing, that produced by English Jews with a flair for the colorful and an aversion for the lachrymose. At the same time, it makes a strong case for the relevance of social history in attaining a richly textured grasp of the Jewish past.

The theme of cultural interaction, so central to the work of Roth and Abrahams, surfaces with equal force in Gideon Libson's exposition of Shelomo Dov Goitein.[28] Libson presents an extensive bio-bibliographical review of Goitein's monumental labors, noting an interesting shift in scholarly direction that bears resemblance to Yitzhak Baer's career. The first phase of Goitein's professional career was devoted to the study of Islam, and more specifically, to cultural relations and interaction between Judaism and Islam. Goitein's interest in the meeting of these two religious cultures reflected his own desire to open "a shutter, perhaps a large window, on the world of the East."[29] Here Goitein was reflecting the pervasive quest for spiritual authenticity, and the concomitant turn to the East of many Germans, particularly German-Jewish intellectuals, in the first decades of the 20th century. Consciously or not, Goitein's search for an Islamic-Jewish "symbiosis" may well have had its roots in his own early attempts to forge a distinct German-Jewish identity. One also wonders whether Goitein's scholarly labors in a later phase of his career reflect a certain frustration, born of contemporary political realities, with the ideal of Islamic-Jewish symbiosis. Did the experience of living in the State of Israel during a period of great military tension between Jews and Arabs alter his perspective, even after his decision to leave Jerusalem for Princeton? Without addressing this question directly, Libson does note that in this later phase Goitein shifted the focus of his research away from the dynamics of symbiosis to the existence of one historical culture (Jewish) *within* a broader one (Islamic). Drawing on the treasure trove of social historical material in the Cairo Genizah, Goitein undertook a systematic investigation of Jewish life in the Mediterranean world. His multi-volume *A Mediterranean Society,* with its Braudelian scope, stands as one of the landmark contributions to Jewish historical scholarship in the 20th century.

Libson observes that Goitein was reticent to use the word "influence" in describing interaction between cultural traditions. Rather, he preferred to speak of "parallels" or "interplay," terms that do not entail the decisive "victory" of one culture over another. This usage hints at the phenomenological approach favored by Moshe Idel in his above-mentioned article. Moreover, a good number of other papers — such as those of Yuval, Myers, Ruderman, and Horowitz — address the issue of influence in Jewish history. Does the term "influence" adequately represent the dynamic and textured interaction of Jews and non-Jews? Or does it presuppose the existence of a world divided between cultural conquerors and victims? Conversely, can we speak intelligently of immanence as a category of historical (as opposed to metahistorical) causality? The answers to these questions shed light not only on the intellectual sensibilities of past scholars but on the cultural/ ideological proclivities of their more contemporary glossators — as we see in the case of David Ruderman and his polemical foil, Robert Bonfil.

Martha Himmelfarb continues the debate over cultural influence in her discussion of Elias Bickerman, the outstanding scholar of Hellenistic-Jewish culture. On Himmelfarb's reading, Bickerman eschewed the crudely hegemonic implications of the term "influence." Instead, he aimed at analyzing what Himmelfarb calls the "restructuring of ancient Judaism." This meant studying "the dynamics of the reception of Greek culture by the Jews: how the Jews transformed Hellenism and how in turn Judaism was transformed."[30] The paths of cultural transmission were bi-directional: neither Judaism nor Hellenism emerged intact, or destroyed, from their encounter. In elaborating on this point, Himmelfarb is careful to note that Bickerman was very much a product of his time. While the theme of a constant cultural negotiation generally operated in his work, Bickerman's analysis of the Maccabees in 1937 marked a departure. His *Der Gott der Makkabäer* described the Jewish reformers of the 2nd century BCE as traitors to the Jewish cause. Under the strain of Nazi threat, Bickerman could not prevent himself from projecting his own damning judgment of Jewish assimilation onto the historical canvas, even when that judgment was at odds with his usual emphasis on the subtle process of restructuring ancient Judaism.

Himmelfarb's conceptual vocabulary bears the traces, deliberately or not, of recent writing in cultural studies. By contrast, Sara Japhet's paper takes a strong stand against recent currents in Bible scholarship which challenge the "valid modern and rational terminology applicable in the historical discipline."[31] In particular, Japhet directs her critique at Philip Davies' *In Search of Ancient Israel,* published in 1992. Japhet intimates that Davies' book reflects a scholarly trend to upend conventional truths in the name of iconoclasm. Thus, for Davies, the basic term "Biblical Israel" possesses no stable meaning; in fact, the Bible is itself a literary source of dubious historical value. Davies prefers to speak of an "historical Israel" which, Japhet argues, is no less arbitrary a construct than "Biblical Israel." Not content to accept a state of terminological caprice, Japhet sets out to rebut Davies' claim that the historical Israel was none other than a group of " 'foreign transportees' of unknown origin and background, brought to Judah under coercion by the Persians for the purpose of agrarian development."[32]

For Japhet, this challenge to the authenticity of historical evidence drawn from the Bible — as well as the very idea of a biblical Israel — suffers from more than methodological defects. It assumes the form of theology, the apparent opposite of history. Davies' theology, according to Japhet, is one of "condemnation" which, though never defined, presumably entails invalidating Judaism and its historical sources. Japhet hints unmistakably that Davies' book is a latter-day religious polemic that is unsupported in the world of critical scholarship. And yet, Japhet's own reading of Davies affirms the importance and value of studying historiography; more than merely a (secondary) source of validation, the *historiographical* text can and must be read as an *historical* text, with all the requisite attention to context on which historians pride themselves.

In light of this charge, Japhet's sharp criticism of Davies should not obscure a proposition that ties together many of the essays in this volume — namely, that extra-scholarly concerns invariably intervene in the production of scholarship. On the whole, this volume represents an attempt to acknowledge and contextualize such extra-scholarly concerns in the work of our predecessors. But this enterprise is far more than merely an antiquarian foray. It constitutes a working through of the present historian's own anxieties, interests, and limitations, a self-analysis of the hidden secrets and more blatant biases that animate the historiographical text. Given the traditional inhibition among students of Jewish history to engage in the hard work of self-analysis, this book is offered as a tentative first step in understanding more fully, to paraphrase R. G. Collingwood, how the Jewish historical mind has itself come into existence.

NOTES

I would like to thank David Goldenberg for his helpful editorial suggestions and criticism of this introduction.

1. R. G. Collingwood, *The Idea of History* (Oxford, 1956), 169.

2. *Ibid.*, 170.

3. Herbert Butterfield, *Man on His Past: The Study of the History of Historical Scholarship* (Boston, 1960), viii.

4. See Reuven Michael, *Ha-ketivah ha-historit ha-Yehudit meha-Renesans 'ad ha-'et ha-hadashah* (Jerusalem, 1993).

5. See Eduard Fueter, *Geschichte der neueren Historiographie* (Munich, 1911); G. P. Gooch, *History and Historians in the Nineteenth Century* (London, 1913); Harry Elmer Barnes, *A History of Historical Writing* (1937. Reprint. New York, 1963); Ernst Breisach, *Historiography: Ancient, Medieval and Modern* (Chicago, 1983); and Horst Walter Blanke, *Historiographiegeschichte als Historik* (Stuttgart-Bad Canstatt, 1991).

6. David N. Myers, *Re-Inventing the Jewish Past: European Jewish Intellectuals and the Zionist Return to History* (New York, 1995), 107.

7. Norman Hampson, *History as an Art: An Inaugural Lecture* (Newcastle-upon-Tyne, 1968), 3.

8. Yosef Hayim Yerushalmi, *Zakhor: Jewish History and Jewish Memory* (Seattle, 1982), 86.

9. Salo W. Baron, *The Contemporary Relevance of History: A Study in Approaches and Methods* (New York, 1986), 95, 98.

10. Robert Liberles, *Salo Wittmayer Baron: Architect of Jewish History* (New York, 1995).

11. See, for instance, Ismar Schorsch, *From Text to Context: The Turn to History in Modern Judaism* (Hanover, New Hampshire, 1994); Jay M. Harris, *Nahman Krochmal: Guiding the Perplexed of the Modern Age* (New York, 1991); or the volume edited by Julius Carlebach, *Wissenschaft des Judentums: Anfänge der Judaistik in Europa* (Darmstadt, 1992).

12. The most reliable guide to the life and thought of Graetz remains Ismar Schorsch's edition of *The Structure of Jewish History* (New York, 1975). For Dubnow, one can profitably consult Koppel Pinson's introduction to Dubnow, *Nationalism and History* (Philadelphia, 1958); Robert Selzer, "Simon Dubnow: A Critical Biography of His Early Years," Ph.D. dissertation, Columbia University, 1970; Sofiia Dubnova-Erlikh, *The Life and Work of S. M. Dubnow: Diaspora Nationalism and Jewish History* (Bloomington, Indiana, 1991); and David H. Weinberg, *Between Tradition and Modernity: Haim Zhitlowski, Simon Dubnow, Ahad Ha-am and the Shaping of Modern Jewish Identity* (New York, 1996). The standard account of Baron's life and work is Liberles' biography mentioned in n. 10.

13. Anthony Grafton, "Jacob Bernays, Joseph Scaliger, and Others," chapter 1.

14. Ibid.

15. For a pre-eminent example, see Abraham ibn Daud's *Sefer ha-Qabbalah,* edited by Gerson Cohen (Philadelphia, 1967). See also Yerushalmi, *Zakhor,* 57–62.

16. Grafton, "Jacob Bernays."

17. I owe this formulation to David Goldenberg.

18. Han-Georg Gadamer, *Truth and Method,* trans. Garrett Barden and John Cumming (New York, 1975), 269.

19. Israel Jacob Yuval, "Yitzhak Baer and the Search for Authentic Judaism," chapter 3.

20. Ibid.

21. David N. Myers, "Between Diaspora and Zion: History, Memory and the Jerusalem Scholars," chapter 4.

22. Derek Jonathan Penslar, "Narratives of Nation Building: Major Themes in Zionist Historiography," chapter 5.

23. This is Ruderman's citation of Bonfil's depiction in "The Historian's Perception of the Jew in the Italian Renaissance: Toward a Reappraisal," *Revue des études juives* 143 (1984), 80.

24. David Ruderman, "Cecil Roth: Historian of Italian Jewry: A Reassessment," chapter 6.

25. Elliot Horowitz, "*Jewish Life in the Middle Ages* and the Jewish Life of Israel Abrahams," chapter 7.

26. Ibid.

27. Ibid.

28. Gideon Libson, "Hidden Worlds and Open Shutters: Goitein between Judaism and Islam," chapter 8.

29. S. D. Goitein, *Ha-Temanim: hisṭoryah, sidre ḥevrah, ḥaye ha-ruaḥ,* ed. Menachem Ben-Sasson (Jerusalem, 1983), 3.

30. Martha Himmelfarb, "Elias Bickerman on Judaism and Hellenism," chapter 9.

31. Sara Japhet, "*In Search of Ancient Israel:* Revisionism at all Costs," chapter 10.

32. Ibid.

ONE

———————

Jacob Bernays, Joseph Scaliger,
and Others

ANTHONY GRAFTON

Historians of scholarship write, for their sins, about their own professional ancestors: other scholars. Historians of art, literature, and philosophy
can happily justify their pursuits by citing the intrinsic interest of their
famous subjects' accomplishments. Historians of scholarship, by contrast,
must morosely identify the dead grammarians they study every time they
give a public lecture or apply for a fellowship. Historians of sexuality spend
their time reading through riotously funny ethnographies and court records. Historians of scholarship, by contrast, disinter long-unused boxes of
notecards from their cobwebbed tombs in ancient file cabinets, and derive
what pleasure they may from discovering long-forgotten errors in unread
footnotes. Historians of science follow the processes by which humanity
gained understanding of the orbits of the planets, the nature of DNA, and
the idiosyncrasies of the fax machine—problems that remain current today.
Historians of scholarship, by contrast, follow the complex, paradoxical, and
drawn-out process by which humanity gradually learned that the past is a

foreign country. But this achievement of intellectuals in Hellenistic Alexandria, 15th-century Florence, and 18th-century Göttingen has little evident relevance to the resolutely unhistorical culture of late 20th-century
America.

Even worse than these problems of audience and rhetoric, moreover, are
the substantive ones. Historians of scholarship set out to identify and study
their betters: to rediscover, by sifting and analyzing the work of great scholars, what it meant in terms of intellectual innovation, provocation, and
controversy to study the past when classical philology and history were the
central intellectual disciplines of the new Dutch universities, in the late
Renaissance or the new German ones in the late Enlightenment. Historians
of science constantly confront the work of greater thinkers than they can
ever hope to be: no sane scholar will claim to have the mind of an Einstein
or a Newton. But historians of scholarship constantly explore the work of
their own colleagues and superiors — the work of philologists and historians
who, unlike them, did work of sufficient originality and interest that it
demands the attention of readers centuries later. Samuel Johnson tried to
defuse the envy of his readers by describing his own trade, that of the
lexicographer, as work fit for a harmless drudge. It is not a *captatio bene-
volentiae* but a grim recognition of existential truth that makes me define the
historian of scholarship as a malevolent drone — one who works obsessively,
not to create something new but to find out what makes warriors and queen
bees tick. Historians of scholarship are doomed, in short, to struggle with
more Oedipal demons than any single hive can contain. This essay deals
with the way that one of the most learned and original historians of scholarship, Jacob Bernays, met — and failed to meet — this challenge.

The son of a controversial and much-loved writer and teacher, Ḥakham
Isaak Bernays of Hamburg, Jacob grew up steeped in traditional Hebrew
learning. At the end of his life, after many years as a university librarian and a
professor of the Greek and Latin classics, he still read the Talmud or other
rabbinic texts for an hour every day.[1] While still a schoolboy, Bernays began
to transcribe unpublished Hebrew manuscripts in the Hamburg library. At
the same time, the Ḥakham insisted that his son grow up steeped in the
secular classics as well. Jacob studied the whole range of Greek and Latin
texts at gymnasium in Hamburg and at the innovative Prussian university in

Bonn. At the university he rapidly became the favorite student of the great Bonn textual critic Friedrich Ritschl, as well as of Ritschl's Jewish wife Sophie, who worried touchingly when Jacob refused to eat anything but bread and butter and fruit at her table.

Bernays began to publish at about the age of twenty. In a pioneering article he showed how one could reconstruct the textual history of Lucretius' poem *De rerum natura* by grouping the extant manuscripts into families—a relatively new idea at the time.[2] The stream of articles and monographs that followed—all of which combined technical brilliance, broad erudition, and a sharp sense for the historically important problem— made his name. Bernays ventured not the first, but the most systematic effort to show that the *katharsis* of pity and terror described by Aristotle as the effect of tragedy was not an aesthetic or moral term, but a medical one. In so doing, Bernays anticipated Nietzsche (who, predictably, became furious when "der Jude Bernays" mentioned this inconvenient fact).[3] Bernays reconstructed, mostly from difficult passages in the late antique commentaries on Aristotle, the nature and purport of the philosopher's lost dialogues. He thus made it possible to attempt something like a critical biography of Aristotle. For good or ill, Werner Jaeger could not have written his *Aristotle* if he had not had Bernays' studies of the language and the transmission of Aristotle's lost texts to disagree with and build upon.[4] Particularly dazzling were the studies in which Bernays showed that late antique Neoplatonists like Jamblichus and Porphyry had quoted rich, forgotten fragments of much earlier philosophical works—like the lost treatise by Theophrastus which, he argued, contained the first account of Jews by a Greek.[5]

Bernays had a gift for friendship and showed almost infinite generosity towards those he respected—who were not many. He collaborated, for instance, with the Prussian ambassador to England, Bunsen, on his elaborate, rather fantastic studies of ancient Near Eastern mythology and history. To more lasting effect, he helped Theodor Mommsen overcome the depression natural in grimy, industrial Breslau and the fatigue caused by a fourteen-hour a week teaching load to produce the greatest of all *Histories of Rome.* Bernays read proofs, offered advice, and drank beer with the great jurist who was turning ancient history upside down.

One revealing case will give a sense of the sorts of scholarly magic Bernays could perform, alone or in company. In a commentary on Aristotle published by Brandes, one of his teachers in Bonn, Bernays found a reference to a grammatical theory ascribed, unintelligibly, to *ho Patraios dous areios*. This he connected, at once, with a remark of the grammarian Hesychius, who had said that the Nabataeans called Dionysus Dousares. The meaningless *dous areios,* Bernays immediately saw, must be a corruption of *Dousareios* — a personal name formed from that of the god, as Dionysius was derived from Dionysus. It was the work of a moment to turn *Patraios* into *Petraios*. Suddenly Bernays had conjured up a forgotten Greek writer, "Dousareios from Petra," the Nabataean city. Further evidence from the Byzantine lexicon of Suidas enabled him to show that Dousareios had belonged to a forgotten group of Greek-speaking rhetoricians and grammarians, men who had cultivated the refinements of Hellenism in the distant rock city.[6] This emendation of two words opened up a lost chapter in cultural history.

The measure of Bernays' achievement is easy to take. He lived in bitter times for German Jews with academic ambitions. Born in 1824, just after the "hep hep hep" movement of 1819 and the prohibition of university careers for Jews, he became a popular Privatdozent at the university in Bonn.[7] However, he had no hope of abandoning this unpaid status — which the son of a poor Ḥakham obviously could not occupy for long — for a permanent chair. The Prussian government proved obdurate not only to his teachers in Bonn but to the influential Bunsen; Bernays, however, refused to convert. He could neither find an appropriate job nor stand to do what he saw as paid hackwork, like compiling the commentary on Lucretius, which the Clarendon Press commissioned from him. Eventually, to avoid starvation, he had to move to barbarous Breslau, where he taught elementary Latin and Greek at Zacharias Frankel's Jewish Seminary (and one advanced course in classics for a time at the university, which gave him teaching status).[8] Only in middle age was Bernays finally called back to Bonn. Even then he became not an ordinarius, but university librarian and professor extraordinarius. Nonetheless, he did win European recognition. The unequalled master of the black arts of scholarship, the emender and interpreter of a thousand obscure texts, Bernays was the only teacher who impressed the Prussian aristocrat Ulrich von Wilamowitz-Moellendorff, less through his learning than through his pride in the nobility of his own Jewish blood. (Wilamowitz later recalled that, with Bernays, everything was genuine; everything had real style — "da war alles echt, hatte alles Stil.")[9]

Bernays died in 1881. Despite his firm position at Bonn, his life ended in despair, in 1881. Bernays held that the new forces of democracy, radicalism, and positivism, joined with the old ones of reaction, antisemitism and religious orthodoxy, would destroy European civilization. He felt sure that the sort of scholarship he and his generation had done would not survive. He was, of course, quite right. In the short run, however, his example would prove a powerful and attractive one. The historian of religion Hermann Usener, who edited Bernays' collected shorter writings, was only one of a number of masters who learned their philological trade by steeping themselves in his work and by trying to emulate his command of multiple forms of evidence and his meticulous attention to revealing detail.[10]

In 1855 Bernays published his first large book, the one with which this essay deals: a biography of Joseph Scaliger, an extraordinarily energetic and productive late-Renaissance humanist.[11] Scaliger, who lived from 1540 to 1609, revolutionized fields of classical studies as varied as Latin textual criticism, Greek epigraphy, and chronology — as I have tried to argue in two substantial volumes of my own.[12] Studying his work has certainly taught me many lessons in humility. If Bernays could reconstruct the lost and repair the corrupt, Scaliger devised the whole instrumentariam of modern scholarship with which his successors, down to Bernays, worked. Arriving in Paris from Agen and Bordeaux, where he had grown up, Scaliger taught himself Greek; it took him all of three weeks, he later recalled, to read the entire text of Homer, compiling his own grammar as he went. Inspired by contact with Guillaume Postel, with whom he briefly shared a bed at a printer's shop, he moved on to study Hebrew. This he learned from the Bible, and well enough that he could dispute in Hebrew with Jews in southern France and northern Italy; they remarked, perhaps not without irony, that he spoke the Hebrew of the Bible, quite a different language from that of *"Rabbotenu zicronam"* (our Rabbis of [blessed] memory). Aramaic, Arabic, and Ethiopic followed.

Still in his early twenties, Scaliger wrote a brilliant commentary on one of the most puzzling and difficult of Latin texts, Varro's *De lingua latina*. His precocious ability to transform scribal gobbledygook into archaic Latin by conjecture startled even the erudite and literate scholars of the mid-16th-century Collège Royal — men like Denys Lambin and Jean Dorat, who had taught the poets of the Pléiade how to emulate classical verse. So did the polyglot erudition with which Scaliger commented on the poems of the late antique schoolmaster Ausonius, drawing on texts as diverse as the *Greek Anthology* and the bilingual dialogues from which the schoolboys of late imperial Rome had learned their Greek. More impressive still was his restoration of the battered text of Sextus Pompeius Festus' Latin lexicon, itself an epitome of an earlier work, which survived only in a single manuscript, much of which had been lost, and in a late epitome by the Christian scholar Paulus Diaconus.

In 1577 Scaliger tried, in a brilliant edition of Catullus, to reconstruct by conjecture the textual history of a classical author. He inferred from identical textual errors in later manuscripts and editions that the lost archetype of Catullus (the medieval manuscript from which all later ones must have descended) must have been written in what he called 'Lombardic' script. The very similar forms of *a* and *u,* tall *i* and *l, c* and *g,* characteristic of this early medieval bookhand, he insisted, had confused later scribes. Only a bold conjectural history of the text could explain the errors shared by later textual witnesses and make it possible to reconstruct an earlier state of the text than they presented. This form of argument would not be revived with such precision and dramatic flair until the 19th-century heyday of German philology, when Karl Lachmann informed his stunned contemporaries how many pages the lost archetype of Lucretius had possessed, and how many lines of verse to the page. Yet even the brilliance of Scaliger's textual history of Catullus pales before the greatest of his editorial efforts: his critical edition of and commentary on the astrological poem of Manilius, which combined tours de force of textual emendation with equally brilliant explanations of the details of Hellenistic astrology.

Scaliger's work as a textual critic — which occupied him until his late thirties — in itself would have ensured him a prominent place in the scholarly pantheon. But he did much more. In the second half of his career, he devoted himself to technical chronology — the discipline, now little known but fashionable in the 16th century, which aimed at establishing the main eras of ancient and medieval history and reconstructing the calendars used in the ancient and medieval worlds. Scaliger's work in this field resulted in two massively unreadable books: the *De emendatione temporum* of 1583 and the *Thesaurus temporum* of 1606. In them he filled more than two thousand folio pages of Latin with computed dates for solar eclipses and planetary occultations, and lists of Egyptian dynasties and Argive priestesses of Hera.

Scaliger drew more heavily on his predecessors than he ever admitted. Many new details of his work, moreover, provoked sharp criticism, some of it justified, from such rival experts as the astronomers Tycho Brahe and Johannes Kepler and the aptly-named chronologer Johannes Temporarius. Still, the structures Scaliger erected have remained, on the whole, astonishingly sound, for four centuries.

Scaliger reconstructed the lost Greek *Chronicle* of Eusebius and used it, deftly and plausibly, to date the main events of Near Eastern as well as Greek and Roman history. He discovered what remain the most important preserved fragments of ancient chronological literature, such as the Egyptian dynasty lists of Manetho. He showed that these were genuine even though they contained what looked, to a 16th-century Calvinist, like wildly improbable statements (for example, Manetho placed the beginning of Egyptian history not only before the Flood, but before the Creation itself). Scaliger steeped himself in the literature of Hellenistic Judaism, becoming the first Christian scholar to recognize — as did the Italian Jew Azariah de' Rossi — that large numbers of Jews in the ancient world had read the Bible and had worshipped not in Hebrew but in Greek, and had created a Greek literature of their own.[13] He made brilliant use of the Passover Haggadah to show that the Last Supper represented an adaptation of the Jewish seder. And he expunged from the historical record, with pungent sarcasm and tungsten-steel philological arguments, a wide range of forged texts — most prominently the letter of Aristeas, which purported to explain the origins of the Septuagint. No one described this massive historical enterprise more effectively than Scaliger himself. With characteristic immodesty he told his students that "I am writing the history of 8,000 years, according to the pagans."

His erudition — unique even in that age of polyhistors, whose common intellectual currency took the shape of back-breaking folios laden with quotations in many languages and scripts — won him all that erudition then could: fame throughout the Republic of Letters, hatred from Jesuits and Puritans alike, and the only research professorship known to have existed between the fall of the Alexandrian Museum and the rise of the Macarthur Foundation. Scaliger held this post for fifteen years at the University of Leiden, the most aggressively modern institution of higher learning in Europe. Though he did not lecture, he created something like an early research seminar, choosing gifted pupils and supervising their work with an iron hand in an iron glove. The ingenious Daniel Heinsius, his favorite, would eventually lapse into alcoholism (his resigned pupils became used to posting a sign in Latin saying, "Heinsius is too hung over to teach today") — but not before he followed Scaliger's hints and devised the theory that the Hellenistic Jews had created their own form of Greek, one in which Greek words bore Semitic senses. Heinsius' thesis provoked sharp and productive debate for decades, even centuries. Still greater success awaited Hugo Grotius. With Scaliger's help, he produced, by the age of fourteen, critical editions of the Latin Aratea and of the obscure late antique encyclopedia of Martianus Capella, *The Marriage of Mercury and Philology*. Later he became, exactly as Scaliger predicted, an able and efficient public official as well as a prolific writer and scholar.

My twenty-year pursuit of Scaliger has been painful, and not only because I continually found myself confronted by his inimitable learning and ingenuity. For my contact with him was never simple or direct. From my first fumbling months of research in 1973 to the last days of proof-reading the second volume of my biography of Scaliger twenty years later, it was Bernays who served as my essential guide through the details of Scaliger's life and work, as well as their political, religious, and intellectual contexts. Bernays' book on Scaliger is a short (70-page) eloquent survey of his hero's life. But it was preceded by a brilliant introduction in which Bernays argued, in detail, that Scaliger was the first real world historian to fuse the Bible and the records of the Near Eastern, Greek, and Roman nations into a single, coherent account of world history. And it was followed, more importantly still, by dozens of excursuses, filling hundreds of pages, which Bernays called his "Giftschrank" (poison cupboard).[14] Here he settled problems of dating, attribution, and interpretation, provided texts and details to substantiate and flesh out the lapidary characterizations in his text, and illuminated many dark corners of late 16th-century intellectual history. Bernays assembled, in mosaic form, what remains the best account of the multiple worlds of scholarship in the late Renaissance, a time in which philologists ruled the intellectual roost. Over and over I have redated a letter from or to Scaliger, seen the biographical relevance of a passing phrase in a technical argument, or discovered a hidden reference to an obscure classical or patristic source — only to find, a day, a week, or a decade later, that Bernays had already made the same find, and recorded it in one of his pullulating appendices.

The book has hardly a misprint to gratify the critical eye; moreover, it is not only rife with solid scholarship but written in a classical German prose. "His majesty J. J. Scaliger stands there alive and gives the epigoni a standard, against which they can measure themselves" — Max Muller's verdict, written just after the book came out, still holds.[15] Even the depressingly familiar fact that thirty years after the book first appeared, when Bernays set out to prepare a new edition, the publisher still had a quarter of the original stock of 600 on hand, offers only modest consolation.[16] For Bernays quarried all the materials that went into this masterpiece himself, unsupported by grants or large public libraries, before the end of his thirtieth year.

Bernays seems slightly out of place as a historian of scholarship. In the first place, he was himself a master, not an epigone, of the art whose development he traced. In the second place, he was a rigorously independent man, in both spiritual and intellectual terms — not the sort of retiring, timorous soul whom one might think of as inhabiting the Oedipal world of scholarly genealogies. He kept up his observance of the Sabbath and the dietary laws even in difficult circumstances — as when, in his twenties, he lived for a while in the Prussian embassy in London, where he could only drink tea. Challenged by his dear friend Bunsen to convert to Christianity — not for careerist reasons but simply, so Bunsen said, because to remain a Jew was to struggle in vain against the great current of world history — Bernays categorically refused. "Jesus of Nazareth himself," he replied, in a letter that became a classic of German-Jewish polemical writing, "born now as a Jew, would not be able to do it [become a Christian]" — at least not as a member of one of the churches of the mid-19th century.[17] He even dared what now seems quite impossible: to tease Theodor Mommsen. Asked by his friend about a problem of interpretation in the satires of Juvenal, Bernays thanked him for the "striking and flattering proof" that Mommsen had not read his essay on the subject, which had appeared in Mommsen's own recently published Festschrift.[18]

In retrospect, Bernays seems a figure far more likely to inspire than to feel the anxiety of influence, the weight of scholarly example. One case, an intimate one, will stand for many parallels. Bernays was one of three brothers; the third one, Berman, remained a faithful Jew, became a merchant, and had a daughter named Martha. She, of course, became Freud's beloved fiancée and, later, his wife. But the second brother, Michael, had a more tormented life and a more complex fate. Like Jacob, he studied at Heidelberg, where he became obsessively interested in German literature. The two young men found some common ground in Edward Gibbon, whose *Decline and Fall* they read together. But Michael eventually succumbed to the mounting political and cultural pressures that Jacob always resisted. He returned to the ancestral city of Mainz, where he announced his conversion to Christianity. He devoted himself to the philological and historical study of German literature. In the end he became, after some hard times, a prominent professor at the University of Munich. The close friend of such prominent antisemites as Heinrich von Treitschke and Richard Wagner, Michael also taught Heinrich Wölfflin and created the discipline now known as Germanistik.[19]

Jacob felt Michael's conversion as a personal wound: he mourned his brother as dead and never spoke of him again, even to their mutual friends, like the poet and Romance scholar Paul Heyse. But he let his rich personal library pass, after his death, to the lapsed younger brother. And Michael clearly spent a lifetime paying tribute, in a variety of ways, to Jacob. He took a deep interest in the history of classical scholarship, as his detailed study of Goethe's relations with the Halle professor and Homeric critic Friedrich August Wolf clearly shows.[20] He was the only Munich professor to offer help and sociability to the brilliant young Jewish palaeographer Ludwig Traube, whose seminar became a center of work on the classical tradition and the history of texts.[21] More strikingly still, Michael emulated, in the realm of German literature, what Jacob had done for Latin. Jacob had grouped the manuscripts of Lucretius into families, establishing a stemma, or family tree, and identifying those that a textual critic must use: Michael did the same for the editions of Goethe's works, establishing that the great poet had often used poor, error-ridden reprints as the basis of the revised editions of his own works. These swarmed, as a result, with missing words and unintelligible remarks that Goethe had not bothered to correct. Michael even arranged the editions into families and drew up stemmata — perhaps a first in the study of printed texts.[22]

Most revealingly of all, to the end of his life Michael felt compelled to return to the interests he shared with his brother. His marvellous essay on the history of the footnote — still the fullest and most enlightening treatment of this absorbing subject ever written — includes a rich analysis of the funniest footnotes ever written, those in Gibbon's *Decline and Fall,* and clearly began from the discussions he and his older brother, who also loved Gibbon's more audacious mock-learned remarks, had held in Heidelberg almost half a century before.[23] True, Bernays did not weigh so heavily on the less gifted of his students as did his English friend Mark Pattison, the biographer of Isaac Casaubon who reviewed Bernays' book on Scaliger in the *Quarterly Review* and then set out to produce his own, never-finished biography. Pattison told a student who, he thought, might edit John Selden's *Table Talk* that he would have to spend at least twenty years memorizing the text and reading the entire literature of the period. The student duly recalled that "he put the thing before me in so unattractive a way that I never did it or anything else worth doing. I consider the ruin of my misspent life very largely due to that conversation."[24] But Bernays showed impatience enough towards those unwilling to follow his precepts and example: for example, he drove the young Hermann Cohen, who had no sympathy for his teacher's rigorous historicism, out of his seminar in Breslau.

What then did Jacob Bernays find in Joseph Scaliger? Why did this man of stiff-necked independence devote himself, in the biography and in a large number of his other writings, to finding heroes to emulate? And does his work on the history of scholarship perhaps reveal some of the tensions common to this tense, aggressive field?

Bernays' motives were both emotional and intellectual. On the first count, readers have realized ever since Bernays' biography appeared that it had something of the character of an allegory. In laying out the main lines of

Scaliger's work and the forces that had shaped his character, Bernays described not only his protagonist but himself as well. He accepted as credible Scaliger's remarkable statements about the rapidity and independence with which he absorbed information — such as Scaliger's boast that he had read Homer in three weeks and made his own grammar of Homeric Greek while doing so.[25] While this may seem highly credulous it is understandable in the light of Bernays' own rapid, self-motivating progress as a scholar. The young man who was already, at the outset of his twenties, reading Joseph Scaliger's Latin letters and studying his annotated books — borrowed, by the happy custom of the time, from the Leiden University Library — felt a kinship with the other prodigy.[26] More important are the other similarities that emerge on comparison: the two mens' refusal to marry; their exile to learned institutions in provincial cities far from their native lands; and above all, their sense of their own nobility.

No facet of Scaliger's fascinating character is more bizarre than his insistence that he belonged to the ancient della Scalla family of Verona — a belief he owed to his father, a brilliant academic con man named Giulio Cesare Bordon. Giulio Cesare, the son of a gifted illuminator of manuscripts, Benedetto Bordon, moved from north Italy to southern France and established himself at Agen. There he passed himself off as a della Scala to the credulous provincial gentry and literati, married the daughter of a local notable and became famous as a natural philosopher and literary critic. His son, Joseph, accepted at his father's knee the belief that he belonged to a noble Italian house, one whose annals stretched back to the time of Theodoric and beyond. He clung to his noble identity as a young traveller in Italy, thrilling himself and his friends as he whispered that he must remain incognito lest Venetian assassins murder him. He repeated his father's dynastic fantasies as a middle-aged scholar in France, even when friends began to report from Italy that another story about his origins was in circulation. And he defended them just as fiercely as an old professor in Leiden, where he insisted on his right to wear, and have his portrait painted wearing, the purple robes of a prince. Scaliger refused to drop his claim to nobility even when his enemies in Italy published his father's doctoral diploma, which clearly bore the name Bordon (he tried, with a brilliantly perverse piece of historical criticism, to show that the document was forged).[27] Even many of Scaliger's

friends and supporters found his attitude puzzling: why not, one of them
asked, simply dismiss the problem? Scaliger and his father had ennobled
their ancestral city by their achievements. Why worry about whether their
ancestors had a claim to nobility by birth as well? Yet Scaliger went to his
death quixotically embattled on this point. And Bernays supported him,
arguing that Scaliger's conduct as a man and as a scholar flowed from his
conviction of his own noble descent and the duties it required of him.

Wilamowitz remarked on what he saw as Bernays' "pride in his nobility":
his sense of himself as one born to a high station.[28] It seems obvious that
Bernays saw in Scaliger someone who shared his high, stern sense of self,
and who followed a rigorous ethical code because he felt he had inherited
the duty to do so. To that extent Scaliger offered him (as Arnaldo Momigliano pointed out in his brilliant article on Bernays) an absolute model of
personal rectitude that no scholar of ordinary descent could have provided.
When Bernays eloquently evoked Scaliger's crushing attacks on fanatical
Calvinists who read the Bible literally and on corrupt Jesuits who refused to
accept that the works of Dionysius the pseudo-Areopagite were forged, he
saw himself, caught between the racism of Protestant Prussia and the ignorance and superstition of the German Catholic population.

But Scaliger mattered for more strictly intellectual reasons as well. In his
biography of Scaliger Bernays stated unequivocally what he believed to be
Scaliger's chief motive for studying the history of his field. Scaliger, he
argued, had devised a method for classical scholarship that remained valid
centuries after his death. His technical work could still supply precedents,
stimuli, and themes for the young philologists of the mid-19th century.
Bernays evidently believed that Scaliger's combination of biblical and classical philology, his insistence on studying Herodotus and the Old Testament
together, offered a model for the study of ancient history that suffered
neither from the excessive classicism of some German philologists nor
from the wild speculation of their enemies, the mythographers and pan-
Babylonist world historians. But Bernays also meant something more specific: that Scaliger had devised and practised exactly the sort of interdisciplinary classical scholarship that the Germans of his own day called
"Altertumswissenschaft" and claimed as their special discovery.

The intellectual revolution that created the new Prussian universities was

touched off by classical scholars such as Christian Gottlob Heyne and Friedrich August Wolf in the later 18th century. Both insisted that philologists
must no longer confine themselves to studying texts; rather, they must
recreate the historical contexts in which the ancients had lived and written,
using everything from the material remains of ancient art to the scattered
evidence of ancient material culture to give their vision of the past color and
solidity.[29] Wolf issued his call for a new scholarship in a densely written,
enthusiastic manifesto, his *Darstellung der Alterthums-Wissenschaft*. This
manifesto, and his brilliant, critical *Prolegomena to Homer*, won him the
fascinated attention of young scholars — like Leopold Zunz, who modeled
his own approach to the study of Jewish texts and traditions on Wolf's
approach to Greece and Rome.[30] It also won him the support of Wilhelm
von Humboldt, who embodied Wolf's theories in his plans for the new
university of Berlin. At Bonn, where Berlin standards were systematically
applied, Bernays mastered the new scholarship and directly experienced
both its rich rewards and its underlying problems and contradictions.

Bernays, however, did something more — and more unusual — than his
predecessors. He insisted that the interdisciplinary study of the past was
neither new nor fully developed in his own time. In his biography of Scaliger, he called the reader's attention to the fact that his hero, a student of
literary and historical texts, had also devoted himself to the study of ancient
inscriptions. Scaliger collected these in notebooks, supervised and encour-
aged the efforts of the Heidelberg scholar Janus Gruter to edit a new corpus
of Greek and Roman inscriptions, and even spent ten months, eighteen
hours a day, drawing up the indices to Gruter's work when Gruter himself
proved unwilling to do so. Bernays' characteristically hyperbolic remark,
"Auch das scheinbar Niedrigste veredelte sich unter seinen Händen," shows
how deeply he respected Scaliger's effort to master all the crafts of scholarship at once.[31] He regretted only that after the middle of the 17th century,
scholars had ceased to follow Scaliger's example and connect the study of
ancient literature with that of the material remains of the ancient world.[32]
Where Wolf and Böckh, in other words, represented themselves as the
creators of a new form of scholarship, Bernays portrayed himself as the
rediscoverer of a lost one.

This argument was not merely rhetorical. One year after Bernays' *Scaliger*

appeared, he published one of the most rigorous and original of all his
technical papers: an analysis of the Greek poem long attributed to Pho-
cylides. This set of moralizing verses, a favorite in Renaissance schools because it seemed so nearly Christian in spirit, had last been studied seriously
by Scaliger. He had argued, at length, that the text must be by a Jew or a
Christian rather than a Greek. Scaliger himself settled for the second hypothesis. Pseudo-Phocylides instructed the reader that "if a beast of your
enemy falls on the way, help it to rise [140]."[33] This injunction to help one's
enemies Scaliger took as a Christian reinterpretation or rewriting of Deuteronomy 22:4, which instructs the Jew to help raise his *brother's* ass or ox if it
falls by the way. But Scaliger also urged erudite young men to continue the
study of Pseudo-Phocylides, saying that they would find plenty of unexplored details there to confirm or challenge his own analysis.[34] In fact,
however, no one accepted Scaliger's challenge: the demonstration that the
text was forged seemed to deprive it of any interest or importance, and it
dropped from scholarly sight in the 17th and 18th centuries.

Bernays, in taking up the gauntlet Scaliger had dropped, did not slavishly
follow his mentor's line. Rather he started out by showing that Scaliger's
analysis of the text's religious character was badly flawed. If Deuteronomy
22:4 instructed the good Jew to help his brother's beast of burden, Exodus
23:5 told him to do the same if the beast of his enemy fell under his yoke.
Bernays concluded: "Wenigstens in diesem Falle erscheint also die 'Fein-
desliebe' als echt mosaisch." Evidently, Scaliger had lacked a "living and
certain" knowledge of the Pentateuch, even if he had noticed his error and
omitted his argument in the second edition of his work.[35] The remainder of
Bernays' analysis, however, moved along rails that Scaliger had laid out and
spiked down.[36]

Scaliger, as we have seen, had proved to his contemporaries that the last
centuries before and the first ones after the beginning of the Christian era
saw the rise of a "Hellenistic" form of Judaism, whose practitioners read the
Torah and performed their liturgy in Greek, not Hebrew. Scaliger argued
that the most prominent Hellenistic writer, Philo, had been so steeped in
Hellenic culture that he had lost contact with Judaism itself: Philo's supposed etymologies of Hebrew terms and explanations of Jewish customs
were largely inventions. Even Christian *tyrunculi,* to say nothing of Jews,

could find the errors in this poor Platonist's efforts to deal with Jewish topics. Scaliger also showed that these Hellenists often had given way to the temptation to invent the texts their tradition did not provide. For example, one of them had forged the letter of Aristeas, which purported to show that the Septuagint deserved more faith than the Hebrew text of the Old Testament.[37] Bernays renewed Scaliger's effort to reveal the peculiarities of the Hellenists' Greek, and continued his effort to identify and produce a literary history of their works; in so doing, Bernays showed once again that he saw Scaliger as a living model for his own work.

Bernays' use of Scaliger clearly shows his distance from the normal preoccupations of German scholars in his time. August Böckh, Karl Lachmann and Theodor Mommsen, for all their differences of method and achievement, agreed in insisting on the novelty of their approaches. No earlier scholar, however erudite, had anticipated their efforts to reconstruct the ancient world as a whole. In the Protestant culture of north Germany, claims to innovation sounded virtuous. In the fiercely competitive German universities and academies, in particular, those who could slaughter their intellectual ancestors stood a better chance of prospering than those who worshipped them.[38] Bernays, by contrast, saw himself as one link in a chain of tradition; and he held that anyone who hoped to join that chain must do so by finding a connection, as Bernays did, to earlier links. It seems only reasonable to identify his attitude as a peculiarly Jewish one: the attitude of one who held that the only way back to canonical texts lay through the whole history of their interpretation, that the best way to form a scholarly life was to ponder the personal examples of great scholars, and that the best way to form a style of inquiry was through the systematic study of one's predecessors. Bernays, the most brilliant of German classical scholars, differed from the rest because he preserved a rabbinic sensibility in the midst of a modern, scientific age. Like all great rabbis, also, Bernays found that he could choose a master without being silenced by doing so. The earlier masters, like Scaliger, spoke not only to instruct but to stimulate; they provided not only rich material to study but also suggestions for further research and incitement to further debate. Discipleship, in Bernays' rabbinic version of it, seemingly did not prejudice independence of thought and frankness of expression.

Or did it? Histories of scholarship, like all other texts, contain silences as well as statements; the silences sometimes speak volumes. Indeed, Bernays said nothing at all in the biography about one especially prominent area of Scaliger's scholarship: his theories about Hellenistic Judaism. Bernays argued, in his own analysis of Pseudo-Phocylides, that the poem was clearly the work of a Jew. The author had desperately wanted to prove, either to his fellow Jews or to cultured Greeks, that the core of Judaism basically matched the teachings of pagan philosophy. Hence his use of a classical meter, but also his omission of vital Jewish tenets, such as the prohibition against worshipping idols. Bernays condemned Pseudo-Phocylides as sharply as Scaliger condemned Philo: Pseudo-Phocylides' poem, like the Hellenized Jewish culture from which it sprang, was doomed to failure because it rested on an effort to conceal its own true essence and tried to pass as something other than what it was. Pseudo-Phocylides fully deserved his eventual fate of scholarly neglect. In fact, Bernays argued, "the history of this little Jewish-Hellenistic product mirrors the fate that deservedly befell the entire Jewish-Hellenistic literature and every other one that resembles it: the fate of failing to influence the spiritual life of peoples, which transforms itself through sharp oppositions and pushes contemptuously to the side all efforts to flatten the concrete by compromise or abstraction."[39] Jewish Hellenism — like the Reform Judaism of the 19th century — falsified the tradition it claimed to preserve.

At this point, as Bernays must have known, his analysis diverged sharply from his master's. For Scaliger did not attribute the defects of Hellenistic Judaism simply to the efforts of individual writers to play down the differences between the Mosaic commandments and the precepts of classical philosophy. He ascribed them, quite directly, to the nature of the Jews themselves. The author of the letter of Aristeas had pretended that twelve Jewish tribes still existed in the age of Ptolemy Philadelphus, centuries after the Exile. He claimed to quote original documents written both by Demetrius of Phalerum and by Ptolemy Philadelphus, even though the supposed letters in question were formally and stylistically identical. Scaliger found it quite easy to explain these obvious "mendacia": they stemmed from the natural Jewish urge to deceive. "Who," he asked rhetorically, "is unfamiliar with the fabrications of the Jews?"[40] The Hellenistic Jews were no less given to invention, to wild attempts to mislead their students and their readers, than the Rabbis of the normative tradition, for whose biblical exegesis and chronological and calendrical hair-splitting Scaliger more than once showed open contempt. In so doing, he founded a tradition of a sort. Later Christian scholars who dealt with similar material found it easy, travelling in his deep wake, to explain the peculiarities of a given Hellenistic text by what August Böckh described as "an impious, rather than pious, deceit, innate to the Hebrews."[41]

Curiously, Bernays never tried, either in his biography or elsewhere, to inquire into Scaliger's diagnosis of the errors of Jewish Hellenism or to follow up its after-effects. He left this unpleasant task to his one gifted pupil at Breslau, Jacob Freudenthal, a pioneering student of Hellenistic Jewish historiography, who confronted directly what his master had ignored. "It is incomprehensible," Freudenthal wrote, that men like Scaliger, Valckenaer, and Böckh should have ascribed the forgeries of the Hellenists simply to "the natural predisposition of the Jewish people."[42] These intolerant philologists had failed to understand the several related but not identical facts that had hemmed in the Greek-speaking Jews: above all, the expressive limits of their dialect of Greek, which made it impossible to reach real literary mastery, and the vicious criticisms to which non-Jews like Manetho subjected them, which forced them to resort to trickery in a desperate, doomed effort at cultural self-defense.[43] Freudenthal was in other ways as well more decisive than Bernays. He moved, over time, away from tradition. He left Frankel's seminar for the University of Breslau, traded up (or down?) from philology to philosophy, and became the author of a magniloquent, enthusiastic biography of Spinoza, whom he eloquently praised as the inventor of historical criticism of the Bible. From this standpoint — one in which he had to invent his own models for conduct as man and scholar — Freudenthal could do more than admire the general greatness and correct specific errors of the great figures of the past. He could bring himself, as Bernays could not, to see their limitations as well as their strengths: to see that they too now belonged to a past that had become irretrievably foreign.

Bernays, by contrast, found in Scaliger a model for both the analysis and the evaluation of Hellenistic Judaism. To do so, however, Bernays had to distort the record, which he knew better than anyone. He never acknowledged that Scaliger had seen Hellenistic Judaism only as an illustration of the general weaknesses of Judaism, as a religion and as a culture. The omission was not accidental. The more closely one examines Bernays' book, moreover, the more gaps and silences one uncovers. Bernays called attention to the fact that Scaliger did not have an educated Jew's command of Hebrew and Aramaic. But he did not describe Scaliger's effort, late in life, to compensate for this weakness by working regularly with a Jewish convert in Leiden. (Scaliger typically remarked that his tutor did not know Hebrew grammar, but admitted that he could recognize, as Scaliger himself could not, Talmudic proverbs and allusions.)[44] Furthermore, Bernays called attention to the fact that Scaliger learned Arabic and Ethiopic. But he omitted Scaliger's own references to the fact that he received assistance with eastern calendars from a remarkable figure of counter-Reformation Rome, the one-time Syrian Jacobite patriarch and later convert to Catholicism, Ignatius Na'amatallah. Ignatius sent Scaliger elaborate treatments in Arabic of the Oriental twelve-year animal cycle and other matters, which Scaliger quoted with lavish endorsements.[45] Bernays lived among Christian friends who prized the rare information he could give them and wanted him to convert for his own sake. He could not endure the fact that Scaliger had resembled his own patrons, like Bunsen or Mommsen, in his limited tolerance for Judaism and in his willingness to work with converts, marginal figures, and informants who looked all too much like a fun-house reflection of Bernays himself.

Most important of all, Bernays could not deal honestly with some of Scaliger's most radical and challenging theories about history and exegesis. Bernays insisted that he himself had no faith in biblical criticism. Historical readings of the Old Testament he dismissed as pseudo-scholarly profanations of a sacred text, based only on wild hypotheses.[46] Scaliger, however, had other views. He not only found but published (and refused to abridge) the Egyptian dynasty lists that plunged the world of European historical learning into a century and more of crisis. Worse still, he speculated in radical ways about the gaps and defects of the Masoretic text of the Hebrew Bible. Scaliger noted that the Masoretic text was relatively late: he dated it to around the time of Gamaliel, whose remark that *masoret seyag la-torah* (tradition is a fence to the law) he took as a reference to the Masoretic apparatus. And he insisted that even this well-preserved official text represented only a version of a lost original. Its language, Hebrew, was not—so Scaliger claimed—a special, holy language, with which God had created the world and in which Adam had named the animals, but the ordinary tongue of ancient Assyria. Neither was its script original or sacred, since the Jews originally had used a different one, much like that of the Samaritans. Only after their return from the Babylonian exile did they transliterate the text into the square Aramic characters used in the extant manuscripts and the printed Hebrew Bible. The Old Testament, like the new, suggested Scaliger, incorporated many errors and showed some worrying gaps. The Masoretes, narrowly Jewish in culture and tradition, had known little or nothing about non-Jewish history. Their vocalizations of non-Hebrew names, for example, were often faulty; much less accurate, Scaliger thought, than those of the more cosmopolitan Alexandrian Jews who had translated the Septuagint. Finally, all texts of the Old Testament referred to stories and texts now lost, such as the story of the young man killed by Lamech, referred to—but not recounted—in Genesis.[47]

Bernays knew that Scaliger took a serious amateur interest in the Bible. He recorded with glee some bold remarks about the New Testament that he found in Scaliger's table talk, the *Scaligerana*. No doubt Bernays relished Scaliger's worried statement that "[T]here are more than 50 additions or changes to the New Testament and the Gospels. It's a strange thing, I don't dare to say it [in print]; if it were a pagan author, I would speak about it differently."[48] But he left Scaliger's efforts to historicize the Old Testament entirely out of account, even though they seem highly relevant to his belief that Scaliger's work retained its relevance in the mid-19th century.

In the end, then, Bernays' *Scaliger* does not do full justice to its subject. Less by misrepresentation than by omission, Bernays fabricated for himself a master who mirrored his own strengths of character and who worked with more than his own sense of purpose, ignoring Scaliger's prejudices and insights when they did not serve his purposes.[49] Those using Bernays' book must do so with due caution, aware that the same passion for his subject that fires his prose sometimes interferes with his analysis. And those who consider his case (as I have, every day for more than twenty years) will probably come away with a deep feeling of uncertainty. If Jacob Bernays could not distinguish between historical fact and personal need, between what the record said and what he wanted to find, can anyone hope to do better? Does his case suggest a gloomy conclusion: that historians of scholarship who are not harmless drudges, stodging away in the records without presupposition, will more likely paint a heroic portrait of a past master, robed in purple, than analyze a past physiognomy, warts, period features, and all? These thoughts disturb me deeply, but I think it may be in keeping with Bernays' heroic side, his willingness to confront deeply uncomfortable truths.

NOTES

1. On Bernays in general see M. Fraenkel, *Jacob Bernays* (Breslau, 1932); A.D. Momigliano, "Jacob Bernays" in *Quinto Contributo alla storia degli studi classici e del mondo antico* (Rome, 1980), 157–180; H. Bach, *Jacob Bernays* (Tübingen, 1974). E.E. Urbach, "The Breslau Years of Jacob Bernays and his Impact upon Jewish Studies," *Jacob Bernays: un philologue juif*, ed. J. Glucker and A. Laks (Lille, 1996), 17–28; J. Bollack, "Un homme d'un autre monde," ibid., 135–226.

2. J. Bernays, "De emendatione Lucretii," *Rheinisches Museum* 5 (1847), 533–587; on the importance of this work see S. Timpanaro, *La genesi del metodo del Lachmann* (Padua, 1985). M. Bollack, "Jacob Bernays ou l'abandon du commentaire," in *Jacob Bernays*, ed. Glucker and Laks, 31–44; J. Glucker, " 'Lachmann's Method' — Bernays, Madvig, Lachmann and others," ibid., 45–56.

3. J. Bernays, *Grundzüge der verlorenen Abhandlung des Aristoteles über Wirkung der Tragödie* (Breslau, 1858), repr. with an introduction by K. Gründer. Hildesheim, 1970.

4. J. Bernays, *Die Dialoge des Aristoteles in ihrem Verhältniss zu seinen übrigen Werken* (Berlin, 1863). B. Effe, "Die Dialoge des Aristoteles: Jacob Bernays und die neuere Forschung," in *Jacob Bernays*, ed. Glucker and Laks, 77–86.

5. J. Bernays, *Theophrastos' Schrift über Frömmigkeit. Ein Beitrag zur Religionsgeschichte* (Berlin, 1866).

6. J. Bernays, "Ein nabatäischer Schriftsteller," *Rheinisches Museum,* 17 (1862), repr. in Bernays, *Gesammelte Abhandlungen*, ed. H. Usener (Berlin, 1885) 2: 291–293. cf. Momigliano's discussion of this article.

7. For the general context see M.A. Meyer, *The Origins of the Modern Jew* (Detroit, 1967).

8. M. Brann, *Geschichte des jüdisch-theologischen Seminars (Fraenckel'sche Stiftung) in Breslau* (Breslau, n.d.); Urbach.

9. U. von Wilamowitz-Moellendorff, *Erinnerungen 1848–1914* (Leipzig, n.d.), 87–88.

10. See H. Usener, "Vorwort," in Bernays, *Gesammelte Abhandlungen,* iii–x, and the painstaking bibliographies that follow.

11. J. Bernays, *Joseph Justus Scaliger* (Berlin, 1855).

12. A. Grafton, *Joseph Scaliger* (Oxford, 1983–93).

13. On Azariah de' Rossi and Hellenistic Judaism see J. Weinberg, "The Quest for Philo in Sixteenth-Century Jewish Historiography," in *Jewish History: Essays in Honor of Chimen Abramsky,* ed. A. Rapoport-Albert et al. (London, 1988), 163–187.

14. Bach, *Bernays,* 128.

15. M. Fraenkel, *Jacob Bernays* (Breslau, 1932), 91.

16. Bach, *Bernays,* 211–212.

17. Fraenkel, *Bernays,* 58–60.

18. Ibid., 163 (Mommsen's funny reply to this comment appears on 163–164); the essay in question appears in *Gesammelte Abhandlungen* 2: 71–80. On the relation between Bernays and Mommsen see L. Wickert, "Theodor Mommsen und Jacob Bernays: Ein Beitrag zur Geschichte des deutschen Judentums," *Historische Zeitschrift* 205 (1967), 265–294, reworked in Wickert, *Theodor Mommsen. Eine Biograpie,* 3: *Die Wanderjahre* (Frankfurt, 1969), 322–342.

19. See *Briefe von und an Michael Bernays* (Berlin, 1907); W. Rehm. *Späte Studien* (Bern and Munich, 1964), 359–458.

20. *Goethes Briefe an Friedrich August Wolf,* ed. (with an exhaustive commentary) by M. Bernays (Berlin, 1868).

21. See F. Boll, "Biographische Einleitung," in L. Traube, *Vorlesungen und Abhandlungen,* ed. P. Lehmann (Munich, 1909), 1; xix.

22. M. Bernays, *Über Kritik und Geschichte des Goetheschen Textes* (Berlin, 1866).

23. M. Bernays, "Zur Lehre von den Citaten und Noten," *Schriften zur Kritik und Literaturgeschichte* (Berlin, 1899), 4:255–347.

24. Quoted in L.A. Tollemache, *Recollections of Pattison* (London, 1885), 5.

25. For a more sceptical view see E.V. Blomfield, "Biographical Memoir of Josephus Justus Scaliger," *Museum Criticum* 1 (1826): 345.

26. Bach, *Bernays,* 51, 80, 95.

27. M. Billanovich, "Giulio Cesare Scaligero e Benedetto Bordon," *Italia Medioevale e Umanistica* 11 (1968).

28. Wilamowitz-Moellendorff, *Erinnerungen,* 88: "Es war eine sonderbare Sorte von Adelsstolz". . . .

29. See A. Grafton, *Defenders of the Text* (Cambridge, Mass. and London, 1991), Chap. 9.

30. Meyer, *Origins of the Modern Jew,* 158–162.

31. Bernays, *Scaliger,* 68.

32. See Bernays, *Gesammelte Abhandlungen,* 71.

33. I cite the translation in *The Sentences of Pseudo-Phocylides,* ed. P.W. van der Horst (Leiden, 1978).

34. Scaliger, *Animadversiones in Chronologica Eusebii,* 95–96, in *Thesaurus Temporum,* 2d ed. (Amsterdam, 1658).

35. J. Bernays, "Ueber das Phokylideische Gedicht," *Gesammelte Abhandlungen,* 192-261 at 198.

36. For the importance of Bernays' work see the review of scholarship in van der Horst's edition, 3–54.

37. Grafton, *Scaliger,* 2:413–420, 510, 707.

38. See W. Lepenies, *Autoren und Wissenschaftler im 18. Jahrhundert* (Munich and Vienna, 1988), 106; G. Walther, *Niebuhrs Forschung* (Stuttgart, 1993), 315–320.

39. Bernays, "Ueber das Phokylideische Gedicht," 254.

40. Scaliger, *Animadversiones,* 133–134.

41. Quoted in J. Freudenthal, *Alexander Polyhistor* (Breslau, 1875), 194.

42. Ibid.

43. See A.D. Momigliano, *Alien Wisdom* (Cambridge, 1975), 116–117.

44. Scaliger, *Epistolae omnes quae reperiri potuerunt,* ed. D. Heinsius (Leiden, 1627), 594.

45. G. Levi della Vida, *Documenti intorno alle relazioni delle chiese orientali con la S. Sede durante il pontificato di Gregorio XIII* (Rome, 1948), 22–25.

46. See, e.g., Fraenkel, *Bernays,* 28–29.

47. Grafton, *Scaliger,* 2:728–737.

48. Bernays, *Scaliger,* 203–205. See also H.J. de Jonge, "The Study of the New Testament," in *Leiden University in the Seventeenth Century: An Exchange of Learning,* ed. Th.H. Lunsingh Scheurleer et al. (Leiden, 1975), 64–109, esp. 76–87.

49. For another case in point—one unconnected with Judaism—see M. Haupt, "Ueber Joseph Scaliger und die von Haase vorgeschlagene Umstellung tibullischer Versreihen," *Opuscula* 3 (Leipzig, 1876): 30–41.

TWO

Subversive Catalysts: Gnosticism and Messianism in Gershom Scholem's View of Jewish Mysticism

MOSHE IDEL

SCHOLEM'S 'HISTORICAL CRITICISM SCHOOL'

Gershom Scholem's contribution to the modern understanding of Judaism in general, and of Jewish mysticism in particular, can hardly be overestimated. It transcends even the role of establishing the modern academic study of Kabbalah. Scholem's opus has illuminated the whole area of Jewish studies with new and fresh insights that penetrate each and every survey in the field in direct and indirect ways. More important, in my opinion, is the establishment of a high standard of scholarship that consists of returning to neglected sources as part of his comprehensive interrogation of the past. Scholem has advanced new views, and has presented a plethora of unexplored texts. Indeed, one of his greatest achievements is his unprecedented katabatic descent into the vast universe of forgotten mystical texts and the anabasis that is characterized by a larger vision, which transcends the details.

The scholarly study of Jewish mysticism is a relatively new academic field.

Covering almost two millennia of literary creativity, thousands of works still remain in manuscript, and most of the printed works are still unexplored or only poorly described. This mystical literature consists of a broad spectrum of mythical, mystical, theosophical and theurgical notions and of different literary genres. The historical picture of the development of Jewish mysticism is still an evolving topic, and nothing like an "ultimate history" has been written. Indeed an explicit sense of being at the beginning pervades the work of Scholem, creator of the modern study of Jewish mysticism. In his latest and most comprehensive survey of scholarship of the field, he duly indicated that "scholarly investigation of Kabbalah is only now emerging from its infancy."[1]

Formulated in 1974, this evaluation still holds some twenty-five years later. The perusal of a huge number of kabbalistic manuscripts, the refinement of methodological approaches, and the historical surveys are still in their initial form. In most cases the tremendous achievements of Scholem have not yet been matched by his followers. It seems that despite the recent surfacing of a great deal of manuscripts and the greater availability of manuscript and printed material already studied by Scholem, it is only rarely, if at all, that subsequent scholars have inspected the huge amount of material Scholem perused in order to formulate his views on Kabbalah. To put it more bluntly, I would be very surprised if the number of manuscripts consulted by Scholem already in the difficult years of the 1930s and 1940s would turn out to be less than that consulted by all the members of his school put together, even in the more calm years of the 1950s and 1960s. Indeed, the two main features of Scholem's writings that contributed greatly to their outstanding originality remained unmatched: (a) he never wrote on books or manuscripts that he had not read; (b) he did not repeat what was already well-known from the studies of other scholars but always advanced his own theory or, at least, added his particular insight. A return to the neglected manuscripts and an emphasis on the necessity of an original conceptual approach, very often critical toward his academic predecessors, recur in many of his writings. It was Scholem's great achievement to have undertaken the promethean task of perusing systematically the vast kabbalistic literature that was available already in the second third of our century. In the difficult conditions of the 1920s and 1930s his perseverance in a systematic reading of everything related to Jewish mysticism was a project more audacious than we can imagine today.

The dominant trend in modern scholarship of Jewish mysticism has been described as the "historical critical school." It is by this term that Scholem defined the school he founded. He enumerated among those who belonged to the school, in addition to himself, the Jerusalem scholars I. Tishby, E. Gottlieb, J. Dan, Rivka Schatz and J. Ben Shlomo.[2] Though Scholem did not explicitly identify himself in this context as the founder of the school, his assessment that the Hebrew University in Jerusalem became, after 1925, "an international center of kabbalistic research"[3] has no other plausible meaning.

Indeed, the emergence of such a school was not a random event. Scholem himself strove toward the crystallization of a group of scholars around him, who would pursue academic studies on Kabbalah. This intention was succinctly formulated in one of Scholem's letters to Walter Benjamin, when he wrote in 1939 that "my studies look very promising, since I had the opportunity of setting up a Scholem 'school' of research."[4]

Benjamin reacted positively, asking Scholem to "Tell me as soon as possible what the Scholem school is all about,"[5] but unfortunately Scholem's answer, if he addressed this last question of his friend at all in a letter, is not extant. The 1974 summary mentioned above seems to be the single formulation describing what "a Scholem school is all about." Therefore, the formation of a school around Scholem was explicitly connected to his views — "my studies" — and to his intentions to create such a school. Scholem could proudly conclude, in 1974, that the school he had set up in 1939 was now a fait accompli.

Certainly, Scholem's formulation in his book *Kabbalah* was a very modest one. In addition to the scholars enumerated above, he could have mentioned three other Jerusalem scholars: the leading classicist Chaim Wirszubski, who contributed to the study of Kabbalah, Christian Kabbalah and Sabbateanism; R.J. Zwi Werblowsky, who wrote a fine monograph on Rabbi Joseph Karo; and Nathan Rotenstreich, a leading Israeli philosopher. Rotenstreich has been drawn strongly to Scholem's vision of Jewish mysticism, he contributed an interesting article on Scholem,[6] and he took an active role in controversies related to the criticism of Scholem's views.[7] One cannot help wondering whether Scholem's description of the "school" should not be read in the context of another of his observations, concerning three groups of German Jewish intellectuals. In his *From Berlin to Jerusalem,* Scholem asserts that "I used to define the three groups around the Warburg library, Max Horkheimer's Institut für Sozialforschung [Institute for Social Research], and the metaphysical magicians around Oskar Goldberg as the three most remarkable 'Jewish sects' that German Jewry produced. Not all of them liked to hear this."[8]

Was Scholem attempting to add a fourth group, or—to use his own term—another sect, active now in Jerusalem, to the three that he discerned earlier in Germany? It is hard to answer this question in a definitive manner. My opinion is that whether or not he intended to produce a new Jewish "group" or sect, he succeeded in doing so.

The success of Scholem's "historical-critical" group was, indeed, enormous. It not only became the dominant school in kabbalistic research for decades, but it was also the most powerful trend in Israeli humanities in general. From an academic point of view, the school strove not only for a detailed mapping of recondite developments of a very complex type of occult literature, but also and, more significantly, for inserting this picture into the center of an understanding of Jewish history. Jewish mysticism was conceived by Scholem and his "historical-critical" school not only as the literature of an elite but, at least from the 16th century, as an important force that has shaped the history of the Jews. Historians of Judaism have adopted the findings of the historians of Jewish mysticism, which became the clue for the understanding of wider developments on the historical plane. As Y. Baer, the greatest of the Israeli historians, has formulated it, Scholem was a metaphysician who, "against his will," was also "a great historian who has fertilized the study of Jewish history more than anyone else in our generation."[9] Unlike Oskar Goldberg, who was characterized as a magical metaphysician, Scholem was an historical one. Indeed, this is one of the reasons for Scholem's impact on Jewish historians.[10]

Given the urgent need to clarify the wide range of biographical and bibliographical data, and to delineate the major historical developments, the main schools, and their fundamental concepts—the more phenomenological approach to kabbalistic literature become a secondary aspect of modern studies. The focus of this school has been, rather, to establish a comprehensive historical picture of the whole range of mystical material in Judaism.

From a methodological point of view, it seems that the philological-historical approach, much more than the phenomenological one, was accepted in the subsequent work of Scholem's school. His proposals for a comprehensive scheme of a history of Kabbalah remained stable, virtually as it was developed by him many decades ago. Furthermore, his phenomenology of Jewish mysticism, formulated in the late 1940s and early 1950s, has dominated the field, often being repeated and remaining largely undisputed. Despite Scholem's explicit acknowledgement that scholarship of Kabbalah is only at its incipient stage, his disciples apparently disagreed with his opinion; they seem to have argued silently with this perception of their master, embracing instead a view that Scholem's and their own findings, as well as their methodological approaches, were rather definitive.

Nevertheless, there are good reasons to rely on Scholem's original views on this topic. Let me exemplify the attitude of two of his followers regarding closure of scholarly discussion. While discussing the early kabbalistic view of prayer—one of the major and most intriguing issues at the initial stages of Kabbalah—Isaiah Tishby, the most important of Scholem's students, wrote in 1961, that "The teachings of the earlier Kabbalists concerning prayer and *kavvanah* have already been exposed in the studies of Gershom Scholem, and I shall do no more than summarize his conclusions and add a little more material."[11]

Similarly, in a discussion of the question of the origins of Kabbalah, one of the most crucial and complex topics in Kabbalah in general, Joseph Dan states that "Scholem has established both the fundamental facts and the principal structures, in whose framework the search for the solutions to questions left by Scholem unanswered, continues."[12]

No major progress in the domain of early Kabbalah was made between 1974—when the above statement by Scholem was made—and Dan's statement in 1982, quoted from his eulogy on the master. The emergence of such certainties regarding the stability to be expected in future studies, which were understood to be oriented by Scholem's approach and findings, is remarkable and illuminates the kind of scholarship employed by Scholem's immediate students. However, Dan's certainty is at odds with the fact that

tens of unknown kabbalistic manuscripts surface each and every year, or
with the fact that even those manuscripts dealt with briefly by Scholem in
the 1930s were not perused again by most of the scholars dealing with early
Kabbalah. As to Tishby's assumption that all that remained to be done
concerning the earliest Kabbalists' view of mystical prayer — a rather enig-
matic mystical practice — was to summarize Scholem's discussions, I can
only express my deep skepticism. There are still unpublished discussions in
manuscripts — two of them extant in Jerusalem — on the nature of mystical
prayer, authored by none other than R. Isaac Sagi Nahor, the so-called
"father of Kabbalah." A quick reading of them immediately suggests that
some of the questions posed in these early kabbalistic discussions were not
addressed even superficially in Scholem's treatments of the subject.[13] Sev-
enty years after Scholem had started his pioneering studies of Kabbalah,
opening this vast body of literature to scholarly scrutiny, his "school" remains interested more in the project of preserving Scholem's historical theories, than in going beyond them, or even criticizing them in a substantial
manner.

As I have stated, Scholem's scrutiny of the sources was based on certain
scholarly presuppositions that informed the selection, interpretation, emphasis on and arrangement of the wealth of kabbalistic material he studied. I
would like to examine here two major categories in Scholem's scholarship,
issues that define to a great extent the dynamics of Jewish mysticism during
most of its stages. Though the following inquiry will be mainly conceptual
and systemic, namely, dealing with the meanings and the roles played by
these two concepts in Scholem's scholarship of Kabbalah, it also has a semantic substratum: in the case of "Jewish Gnosticism" I shall try to show
that Scholem has stretched the concept that underlies this term beyond
reasonable boundaries, while the term "Messianism" was defined in a very
restricted way, as apocalypticism.

The two major catalysts for the dynamics of Jewish mysticism as envisioned by Scholem were gnosticism and messianism. In his estimation,
apparently they represent two different religious mentalities. The first is
concerned with the divine autogenesis and its crises and with redemption of
the individual; it is an escapist religiosity. The second focuses on the future
of the collective or of the community, a transformation of the society within

an eschatological history, replete with apocalyptic elements. Nevertheless, both were conceived of, either separately or together, as contributing to Jewish mystical concepts and energies that have played a dynamic role on the stage of Jewish history. I shall focus my analyses below on these major catalysts because they have influenced most important forms of modern Jewish historiography, visible far beyond the boundaries of the field of kabbalistic studies. Indeed, it would not be an exaggeration to describe Scholem's historiography based upon these two catalysts, as permeating crucial segments of the modern intellectual history of Judaism. This is a dominant paradigm, established by a prestigious scholar of Jewish mysticism; but it transcends this field, embracing scholars in other domains and affecting many of the leading surveys of Judaism.

Scholem portrayed gnosticism as the primary trigger for shaping the spiritual physiognomy of the Kabbalah, from its appearance as an historical force at the end of the 12th century, to the expulsion of the Jews from the Iberian Peninsula at the end of the 15th century, and reverberating even later on. In fact, he conceived of gnosticism as the major source of religious creativity.[14] Messianism plays a central role in Scholem's historical picture of Kabbalah in the 16th and 17th centuries alone.[15] Though substantially different from one another, these two major catalysts share a main feature: the coming to the fore in Jewish mysticism as a result of external influences or events imposed from outside. In the case of gnosticism (radically opposed to classical Judaism)[16] the influence is that of an alien type of thought. Messianism develops from the result of a huge historical upheaval, the expulsion of the Jews from the Iberian Peninsula, which provoked a profound discontinuity between the earlier forms of Kabbalah and the later ones. In both cases, ruptures in the inner development of Jewish mysticism were vital elements in Scholem's reading of the history of Kabbalah.[17] Yet Gnosticism and messianism are, however, much more than catalysts or triggers of certain types of mysticism. They became, according to Scholem, part and parcel of the texture of Kabbalah, even major components of the fabric or conceptual infrastructure of this type of mysticism. They have contributed decisive components to the religious mentality of the kabbalists. One may even ask what would remain from the Kabbalah as portrayed by Scholem and his school if these two elements would disappear? Are not these catalysts so strong that they do not leave sufficient room for a certain kind of mysticism that has its own *raison d'etre*?

The expulsion of 1492 brought together the already existing kabbalistic gnosticism with the allegedly non-kabbalistic messianism, more precisely, Jewish apocalypticism. The *hieros gamos* took place, according to Scholem's historiography, in Safed, especially in the mystical system of R. Isaac Luria Ashkenazi, and the main offspring was none other than Shabbetai Ṣevi's messianic movement. In other words, whereas the Spanish Kabbalah represents the silent growth of kabbalistic gnosticism, the post-expulsion history of this mystical lore represents not only a further expansion of the gnostic elements, but also their projection onto the historical scene as a powerful ideology. It is the acceptance of the importance of the two catalysts as central factors in the history and phenomenology of Kabbalah that defines Scholem's historical critical school.

SCHOLEM AND HIS SCHOOL ON GNOSTICISM

The thesis that gnosticism had influenced kabbalistic literature emerged already during the Renaissance, as part of an attempt by some authors to distance their views from the influence of Kabbalah, because of the stigma attached to them by their affinity to this lore.[18] Scholem, consciously or not,[19] adopted this thesis in the late 1920s,[20] though it is absent in his earliest writings.[21] He used the term "gnosticism" in two major contexts: in order to point to a religious phenomenon with which some phases of Jewish mysticism were in historical and literary contact and, in addition, in order to compare, phenomenologically, religious structures that can be summarized as mythocentric systems, which may have been historically independent. Let me consider the first usage, which is related to a double use of the phrase "Jewish gnosticism" in Scholem's writings.

It is possible to discern two major, and different, uses of the term "Jewish gnosticism" in Scholem's studies when related to historical filiation between kinds of religious literature:

(a) It is the collective name given by him to the *Hekhalot* literature: "The historian of religion is entitled to consider the mysticism of the Merkabah to be one of the Jewish branches of Gnosticism."[22] In this context, Jewish gnosticism is portrayed by Scholem as conservative and consonant with the Rabbinic tradition, a fact expressed by his coining the phrase "Rabbinic gnosis." His sense of gnosticism is related to the ideas, considered by Scholem as the "fundamental characteristics of Gnosticism,"[23] such as the ascent of the soul, the world of the *Merkavah* as pleromatic, and the revelation of esoteric knowledge. As to the origin of these ideas, Scholem admits that the Jewish apocalyptic writings "evidently form a plausible transition to both Jewish monotheistic Gnosticism and the heretical Gnosticism that tended toward dualism."[24] Elsewhere in his writings, we learn that Scholem envisioned this transition as the result of some "second century Jewish converts to Christianity . . . who apparently conveyed aspects of Merkabah mysticism to Christian Gnosticism."[25] Scholem's major assumption is not entirely clear. Is it that apocalyptic literature served as a common source for both Jewish and Christian forms of gnosticism, one monotheistic and conservative, the other radical and heterodox, or that theories closer to the *Hekhalot* thought, were more critical in establishing a plausible link between Hebrew mystical literature and gnostic writings? In this latter sense, Scholem approached the hypothetical history of a crucial concept in *Hekhalot* literature, *Yoṣer Bere'shit,* emphasizing that it is a "thoroughly monotheistic conception and completely lacks the heretical and antinomian character it assumed when the Creator God has been opposed to the true God."[26] At the same time, Scholem also spoke about "gnostic theosophy" in the context of *Hekhalot* thought.[27] Therefore, the two forms of gnosticism, the orthodox and the heterodox, stem, roughly speaking, from similar spiritual sources, though their subsequent developments were palpably different. Scholem emphasizes the fact that there are only a few references in the *Hekhalot* literature to gnostic myths, and indeed to myths in general.[28] If that is so, we may infer that besides the divergences between the two forms of gnosticism in matters of theology—monotheistic versus dualistic—there is also a difference in the way the two types of gnosticism express themselves: the former is utterly mythical while the other is less inclined to use myths as a central form of expression.

Historically speaking, Scholem regards the creative period of this type of Jewish gnosticism as being over already at the end of the 3rd century,[29] while the ecstatic practices of this literature evolved somewhat later.[30] This scheme of dating was connected to his view that during this period Rabbinism was in "sharp conflict with 2nd-century gnosticism."[31]

Scholem's systematic use of the phrase "Jewish gnosticism" for an ancient Jewish phenomenon has provoked strong critiques from such scholars of late antiquity as David Flusser,[32] Michel Tardieu,[33] Ioan P. Couliano[34] and, in a more veiled manner, Hans Jonas.[35] Scholem reacted only very tersely to these critiques,[36] maintaining that for him "it does not seem to matter greatly whether phenomena previously called gnostic are now designated as 'esoteric,' and I for one cannot see the use of the newly introduced distinctions (for example, gnosis — Gnosticism and the like)."

However, this cavalier reaction does not attenuate the claim that not every esoteric rite that intends to elevate the soul to the upper world is a gnostic phenomenon. In any case, the assertion that imprecise use of the term was accepted in the earlier decades of our century is not completely accurate. Among scholars of late antiquity, like H. Jonas, it was not acceptable — as we can learn from a survey of the definition of gnosticism written in the mid-1930s.[37]

What seems to me the important point, however, is the fact that the very broad definition of gnosticism and Jewish gnosticism that characterizes Scholem's discussions of the ancient Jewish mysticism, does not fit the way Scholem himself understood the nature of Jewish gnostic traditions that informed early Kabbalah.

(b) "Jewish gnosticism" also refers to those traditions that reached some of the 12th-century Jewish masters in Provence and Spain, who combined them with Neoplatonic ideas and thereby created Kabbalah: "The Kabbalah, in its historical significance, can be defined as the product of the interpenetration of Jewish Gnosticism and neoplatonism."[38] In Scholem's estimation, the "Gnostic tradition contained in the Bahir" is the main source for what he assumed was the Jewish gnostic and neoplatonic synthesis in Provence.[39]

When addressing the question of the emergence of Kabbalah, Scholem understood "Jewish gnosticism" as consisting of traditions that varied drastically from the conservative Rabbinic attitudes, and even as having strong antinomian components. Indeed, he attributed only a limited role to the *Hekhalot* literature in the group of sources that shaped the early Provençal Kabbalah. Furthermore, there can be no doubt that he had in mind other formative sources and traditions, which were probably transmitted in Hebrew and preserved for centuries before they encountered Neoplatonism in Europe. While the ascent of the *Merkavah* and the nature of this realm are the "gnostic" components of the ancient Jewish mystical literature, and its mythical part is negligible, the opposite seems to be the case regarding the traditions Scholem presumed in connection to the emergence of later Kabbalah. Here, the term "Jewish gnosticism" points to a strong mythical mentality, which emphasizes, at the same time, a complex theosophy. Therefore, there is only a limited overlapping between the concepts that inform the term "Jewish gnosticism" when it is used in the two different historical settings. This incongruity in Scholem's terminology has apparently passed unnoticed by the Scholem school, as far as I am acquainted with it, and it deserves a more detailed examination.

One of the basic assumptions of Scholem's phenomenology of Jewish mysticism is the gnostic nature of medieval Kabbalah. According to most of his statements, he envisioned the emergence of the medieval type of Jewish mysticism named Kabbalah to be the result of the vivification of rabbinic Judaism through gnostic traditions that stem from the Orient.[40] This gnostification of the thought of some segments of the Jewish elite was crucial for all the later developments of Kabbalah as understood by Scholem. The antinomian elements of this component of Kabbalah were to lead, in certain historical circumstances, to the explosion of halakhic, namely normative, Judaism. The dialectic of the normative on one hand, and the latent, sometimes explicit antinomian elements on the other, can be understood as the competition between two Jewish religious modalities. Finally, at the end of an important development in the history of Kabbalah — the supposed dissemination of Lurianic messianism[41] in the Sabbatean movement — the gnostic elements came to the fore and exploded the frame of normative Judaism.[42] According to Scholem, the gnostic elements found in Lurianic theosophy[43] are still evident in Hasidism, as his critique of Martin Buber convincingly shows.[44]

A process of gradual gnostification was conceived by Scholem as having a double importance. On the one hand, it contributed to a spiritual revival of static rabbinic Judaism and thus the deepened meaning of the rabbinic corpus of legends and commandments. On the other hand, as I have mentioned above, the gnostification caused an inner tension between the spiritualists, in this case the kabbalists, and the conservatives, in this case the halakhists. The dialectic of intensified spiritualization and the tensions provoked by such a process was one of the major postulates of Scholem's phenomenology of Jewish mysticism.[45]

Scholem assumed that the gnostic elements were active already at the very beginning of Kabbalah. He wrote that the "gnostic way of seeing things likewise penetrated their prayer mysticism,[46] without being able to overcome it entirely."[47] Thus, the emergence of the tension between the gnostic *mythologoumena* and rabbinic anti-mythic culture does not require any assumption of an inner, organic development in the bosom of Judaism but merely the surfacing of material already present in its ancient sources.[48]

It is worth repeating that gnosticism as a source of medieval Kabbalah was conceived by Scholem as a religious mentality, ultimately alien to and alienated from the "classical" biblical and rabbinic forms of Judaism. "Jewish gnosticism" — of foreign extraction, though probably sometimes influenced by some Jewish *mythologoumena*, and stemming from putative heretical Jewish circles — played the role of the catalyst of an allegedly hypertrophic rabbinism, entrenched in ritualism, by contributing mythical and theosophical traits to rabbinic thought.[49] In his authoritative *Major Trends,* Scholem indicated that "it was Gnosticism,[50] one of the last great manifestations of mythology in religious thought, and definitely conceived in struggle against Judaism[51] as the conqueror of mythology, which lent figures of speech to the Jewish mystic."[52]

In an even more suggestive, and in my opinion also representative, formulation Scholem declares "Foreign mythical worlds are at work in the great archetypal images of the Kabbalists even though they sprang from the depth of an authentic and productive Jewish religious feeling. Without this mythical contribution, the impulses of the Kabbalists would not take form. Gnosis, one of the last great manifestations of myth in religious thinking, conceived at least in part as a reaction against the Jewish conquerors of myth, gave the Jewish mystics their language."[53]

Fond of paradoxes, Scholem also envisioned this situation as a paradox that could hardly be exaggerated: he conceived of gnostic mythology as a religiosity "whose whole meaning and purpose of those ancient myths and metaphors, whose remainders the editors of the book of *Bahir,* and therefore the whole Kabbalah, inherited from Gnostics, was simply a subversion of a law which had, at one time, disturbed and broken the order of the mythical world."[54]

What precisely is anti-rabbinic in the early kabbalistic writings was, as far as I know, never discussed by Scholem. Furthermore, his vision of rabbinism is not always clear. Indulging in generic terminology — myth, rabbinism, gnosticism or law — Scholem's depiction of gnosticism as one of the main sources of Jewish mysticism (as we have seen above, Scholem mentions the whole of Kabbalah as influenced by gnosticism via the *Bahir!*), characterized most of the subsequent scholarship on Kabbalah. Though Scholem never devoted a detailed study to the precise nature of the gnostic influence, or to the channels through which it allegedly passed into medieval Kabbalah, and while he never discovered any *verbatim* quotations from gnostic sources in Kabbalistic texts — his views were widely accepted and repeated by modern scholars. Yet, one can question the precise meaning of Scholem's view regarding the historical or phenomenological relationship between historical gnosticism and medieval Kabbalah. In my opinion, his writings point to an influence of alien myths, described as being of gnostic origin, on the historical development of Kabbalah. However, one way to clarify Scholem's view on the subject would be to see how he was understood by his own school. After all, his students and colleagues had direct contact with the master, they have continued to elaborate upon his theories and they could, therefore, serve as faithful witnesses of his intentions, when they were not articulated clearly enough. With this in mind we turn to one of Scholem's main disciples, Isaiah Tishby, who described one of the key concepts of Kabbalah, the sefirotic theosophy, as follows:

> As far as the doctrine of the *sefirot* is concerned, *it can be established without a doubt* that there is some reflection here of a definite gnostic tendency, and that it did in fact emerge and develop from a *historico-literary contact with the remnants of Gnosis,* which were preserved over

a period of many generations in certain Jewish circles, until they found their way to early kabbalists, who were *deeply affected* by them both spiritually and intellectually.[55]

As we learn from this quotation, confidence in Scholem's theory was so great that the gnostic thesis was considered to be a proven fact, one that "deeply affected" Kabbalah. Indeed, Tishby tells us that "the growth of the *sefirot* doctrine from contact with the remnants of Gnosis was proved and analyzed at length by G. Scholem."[56] There is no hesitation here concerning a major assessment of an issue that "deeply affects" the very nature of the main form of Kabbalah.

The kabbalistic views on evil, another topic which may indeed be important but was certainly overemphasized in modern scholarship, were also deemed to be influenced by gnostic sources.[57] Scholem assumed that the kabbalistic views of the origin of evil derived from a zoroastrian source, and that they reached the medieval kabbalists through the mediation of gnostic sources.[58] Tishby, who wrote the main study of the kabbalistic doctrine of evil, formulates this view as follows:

> The theory that evil and the dark, "left-sided," forces were derived from a separate emanation, is an ancient one and it *certainly* stems from Iranian dualistic systems, and from there it came to the Gnostic movement. . . . It is clear that such a doctrine had necessarily changed its extreme dualistic nature when it penetrated into Jewish circles.[59]

The certainty regarding the Zoroastrian source in this quote is remarkable. In support of it there is nothing more than a similar statement of Scholem's which, to the best of my knowledge, is not corroborated by any textual, historical or philological analysis. Fifty years after these sweeping statements were formulated, not even one pertinent source has been discovered that substantiates these claims. I wonder why it was necessary to assume such an extreme dualism from the very beginning, only in order to determine that it was later on transformed in the Jewish milieu. A sounder historical and philological approach would be to look at the origins of the more moderate explanations of the sources of evil, as they are present in the kabbalistic sources, instead of speculating about such a complex, and com-

pletely unproven, Zoroastro-gnostic-kabbalistic nexus and its alleged modi-
fications.[60] Thus, I propose, following Tishby, to see Scholem's view of the
kabbalistic concepts of God and evil as stemming, at least to a considerable
degree, from historical gnostic sources, and the historical affinities between
medieval Kabbalah and the ancient sources as no more than a matter of
phenomenological resemblances.

Even more interesting is the picture of the emergence of Kabbalah. As
J. Dan has indicated, Scholem viewed the acceptance of the ancient gnostic
mythology in southern France and northern Spain as facilitated by the
"great impact of the Catharist religious insurrection."[61] This fascinating
explanation emerges from a few explicit statements in Scholem's vast opus[62]
and allows for the impact of the ancient gnostic theories on the emergence
of Kabbalah. In its medieval form, gnosticism as Catharism created a proper
spiritual background in Provence for the surfacing and acceptance of ancient gnostic themes in rather conservative circles of rabbinic Judaism. European Catharism became a real *preparatio evangelica* for the "eastern Juda-
ized gnostic sources." To summarize: both the kabbalistic theory of the
divine sefirotic realm and the kabbalistic conception of evil were informed,
according to the dominant view in modern Kabbalistic scholarship, by non-
Jewish gnostic sources. These inspired a later, rather elusive entity named
"Jewish gnosticism," which influenced the earliest kabbalistic texts, both
historically and literally.

There can be no doubt, however, that in addition to attributing a historical role to ancient gnosticism for the formation of the specific physiognomy
of Kabbalah, Scholem also believed that ancient gnosticism and Kabbalah
had phenomenological resemblances between them that stemmed from independent developments, and that resulted from similar directions motivated by an inner tendency to create myths.[63] However, even these independent developments are somehow related to the formative impact of the
gnostic *mythologoumena* that had penetrated the first stratum of kabbalistic
writings. In any case, the numerous phenomenological statements, which
do not suggest an historical filiation between Kabbalah and ancient gnosticism, do not detract from the more historical nexus that Scholem indeed
believed existed between gnosticism and Kabbalah. His relatively moderate
approach to the gnostic theory in his earlier years evolved, in his later

writings and in those of his followers, into a certainty regarding the real impact of gnostic themes. An interesting and attractive theory, speculative from both historical and philological points of view, had become canonical.

What is fascinating, however, is not only the gnostic paradigm itself as installed by Scholem in the guise of a conservative esotericism, but also the wide reception this paradigm has had in intellectual circles in our time. Conversely, it is instructive to note the almost total absence of more sceptical or openly critical attitudes toward such a speculative theory among scholars. Let me describe the type of phenomenology that has been so easily accepted: Kabbalah, deemed by the kabbalists as the most conservative form of Judaism, has been conceived by modern scholars as suffering from an alienation from classical rabbinism, because of its anti-rabbinic mode of religiosity. Invoking ancient anti-Jewish myths in order to solve the problem of Jewish survival is an academic *grand tour de force,* which may preoccupy the future sociology of knowledge. By downplaying the importance of the *Hekhalot* literature and the rabbinic material for the actual development of Kabbalah, Scholem has "opened" the gate of scholarly imagination by presuming the surfacing and the survival of gnosticism, a world that had vanished many centuries ago. A bizarre world has been resurrected in describing Kabbalah as a belated, and most viable, medieval reverberation of gnosticism.

Let us ponder now the sharp discrepancy between the two meanings of Scholem's "Jewish gnosticism." The old one was conservative and perhaps located at the core of the Jewish establishment, as Scholem put it. The other one, which reached Provence, was anarchic, potentially antinomian, attempting to take revenge for the alleged, primordial victory of rabbinism over myth, and therefore, was hardly a tradition at the core of Jewish culture. A long series of fascinating questions may be raised if we become aware of the complexity of the different concepts represented by Scholem's use of the same term. What, for instance, is the relationship between the conservative Jewish gnosticism and the mythical, rebellious one? Are they part of one line of tradition, which dramatically changed from conservative to radical just after the suppression of non-Jewish gnosticism by the Christian Church? Scholem has never addressed this question.

If no historical line links the two and if they are so substantially different from each other, what is the ultimate source of the rebellious "Jewish gnosticism" that reached the medieval kabbalists? Was it the result of the influence of anti-Jewish gnosticism on Jewish circles or of heretical Jewish groups that had existed in late antiquity? And why would the early kabbalists, who were rabbinic leaders, accept such traditions, which are, religiously speaking, so problematic? And if such anti-establishment views emerged in some marginal groups in late antiquity, how and why did such traditions move to the center in the Middle Ages in one of the most orthodox and creative Jewish circles? All these questions are still to be addressed critically by the Scholem school. Meanwhile, we hear innumerable repetitions of Scholem's views that have transformed an extremely hypothetical proposal into a "fact" that "was established without doubt," as Tishby asserted. Scholem designated his school as that of "historical criticism" but there is little history and even less criticism in the way the above hypothesis has been embraced and repeated.[64]

One last, basically semantic question: why use the same term "Jewish gnosticism" in order to refer to two different religious phenomena, one non-mythical and conservative and the other mythical and rebellious? Such a use seems to point to an inner need of Scholem's historiography: it ensures the presence of the gnostic elements throughout the entire history of Jewish mysticism, which has thereby become a "branch of gnosticism" either historically or phenomenologically. It may be that Scholem was not aware of the discrepancies between his visions of two different "Jewish gnosticisms," or again, that I have misunderstood him. However, if I am not misrepresenting him, there remains a profound problem of addressing different religious views by the same term.

The strong emphasis upon questions that were central for gnosticism become central for the understanding of Kabbalah as well. As seen above, the problems regarding the sources and the nature of evil, theosophy and esotericism are the great protagonists in the drama of modern scholarship on Jewish mysticism. The nature of the mystical experience or the different Jewish mystical techniques played only a secondary role in this form of scholarly endeavor. By gnostifying Jewish mysticism, modern scholars, to a great extent, have gnostified the agenda of Kabbalah scholarship.[65] This is one of the reasons for the exclusion of a major trend of Kabbalah from the phenomenological approach that has been perpetuated in Scholem's school: the ecstatic Kabbalah, which has nothing to do with historical gnosticism and its myths.[66]

SCHOLEM AND HIS SCHOOL ON MESSIANISM

Messianism has ancient Jewish roots. Long before the emergence of historical Kabbalah, it had become part and parcel of the rabbinic spiritual universe. Moreover, messianism was much more than an abstract idea; a whole range of messianic texts was composed in Hebrew, between the 7th and 9th centuries, in the wake of the great victories of the Muslims in the Orient and in North Africa, and they were added to the already existing rabbinic apocalyptic material.[67] These testify to the intensity of the messianic aspirations prevalent in some Jewish circles during that period, eschatological feelings which apparently were nourished by the hope that the Christian empire, or the Christian religion, was coming to an end. In the 11th and 12th centuries messianic tensions were felt in Jewish circles too, and continued well into the second half of the 13th century. Maimonides' attempts to regulate the intensive messianism of some of his contemporaries bears evidence to the dangers that some elitist circles felt the eschatological ferment might provoke.[68]

Nineteenth-century Jewish scholarship was much more interested in matters related to Jewish Kabbalah than to Jewish messianism. To a certain extent, it shared Maimonides' fears of apocalypticism. Some of the first scholars of the kabbalistic literature were even positively inclined to their subject-matter, as is evident in the cases of M. Landauer and A. Jellinek.[69] Yet, even they did not display a sympathetic attitude toward messianism. It seems that to a great degree they conceived the two spiritual phenomena as separate issues, which may overlap in some cases but cannot be essentially related to each other. Some of their contemporaries, like Heinrich Graetz and Moritz Steinschneider, did assume that a certain correlation exists but their attitude to both mysticism and messianism was negative.[70] Since the beginning of the 20th century, there have been three major approaches to understanding the possible affinities between them:

First, there is no important messianic element in Jewish mysticism, the latter being described without resorting to substantial discussions of messianism. This is the case in the writings of Martin Buber, S. A. Horodetzky, Hillel Zeitlin and Abraham Y. Heschel. In the studies of two major scholars of Kabbalah, Alexander Altmann and Georges Vajda, the messianic elements are only rarely discussed. In general, these scholars were concerned more with the speculative aspects of Kabbalah.

Second, there is no important need to refer to mystical thought in order to understand messianism. Scholars who devoted lengthy analyses to Jewish messianism did not address the problem of an essential link and they proceeded to describe messianism as a separate realm. Such an approach is evident in the writings of David Castelli, A. Posznanski, A. Z. Aescoli, Yehudah Even Shemuel and Abba H. Silver.

Third, it is Gershom Scholem's school that has examined in detail the relationship between Jewish mysticism and messianism, establishing significant affinities between the two phenomena. Following his lead Isaiah Tishby, Joseph Dan, Rivka Schatz, Yehuda Liebes, R. J. Zwi Werblowsky and I all have elaborated upon this messianic-kabbalistic link in a long series of studies. These affinities have become the focus of academic research in the last generation of scholars whose work established it as such in the leading center of Jewish studies, the Hebrew University in Jerusalem. No doubt this view represents a distinctly Israeli phenomenon, as it is clear from the affiliation of most of its major exponents. Scholem's descriptions of the relationship between messianism and Jewish mysticism assume the existence of three different phases, which are delineated in his historiography and phenomenology in a very distinct manner.[71]

In the first phase — namely between 1180 and 1492 — Kabbalah was assumed to be indifferent toward messianism. If the latter means speculations as to the nature of the eschaton, that is, strong apocalyptic aspirations and beliefs that the end is near, then the kabbalists during the first 300 years of its development, according to Scholem, had certainly turned their backs on such a preoccupation. They preferred instead to focus attention on the processes related to the emanational type of creation, or to the nature of theosophical processes; salvation was sought in the contemplative return of the individual to the beginning rather than by attempts to hasten the end.

In the second phase — after the expulsion from Spain — messianism gradually became part of the core of kabbalistic thought. This is portrayed as the result of the trauma of the brutal expulsion from the Iberian Peninsula.[72] There are three major stages of mystical messianism in this second phase:

1. Between the expulsion and the emergence of the Lurianic Kabbalah, namely 1492–1570. In this stage, there are, according to Scholem, two major types of relationship: either Kabbalah was still divorced from messianic thought though kabbalists were deeply involved in messianic propaganda,[73] or, in other discussions of Scholem, these two types of thought were described as having been combined though nothing original emerged from such a combination.[74] It is not so simple to decide which of these two views is the more representative of Scholem's thought.

2. Between 1570 and the emergence of Sabbateanism, around 1660. In this period Kabbalah, in its Lurianic version, absorbed messianic concerns as a pressing topic which became part and parcel of this kabbalistic system.[75] In other words, Kabbalah became imbued with eschatological issues, though the advent of the messianic figure himself is marginal for the Lurianic corpus. It is rather an implicit messianism, embodied in the kabbalistic concept of *Tikkun*,[76] and is unparalleled by anything similar in the previous versions of Kabbalah. By and large, kabbalistic messianism is based on the assumption that the cumulative efforts of the whole Jewish nation to mend or repair the primordial metaphysical catastrophe within the divine realm — by means of the performance of the commandments according to their kabbalistic intentions — are paramount for the advent of the redemption.

3. During the third and fourth decades of the 17th century, the Lurianic version of messianism was disseminated among the masses, and in turn fueled the Sabbatean and the Frankist movements, which constitute acute forms of messianism. During this stage, messianism was not only a kabbalistic and relatively esoteric form of mystical ideology or lore, but also a mass-movement that moved to the center of Jewish life all over the Jewish world. It is important to emphasize that Scholem stressed, time and again, the gnostic nature of some aspects of Sabbatean thought.[77] It is this religious phenomenon that embodied the convergence of the two catalysts we are discussing here.

In the third phase — the Hasidic brand of mysticism — messianism was neutralized due to fears of the deleterious consequences of the messianic outburst in Sabbateanism and Frankism. In its place, according to Scholem, a new form of eschatology emerged: a quest for individual redemption, which was nonexistent in Judaism before the middle of the 18th century.[78] The major move in Hasidism is, therefore, the replacement of the Lurianic *Tikkun* fraught as it is, according to Scholem, with messianic cargo, by the concept of *devequt,* which lacked any messianic connotation.[79]

These three phases of changing relations between mysticism and messianism may be classified as indifference (sometimes meaning also neutralization), synthesis, and neutralization. Each phase, according to Scholem's historiography, is well-defined in chronological terms and in the instance of the last two cases, the particular relations between messianism and mysticism were conditioned by specific historical events. For Scholem, to the extent that messianism penetrated Jewish mysticism, it was part of the need to respond to the challenges of history, but not so much the result of the inner development of either Kabbalah or messianism.

The messianic concepts in Judaism in general, and in Kabbalah in particular, interested Scholem deeply. The visible testimonies of this long-standing concern are the essays on messianism, which constitute a book, and his monumental *Sabbatai Sevi.* Although messianism was much more important for Scholem's overall vision of the history of Jewish mysticism, and for Jewish history in general (understood as the concatenation of important public events), gnosticism was nevertheless more important for his phenomenology of almost all the important stages of this mystical lore.[80]

The problem with Scholem's discussion of the evasive Jewish gnosticism is the difficulty inherent in proving an historical filiation between ancient subversive ideas and medieval ones, especially in light of the vagueness that is so characteristic of Scholem's use of the term gnosticism in referring to a religious phenomenon. In the case of messianism, the problem is quite different: the relation between these two constituents of Jewish religion, Kabbalah and messianism, is very simple. However, Scholem has chosen to restrict the meaning of messianism to too narrow a concept — that of apocalypticism — neglecting the other, non-apocalyptic forms of messianism.[81] The attempt to restrict the impact of this apocalyptic messianism on Kabbalah to the post-expulsion period led to the neglect of crucial messianic elements in early Kabbalah: Abraham Abulafia's Kabbalah, which was written by someone who conceived himself to be a messianic figure and which has contributed to a spiritual version of messianism,[82] on the one hand, and of some important aspects of the Zoharic messianic thought, on the other.[83] Therefore, while gnosticism — even if we use the term in a pure phenomenological sense — permeates, according to Scholem's historiography, almost the entire spectrum of Jewish mysticism, the gamut of messianic concepts was drastically reduced to only one of its manifestations, apocalypticism, active in Kabbalah only for a limited period in time, namely between the 16th and the 18th centuries.

A COMPARISON BETWEEN THE TWO CATALYSTS

Let me compare the dynamics of the influence of the two catalysts. It seems that a common assumption informs the way Scholem portrayed both of them: at the beginning, both Jewish gnosticism and messianism coexisted peacefully with other elements of Jewish mysticism. However, at a certain moment, both became explosive factors that changed the course of the developments of this mystical lore. Early Kabbalah absorbed the gnostic *mythologoumena* that eventually exploded into an elaborate antinomian articulation, while messianism, especially in its apocalyptic form, entered Kabbalah only later, after the expulsion, and created the climate for the Sabbatean movement. Thus a two-phase development is identifiable in both Jewish gnosticism and messianism: a more moderate version of a phenomenon first appeared, which later became a more subversive factor. According to Scholem, both catalysts marked crucial turning points in the history of Jewish mysticism. But what exactly are the possible implications of the role of these catalysts at the turning points in the history of Jewish mysticism?

One conclusion may be that the inner logic of Jewish mystical texts was not conceived of, in Scholem's eyes, as sufficient for properly understanding the dynamics of the mystical material he was exploring. The external elements have provided the clues for the fateful departures from extant types of mystical thought. Therefore, Kabbalah research developed much more in the direction of attempting to determine the dominant external conditions that shaped the tradition than in clarifying the inner consistency of the various developments of this mystical system.

A second conclusion may be that the non-conformist nature of these catalysts is obvious and very striking. It is precisely that subversive facet, the aspect that does not accord with the rabbinic conservative mind, that changes the course of Jewish history. Scholem always presented these vitalistic elements in a positive light, while he considered the conservative factors as inertial and hypertrophic. He portrayed the rabbinic establishment as repressive, stating that there was a tendency of classical Judaism "to liquidate myth as a central spiritual power."[84] Elsewhere, he conceives of the Hasidic "neutralization" of Sabbatean messianism as an abdication of the realm of messianism, or, again as a liquidation of the historical force that was based upon the "sense of imminent catastrophe."[85]

This repressive conception concerning both the early and the later attitudes in Judaism towards vitalistic elements is a leitmotif of Scholem's lifetime project, begun as an attempt to discern the forces that allowed for the continuation of the Jewish nation.[86] Scholem chose to stress the paramount importance of the subversive and the catastrophic,[87] neglecting a careful inspection of the spirituality of the conservative forces which, in my opinion, can easily be detected in texts. Though he admitted from time to time that this issue too should be investigated,[88] he never embarked on such a project himself.[89]

However, we should not forget that the conservative elements in Jewish religion have survived independent of these subversive catalysts, a fact of paramount relevance for Scholem's project of explaining the survival of Judaism. The more vital forms of Judaism in later generations were far removed from the two forms of Kabbalah, gnostic or messianic. This is a crucial fact that conspicuously demonstrates a more modest role played by these factors in sustaining the spiritual life of the Jews than what Scholem assumed. Whether he was correct in emphasizing the centrality of the antinomian factors and disruptive events of the 17th century for the emergence of some modern forms of Judaism like Enlightenment, Hasidism and reform is still an open question.[90] Yet, it is important to mention that subversive catalysts tend to create centrifugal tendencies, and that the emphasis on them as positively creative is part of a certain axiology which prefers one type of religiosity over another. An intensive search for the antinomian and the catastrophical permeates important segments of the Scholemian school, as R. J. Zwi Werblowsky has already noticed.[91] In fact, despite his search for the vital forms of religiosity that sustained Jewish life throughout centuries, Scholem focused his research, to a great extent, upon the crises that endangered Judaism as potential catalysts of changes.[92]

In order to understand better the complex dynamism of a certain religiosity, it would be better to strike another balance between the centrifugal and centripetal elements; the same is true of Jewish mysticism. Especially interesting would be an effort, still requiring detailed analysis, to discuss the kabbalistic antinomianism as partly the result of an inner development — one based on the logic of the kabbalistic symbolic systems[93] — rather than as the importation of ancient tensions into a medieval mystical discipline. After all, non-conformist ideas can emerge without any external influence, as the effect of certain inner spiritual processes. Moreover, a "heresy" like that of David of Dinant, for example, can be motivated by philosophy. In any case, the many, variegated heretical movements in Christian Europe testify that we should not merely invoke Bogomilism or Catharism in order to explain their emergence and their various developments. When taking a closer look at Judaism, it is easy to determine that the spiritualistic approach of Bahya ibn Paquda or the eccentric anomian theories of Abraham Abulafia have nothing to do with gnosticism, either historically or phenomenologically. Indeed, their radical religious views are nourished, respectively, by Sufi and medieval philosophical views. Therefore, I see no reason to resolve the very few instances where it is possible to detect some tensions between different, or opposing views in Judaism by recourse to the thesis of a formative influence of an ancient, vitalistic and militant gnosticism.

Were the gnostic elements responsible for the tensions created by Kabbalah, they would appear at the emergence of this historical phenomenon and not later. Scholem's historiography does leave the impression — one that seems to me generally correct — that the later stages of Kabbalah were much more critical *vis à vis* the more traditional form of Judaism than the earlier ones. However, I am not aware of an additional claim in Scholem's writings, namely that earlier stages of Kabbalah reflect tensions between the alien and the traditional elements. Indeed, those tensions have appeared only during the relatively later phases of the evolution of Kabbalah and, in my opinion, as the result of mainly, though not exclusively, inner developments which explicated — (in rather unexpected ways) some assumptions inherent in earlier texts and forms of symbolism.

CONCLUSION

Scholem's heavy reliance upon ruptures and discontinuities when dealing with the development of medieval forms of Jewish mysticism is highly interesting. At least in so far as the penetration of messianism in Kabbalah is concerned, it assumes, implicitly, that the course of Jewish mysticism reflects that of Jewish history.[94] Confronted by conspicuous cases of ruptures in their social and economic life, the Jews had to rebuild their communities time and again in new circumstances. This rebuilding consisted not only in a need to move from one geographical area to another, but also in more radical changes like the necessity to adjust their religious *modus vivendi* to entirely new problems. Living in northern Europe is very different from living in Southern Europe with respect to the customs that Jews observed. To mention here only one example: the late occurrence of Sabbath in Northern Europe required other arrangements and details of behavior in comparison with the South. Thus, the Ashkenazi customs often differed from the Sephardi ones.[95]

But a heavy reliance on the Jewish historical context for interpreting the nature and the processes related to Jewish mysticism is misleading, for a few important reasons. Certainly, the ability for change is vital in order to be able to adjust to a new environment, and no doubt the Jews have changed, both in terms of their behavior and in the content of their thought, be it halakhic, philosophical or mystical.[96] However, such a study should not ignore continuities of thought and praxis.[97] After all, what has unified the disparate Jewish communities was mainly their common cultural heritage, which not only preserved the spiritual specificity of a certain community in a different religious and cultural environment, but also safeguarded a degree of unity between all remote communities. No less characteristic of Judaism than its cosmopolitanism is its conservatism, considered as another, complementary and basic feature of Jewish culture. If their relative openness has facilitated the adjustment of some Jews to new environments, conservatism has enabled them to maintain and elaborate upon their peculiar culture. Evidently, the detection of external influences is a major avenue to approaching the historical development of Jewish culture. Yet, the general assumption of alien influences does not always answer questions about the peculiar nature of the culture that has absorbed them, or precisely how these influences have been adopted and adapted, or why they were adopted at all, and finally about what happened to this culture after so many cultural changes.

Moreover, there is no need to assume that all the forms of a certain type of thought, in our case Kabbalah, necessarily or even dramatically changed. In order to understand change we need to understand some stable elements beyond change; otherwise we remain with disjointed members of an organism that lacks inner cohesion. In the case of Kabbalah, there are sufficient reasons to assume that it is a more conservative kind of mysticism, in comparison to the other monotheistic types of mysticism. The Jewish mystics were, roughly speaking, a learned group, some of them outstanding polymaths. This seems to be obvious in the case of persons like Abraham ben David, Naḥmanides, Shelomo ibn Adret, Joseph Karo, the Gaon of Vilna, or Isaac Yehudah Safrin of Komarno. Their deep immersion in classical Jewish texts involves not only a profound erudition in very broad areas of Jewish literature — biblical, halakhic and midrashic writings — but also the necessity to study in depth and, from time to time, even to comment extensively upon the canonical texts of Jewish mysticism: *Sefer Yeṣirah,* the book of *Bahir* or the Zoharic literature. More than Christian and Muslim mysticism, Kabbalah was informed by a scholastic approach to mystical sources. Moreover, it was an intertextual type of literature, attempting to resolve the divergences, the conceptual discrepancies and the tensions between different layers of Jewish religious writings and even between the various types of kabbalistic thought.

Nevertheless, even when questioning the overemphasis on the discontinuity — so evident in Scholem's history of Kabbalah — one should not negate the obvious and unquestionable fact that culture in general, and in our case Kabbalah, changes, sometimes very dramatically. It is, however, preferable to evaluate change in a careful way, after considering persuasive evidence, without relying on impressionistic speculations,[98] fascinating as they may be in themselves, but repeated unthinkingly. There can be no dispute as to the importance of Neoplatonic,[99] Aristotelian,[100] Sufi,[101] Christian,[102] Hermetic[103] or other demonstrably influential types of thought,[104] on the various stages of Jewish mysticism and on messianism as well.[105] This multiplicity and variety of the sources and of Jewish spirituality should never be reduced arbitrarily by scholars to two main, subversive catalysts,[106] messianism and gnosticism alone. Forces of continuity and conservatism must be carefully calibrated with those of radical rupture and discontinuity before a fuller and more balanced understanding of the history and phenomenology of Kabbalah can be achieved.

NOTES

A short version of this paper was originally delivered as a lecture in 1992 at a conference organized by Einstein Forum in Berlin. It appears in a German translation in *Gershom Scholem: Zwischen den Disziplinen*, ed. Peter Schäfer and Gary Smith (Frankfurt am Main: Suhrkamp, 1995), 80–121.

1. Gershom Scholem, *Kabbalah* (Jerusalem, 1974), 203.

2. Ibid.

3. Ibid.

4. *The Correspondence of Walter Benjamin and Gershom Scholem, 1932–1940*, ed. Gershom Scholem, trans. G. Smith and Andre Lefevere (New York, 1989), 261.

5. *Correspondence*, 263.

6. See his "Symbolism and Transcendence: On Some Philosophical Aspects of Gershom Scholem's Opus," *Review of Metaphysics* 31 (1977–78), 604–614.

7. See, for example, the exchange between him and Yehuda Liebes in *Peʿamim* 52 (1992), 140–144 (Hebrew).

8. *From Berlin to Jerusalem: Memories of My Youth,* trans. Harry Zohn (New York, 1988), 131.

9. See Y. Baer, "The Theory of the Natural Equality of Early Man according to Ashkenazi Hasidism," *Zion* 32 (1967), 129 (Hebrew). See also Moshe Idel, *Kabbalah: New Perspectives* (New Haven, 1988), 11–13.

10. I have dealt with Scholem and Jewish history in several studies, most recently in "Mystique juive et histoire juive," *Annales: Economies, Societés, Civilisations* 49 (1994), 1223–1240.

11. *The Wisdom of the Zohar,* trans. David Goldstein (Oxford, 1989), 3: 946.

12. Yosef Dan, "The Historical Perception of the Late Professor Gershom Scholem," *Zion* 47 (1982), 167 (Hebrew). See also below, note 19.

13. See, for example, M. Idel, "On the Mystical Intention during the Eighteen Benedictions according to R. Isaac Sagi-Nahor," in *Ephraim Gottlieb Memory Volume,* ed. A. Goldreich and M. Oron (Tel Aviv, 1993), 25–52.

14. See Harold Bloom's introduction to Scholem's *From Berlin to Jerusalem* (New York, 1988), xx. See also p. xxi: "[Scholem] longed for a wholly Gnostic Kabbalah, and indeed for a Gnostic Judaism, though he was wary of expressing this desire too overtly." See below my discussion of the fact that Scholem assumed that almost all the important stages of Jewish mysticism have gnostic elements. See also below, note 65.

For analyses of Scholem's view of gnosticism see David Biale, *Gershom Scholem, Kabbalah and Counter-History* (Cambridge, Mass., 1979), 113, 128–133, 137–143, and his article on Scholem in Mircea Eliade, *Encyclopaedia of Religion* (1987), 13: 119–120, especially his statement that "Scholem identified the central myth of Kabbalah as Gnostic." See also Joseph Dan, *Gershom Scholem, The Mystical Dimension of Jewish History* (New York, 1987), 41–44.

15. See below, "Scholem and His School on Messianism."

16. See the text quoted in note 54.

17. See Bloom (above, note 14), xx and Marcus' essay (below, note 94).

18. See Moshe Idel, *Kabbalah: New Perspectives* (New Haven, 1988), 2–6; Gedaliahu G. Stroumsa, "Gnosis and Judaism in Nineteenth Century Christian Thought," *Journal of Jewish Thought and Philosophy* 2 (1992), 45–62; Daniel Abrams, *The Book Bahir, An Edition Based on the Earliest Manuscripts* (Los Angeles, 1994), 4–7.

Recently, Joseph Dan has made the claim that there is no significant relation between ancient gnosticism and Kabbalah, but postponed his detailed exposition for a later article. See his "Jewish Gnosticism?" *Jewish Studies Quarterly* 2 (1995),

309–328. Characteristically enough, he prefers to ignore studies written on the issue by others, some of them mentioned above in this note (see also below, note 43), and to mention his own former position adopted from Scholem. See also below, note 36. For a critique of Scholem's view of gnosticism and of Dan's description of Scholem, sometimes also along the lines delineated in some of my former studies, see now Nathaniel Deutsch, *The Gnostic Imagination, Gnosticism, Mandaeism, and Merkabah Mysticism* (Leiden, 1995).

19. See Scholem, *Kabbalah,* 202; for Nahman Krochmal's view of gnosticism and Kabbalah, and its possible impact on Scholem, see Biale, *Gershom Scholem,* 134.

20. It may be important to mention that in the same period some articles of Alexander Altmann attempted to show the influences of gnostic *mythologoumena* on midrashic literature; see, for example, his "Gnostic Themes in Rabbinic Cosmology," in *Essays Presented to J. H. Hertz* (London, 1942), 28–32; idem, *The Meaning of Jewish Existence: Theological Essays 1930–1939,* ed. Alfred Ivry (Hanover, 1992), 117–132, and see P. Mendes-Flohr's introduction, where he portrays the existential background of this concern with gnostic religiosity in the middle of the 1930s; *ibid.*, xlv–xlvii.

21. See Biale, *Gershom Scholem,* 133.

22. Gershom Scholem, *Origins of the Kabbalah,* trans. A. Arkush, ed. R. J. Zwi Werblowsky (Princeton, 1987), 21. See also Scholem, *Jewish Gnosticism, Merkabah Mysticism, and Talmudic Tradition* (New York, 1960), 10: "The texts of Merkabah mysticism that have so far come to our knowledge also display what I have called an orthodox Jewish tendency, and are in no way heretical. . . . If what these texts present is Gnosticism — and their essentially Gnostic character cannot in my opinion be disputed — it is truly rabbinic Gnosis. . . . Indeed all these texts go to great lengths to stress their strict conformity, even in the most minute detail, to halakhic Judaism and its prescriptions." If the term "Jewish Gnosticism" was used in order to describe a Jewish form of the larger phenomenon of gnosticism, why did Scholem use the two phrases, "Merkavah mysticism" and "Jewish Gnosticism," in the title of the same book? Do they point to distinct religious orientations or different types of literature, or to two distinct branches of one phenomenon? I was unable to find any clarification for the occurrence of these two phrases together. This fact seems to be an interesting example of the special concern of Scholem to point to the gnostic nature of this early form of Jewish mysticism. See, especially, his *Jewish Gnosticism,* 83, where he speaks about the need of a "proper insight into Merkabah mysticism and Jewish Gnosticism."

23. *Origins of the Kabbalah,* 22; idem, *Major Trends in Jewish Mysticism* (New York, 1967) 48; idem, *'Od Davar, Explications and Implications* (Tel Aviv, 1989) 2:181 (Hebrew).

24. *Origins of the Kabbalah,* 22. The phrase "monotheistic gnosticism" appears already in *Major Trends,* 48; see also his *Kabbalah,* 22.

25. *Kabbalah,* 376.

26. *Origins of the Kabbalah,* 22. See also his *Major Trends,* 64; *On the Kabbalah and its Symbolism* (New York, 1973), 107; and *Jewish Gnosticism,* 2–3. Scholem indeed adduced an additional thesis, in the name of M. Friedlander (see *Jewish Gnosticism,* 3; *Kabbalah,* 22.), to the effect that there were Jewish heretical sects, which might have been the source of some of the gnostic ideas, but I wonder to what extent it represents his own primary view on the subject. See, however, *ibid.,* 21 where Scholem asserts that the "semi-mythological speculations of the Gnostics which regarded the qualities as 'aeons' were not admitted into the rabbinic tradition of the Talmud or the Midrashim, but they find a place in the more or less heterodox sects of the *minim* or *ḥizzonim.*" Therefore, the gnostic influence on the Jewish circles was reduced to heterodox sects, which accepted, rather than generated, the mythological *theologoumena.* In his essay on "Judaism and Gnosticism" Scholem speaks about two forms of ancient Jewish gnosticism: one orthodox and the other heretical, Samaritan; See Scholem, *'Od Davar,* 176–178. See Dan, *Gershom Scholem,* 46, to the effect that Scholem presupposed the existence of Jewish heterodox sects as the origin of some material that reached the gnostics. On this point, namely the possible existence of Jewish *mythologoumena* that informed also the *Hekhalot* literature, I am in complete agreement with Scholem; I differ from his view insofar as the origins of Kabbalah are considered, as he saw them in antinomian circles.

27. *Origins of the Kabbalah,* 23.

28. *Ibid.,* 21. See, however, *Major Trends,* 73.

29. *Origins of the Kabbalah,* 23.

30. *Major Trends,* 51. See, however, his own comments in *Origins of the Kabbalah,* 248. And compare, Idel, *Kabbalah: New Perspectives,* 320 n. 112.

31. Scholem, *On the Mystical Shape of the Godhead* (New York, 1991), 148.

32. David Flusser; "Scholem's recent book on Merkabah Literature," *Journal of Jewish Studies* 11 (1960), 59–68.

33. M. Tardieu and J. D. Dubois, *Introduction à la littérature gnostique* (Paris, 1986), 33.

34. Ioan P. Couliano, *The Tree of Gnosis,* (San Francisco, 1992), 42–43.

35. Hans Jonas, "Response to G. Quispel's 'Gnosticism and the New Testa-

ment,'" in *The Bible in Modern Scholarship,* ed. J. Philip (Nashville, 1965), 279–293.

36. See *Origins of the Kabbalah,* 21 n. 24; *'Od Davar,* 181. See also Scholem's *Jewish Gnosticism,* 1–2, and Dan's attempt to defend Scholem's use of the term in *Gershom Scholem,* 42–46; there, Dan mentions some unnamed Christians scholars who assume that the source of gnosticism "as a whole" is in Judaism (45)!

37. See R. P. Casey, "The Study of Gnosticism," *Journal of Theological Studies* (1935), 45–60.

38. *Kabbalah,* 45, 98.

39. *Ibid.* 45, 315. See also *Origins of the Kabbalah,* 46–48, and especially 48 where Scholem describes the difference between the earlier *Hekhalot* concepts, which were well-known to Yehudah Barceloni, and the earlier, medieval Kabbalah, as the result of the "reappearance, in the heart of Judaism, of the Gnostic tradition." Therefore, the ancient Jewish esoteric sources that constitute the ancient "Jewish Gnosticism" are conceived now as not gnostic, or at least not gnostic enough in comparison to the Jewish gnosticism that informs the medieval Kabbalah. This could have been a compelling instance where Scholem needed to clarify the differences between the two forms of Jewish gnosticism, but instead he preferred simply not to use the phrase "Jewish gnosticism" here for the *Hekhalot* texts, though elsewhere he used the phrase "Merkabah gnosis" (*Origins of the Kabbalah,* 23, 24.)! Earlier in the same work, we face an inverse, though nevertheless similar, situation: Scholem writes that "the forms of Jewish mysticism that appeared in the Middle Ages from around 1200 onward under the name 'Kabbalah' are so different from any earlier forms, and in particular from Jewish gnosis of Merkavah mysticism and German Hasidism of the twelfth and thirteenth centuries, that a direct transition from one form to the other is scarcely conceivable" (6–7).

An issue of importance in the first quote is the idea of the "reappearance." According to this term, the gnostic tradition was on the margin of Judaism, and moved to its center in Provence. However, what is also implied is the fact that these traditions were, at one time, at the center. Unfortunately, this crucial point was not elaborated by Scholem.

40. See M. Idel, "Rabbinism versus Kabbalism: On G. Scholem's Phenomenology of Judaism," *Modern Judaism* 11 (1991), 281–296.

41. On this issue see Scholem, *Sabbatai Ṣevi: The Mystical Messiah, 1626–1676,* trans. R.J. Zwi Werblowsky (Princeton, 1973), 7–8, 24–68 and note 62 below, and M. Idel, "'One from a Town, Two from a Clan' — The Diffusion of Lurianic Kabbala and Sabbateanism: A Re-Examination," *Pe'amim* 44 (1990), 5–30 (Hebrew). English version in *Jewish History* 7. 2 (1993), 79–104.

42. Scholem, *Sabbati Sevi,* 311–312.

43. On the gnostic aspect of Lurianism see Scholem, *Major Trends,* 276–277; Isaiah Tishby, "Gnostic Doctrines in Sixteenth Century Jewish Mysticism," *Journal of Jewish Studies* 6 (1955), 146: "The gnostic character of the main trend of the medieval Jewish mysticism known as Kabbalah, is now a well known and well established fact, thanks to the researches of Prof. Scholem." For a critique of Scholem's attempt to find in Lurianism parallels to ancient gnostic motifs see the important article by Charles Mopsik and Eric Smilevitch, "Observations sur l'oeuvre de Gershom Scholem," *Pardes* 1 (1985), 38.

44. *The Messianic Idea in Judaism,* (New York, 1971) 240–241.

45. *On the Kabbalah,* 12–13.

46. Scholem is referring here to the first kabbalists, Ya 'aqov ha-Nazir and Abraham ben David.

47. *Origins of the Kabbalah,* 247; see also *Kabbalah,* 98, but compare what he has written in *Origins of the Kabbalah,* 248.

48. See Scholem, *On the Kabbalah,* 120; see also 97–98, where Scholem writes: "Apart from certain basic features whose importance I do not wish to minimize, the gnosis of the Kabbalah developed independently from within. There is no need to choose between a historical and a psychological explanation of the origin of the Kabbalah; both elements played a part." Therefore, there are "basic features" of importance that are the result of historical influence, which may have been the origin of the tensions between early Kabbalah and the traditional Jewish sources. See also below, notes 53 and 67. Unfortunately, Scholem did not explicate in detail the nature of these tensions and he took it for granted that a mythical form of thought cannot be grafted successfully onto rabbinic literature. Indeed, in gnosticism there is a dominant preference for myths but a reticence towards rituals, though they are still mentioned from time to time. See J. M. Sevrin, "Les rites et la gnose, d'après quelques textes gnostiques coptes," in *Gnosticisme et monde hellenistique* (Louvain-la-Neuve, 1982), 440–450. The only scholar who paid attention to the possible tension between ancient and medieval forms of "Jewish mysticism" as used by Scholem is Harold Bloom, whose solution differs from that proposed here. See his introduction to *Gershom Scholem,* ed. H. Bloom (New York, 1987), 4–5.

49. See Idel, "Rabbinism versus Kabbalism," 281–296.

50. In this context it is obvious that gnosticism is not merely mythology, but a very specific branch of mythical thought, in contact with but nevertheless opposing Judaism.

51. On the struggle between Judaism and gnosticism see below, note 54.

52. *Major Trends,* 39.

53. *On the Kabbalah,* 98. It seems obvious that Scholem considered historical gnosticism, and not only the phenomenological parallelism, as significant for the emergence of the early Kabbalah. See above, note 48. In fact, this can be easily shown even by a superficial inspection of the sources adduced by Scholem when discussing the origin of Kabbalah; they are, in the great majority of the cases, brought from the gnostic literature, while ignoring other forms of ancient esoteric literature that have some conceptual parallels to gnosticism. For example, Philo's writings, or the *Chaldean Oracles* — which were analyzed in such a brilliant manner by Hans Lewy, Scholem's distinguished colleague in Jerusalem — never appear in Scholem's writings as a possible important source for Kabbalah. It should be mentioned that the introduction of the alien elements into Jewish mysticism, as expressed in this quote, uses an explicit Jungian phrase: "archetypal images." See also *On the Kabbalah,* 101. Compare, however, J. Dan's assumption that despite the frequent presence of Scholem at Ascona, he was not influenced by Jungian thought; see his forword to *On the Mystical Shape of the Godhead,* 7. See also Scholem, *Major Trends,* 228.

54. *Major Trends,* 35. Elsewhere, Scholem defines Gnosticism as "metaphysical anti-Semitism"; see *The Messianic Idea in Judaism,* 104. According to Bloom, Scholem later on retreated from this negative evaluation of Gnosticism; see Bloom, intro. to Scholem *From Berlin to Jerusalem,* xi.

55. Tishby, *Wisdom of the Zohar* 1:236. Emphasis added.

56. *Ibid.,* 1:252 n. 17. Unfortunately, in those of Scholem's studies with which I am acquainted, there is no lengthy analysis of this issue, only some remarks.

57. The fascination of modern scholarship of Kabbalah with the problem of evil and its role in Jewish mysticism is worthy of separate analysis; it may betray the fascination with evil that is characteristic of the gnostics themselves. See, for example, Scholem, *On the Kabbalah,* 98–100; *Kabbalah,* 122–128, and Tishby, *Wisdom of the Zohar;* see also below, notes 59 and 60.

58. See Gershom Scholem, *Kabbalot R. Ya'aqov ve-Yiṣḥaq ha-Kohen* (Jerusalem, 1927) 31 (Hebrew).

59. *The Doctrine of Evil and the "Kelippah" in Lurianic Kabbalism* (Jerusalem, 1942), 16 (Hebrew). See also Tishby, "Gnostic Doctrines," *JJS* 6 (1955), 146, where he argues that "the gnostic character of the main trends of the medieval Jewish mysticism, known as Kabbalah, is now a well-known and well-established fact. . . . These systems exhibit gnostic traits in the whole field of theology: in their doctrines of God, creation, evil, man, salvation, and redemption. They amount, in fact, to a gnostic transformation of Judaism."

I would like to point out the similarity between the conception of medieval Kabbalah as derived from ancient gnostic forms of thought, and Jung's view of alchemy as the medieval inheritor of ancient gnosticism. In both cases the vitality of gnostic religiosity is taken for granted and the efforts of scholars are directed toward the discovery of the impact of ancient lore in the Middle Ages. See Carl G. Jung's statement that "the possibility of a comparison with alchemy, and the uninterrupted intellectual chain back to gnosticism, gave substance to my psychology," in *Memories, Dreams, Reflections,* ed. Aniela Jaffe, trans. R. and C. Winston (New York, 1965), 205. In both cases, gnosticism served as the source of a vitality that underwent a strong metamorphosis, becoming either alchemy or Kabbalah; symbolic hermeneutics are crucial for the retrieval of the meanings inherent in these latter reverberations. Interestingly enough, Jung was described by several thinkers as a modern gnostic: see Maurice Friedman, *To Deny Our Nothingness* (New York, 1967), Chapter 9 and the references collected by Robert A. Segal, in *The Poimandres as Myth: Scholarly Theory and Gnostic Meaning* (Berlin, 1986), 149–150 n. 37. Compare below, note 65.

60. See M. Idel, "The Evil Thought of the Deity," *Tarbiz* 49 (1980), 356–364 (Hebrew). In this article I attempted to point out the possibility that not the gnostic, but the Zurvanic view of the origin of evil, has influenced Kabbalah.

61. J. Dan, *The Mystical Dimension of Jewish History,* 136.

62. See Scholem, *Kabbalah,* 45, 345.

63. *On the Kabbalah,* 97–98.

64. *Kabbalah,* 203.

65. See Harold Bloom's characterization of Scholem as a "Gnostic Jew" in *Gershom Scholem,* ed. Harold Bloom, 216 and see above, note 59. Especially interesting is Bloom's comment that Scholem's "Kabbalah was Gnostic and not Neoplatonic." See also the view of Scholem that both gnosticism and Platonism are of Jewish extraction, as told by Scholem to Bloom, *ibid.*, 216.

66. See my "The Contribution of Abraham Abulafia's Kabbalah for the Understanding of Jewish Mysticism," in *Gershom Scholem's Major Trends in Jewish Mysticism, 50 Years After* ed. P. Schaefer and J. Dan (Tuebingen, 1993), 117–143.

67. Though Scholem considered apocalypticism as "not a foreign element" to halakhah, he nevertheless regarded it "as a kind of anarchic breeze." See *The Messianic Idea,* 21, and 19–20; it is interesting to note that Scholem envisioned Jewish apocalypticism as having some "inherent mythology" (*ibid.*, 20), thereby creating an intrinsic affinity between the main feature of gnosticism as mythical, on the one hand, and apocalypticism on the other; see the analysis of Biale, *Gershom Scholem,* 153–154.

68. See Biale, *Gershom Scholem,* 148–152; on Maimonides' eschatology, including a critique of Scholem's understanding of Maimonides' thought on this issue see Aviezer Ravitzky, "Maimonides on the Messianic Era" in *Messianism and Eschatology,* ed. Zvi Baras (Jerusalem, 1984), 191–220 (Hebrew).

69. See Idel, *Kabbalah: New Perspectives,* 7–9.

70. The survey of the 19th century attitude to messianism in Jewish scholarship is still a desideratum.

71. Scholem never divided his historical conception of kabbalistic messianism in three well-distinguishable periods; the following scheme is the result of my combining the relevant topics in a certain order. On Scholem's view of messianism in general see Biale, *Gershom Scholem,* 71–93; and the essays of Robert Alter and W. D. Davies in *Gershom Scholem,* ed. Harold Bloom, 21–28, and 77–97 respectively. See also Scholem, *The Messianic Idea in Judaism,* 202.

72. *Ibid.,* 41–43.

73. *Ibid.,* 41.

74. Gershom Scholem, *Devarim be-Go* (Tel Aviv, 1976), 205 (Hebrew); idem, *Sabbatai Sevi,* 18–20.

75. Scholem wrote about Lurianism, for example: "this latter Kabbalah, as it developed in classical forms in Safed in Palestine in the sixteenth century, was in its whole design electric with Messianism and pressing for its release; it was impelling a Messianic outburst." See Scholem, *The Messianic Idea in Judaism,* 59. The deterministic vision of the history of Kabbalah, within which messianism played such an important role, is evident also in some of Scholem's other discussions. See, for example, *Major Trends,* 287: "The spread of Lurianic Kabbalism with its doctrine of *Tikkun* . . . this doctrine could not lead but to an explosive manifestation of all the forces to which it owned its rise and its success." See also *Major Trends,* 284.

76. See Scholem, *The Messianic Idea in Judaism,* 13; idem, *Major Trends in Jewish Mysticism,* 246.

77. *The Messianic Idea in Judaism,* 103ff, 132ff, 162ff, 231, 235, 241.

78. See Scholem, *'Od Davar: Explications and Implications,* (Tel Aviv, 1989), 2:271 (Hebrew) and his postscript to *The Messianic Idea in Israel* (Jerusalem, 1982), 259–260 (Hebrew).

79. *The Messianic Idea in Judaism,* 186–187, 216–217.

80. See Scholem's view that the concept of emanation was deleterious for the spiritual constitution of Kabbalah, in his *'Od Davar,* 36. Therefore, though he admitted the merger between Neoplatonic and gnostic elements, only the latter elements are seen as positive in Scholem's eyes. If we remember that he was inclined also to restrict the importance of messianism during the first phases of the

Kabbalah, we can see how the role of gnosticism implicitly was built up so that it was presented as informing the whole range of Jewish mystical phenomena.

81. See Biale, *Gershom Scholem,* 154. On the symbiosis between apocalypticism and messianism as a major characteristic of Western culture see Jacob Taubes, *Abendländische Eschatologie* (Bern, 1947), and Couliano's analysis in his *The Tree of Gnosis,* 256–259.

82. See Idel, *Studies in Ecstatic Kabbalah,* (Albany, 1989), 45–61 and "The Contribution of Abraham Abulafia," 138–141.

83. See Yehuda Liebes, "The Messiah of the Zohar," in *The Messianic Idea in Israel* (Jerusalem, 1982), 87–236 (Hebrew). See also Biale's remark that in *Sefer ha-Temunah,* written in the 14th century, there is a strong eschatological element, *Gershom Scholem,* 156.

84. *On the Kabbalah,* 88. I assume that "myth as a central spiritual power" is a fine formulation of Scholem's total vision of Kabbalah, a vision I propose to call mythocentric. See also Biale, (above, note 14).

85. *The Messianic Idea,* 202, 217. Compare also the use of the phrase *ḥissul ha-ḥissul,* the liquidation of liquidation, introduced by Scholem when discussing the need to do away with the *Wissenschaft des Judentums* approach to Jewish creation. See Scholem, *Devarim be-Go,* 399. The accompanying phrase *hapallat ha-hapallah* is reminiscent of Averroes' classic writing *negatio negationis* but also of Hegel's negation of the negation.

86. See Scholem, *From Berlin to Jerusalem,* 172.

87. Harold Bloom has described Scholem as having "an obsession with the imagery of catastrophe." See his "Scholem: Unhistorical or Jewish Gnosticism," in *Gershom Scholem* (note 65 above), 217.

88. *On the Kabbalah,* 121.

89. The most important discussion of the conservative nature of mysticism, but not of non-mystical Jewish spirituality, can be found in *On the Kabbalah,* 5–31. See also *ibid.,* 125.

90. See Jacob Katz, "On the Connection between Sabbatianism, the Enlightenment and the Reform," in *Studies in Jewish Religious and Intellectual History Presented to Alexander Altmann,* ed. S. Stein and R. Loewe (Alabama, 1979), 83–100.

91. R.J. Zwi Werblowsky, "Reflections on Gershom Scholem's Sabbatai Sevi," *Molad* 15 (1957), 539–547 (Hebrew). See also Scholem's response, without identifying the name of the addressee, printed in a shorter version in Scholem, *'Od Davar,* 98–104.

92. See the critique of Baruch Kurzweil, *Be-Ma' avaq 'al 'Erkhe ha-Yahadut*

(Tel Aviv, 1969), 99–243 (Hebrew), and Eliezer Schweid, *Judaism and Mysticism according to Gershom Scholem,* trans. D. A. Wiener (Atlanta, 1985) and the studies mentioned above, note 90.

93. I hope to be able to develop this idea in a detailed study of the mystical interpretations of the prohibition of incest.

94. On the importance of ruptures in modern scholarly historiography see the important article of Ivan Marcus, "Beyond the Sefardi Mystique," *Orim* 1 (1985), 35, 46–47.

95. See I. Ta Shma, "Law, Custom and Tradition in Early Medieval Jewish Germany: Tentative Reflections," *Sidra* 3 (1987), 85–161 (Hebrew).

96. Indeed, it is a major requirement of the study of Jewish thought, and perhaps — as Prof. S. Pines has emphasized it — the most cosmopolitan one in general, to be able to do justice to this type of thought. Therefore, the study of external influences is decisive for a better understanding of Jewish religion. See Warren Z. Harvey's introductory survey in *Shlomo Pines Jubilee Volume,* eds. M. Idel, W. Z. Harvey, and E. Schweid (Jerusalem, 1988), 1:4–6 (Hebrew).

97. See, for example, my discussion of the issue of the Golem and related topics in Idel, *Golem: Jewish Magical and Mystical Traditions on the Artificial Anthropoid* (Albany, 1990).

98. See, for example, Scholem's assumption that Luria's innovative kabbalistic theories were responding to the trauma of the expulsion of the Jews from Spain, so that the emergence of the Lurianic view of *Ṣimṣum* is to be understood in such a reactive way; *Major Trends,* 241–247; *On the Kabbalah,* 110–111. However, it seems that we can better understand the Lurianic concept not as an innovation but as a continuation of much earlier kabbalistic views; see M. Idel, "On *Ṣimṣum* in Kabbalah and in Scholarship," in *Lurianic Kabbalah,* ed. R. Elior and Y. Liebes (Jerusalem, 1992) 59–112 (Hebrew).

99. Scholem, *Origins of the Kabbalah,* index, s.v. *Neoplatonism.*

100. See Idel, *Studies,* 4–18.

101. *Ibid.,* 73–83, 106ff.

102. Yehuda Liebes, "Christian Influences on the Zohar," *Jerusalem Studies in Jewish Mysticism,* 2 (1983), 43–74 (Hebrew). English (shorter) version: *Immanuel* 17 (1983–84), 43–67. In fact, some of the Neoplatonic sources mentioned by Scholem (see above, note 86) also have reached medieval Kabbalah by means of Christian mediation.

103. See M. Idel, "Perceptions of the Kabbalah in the second half of the 18th century," *Jewish Thought and Philosophy* 1 (1991), 83–90; idem, *Kabbalah: New Perspectives,* 40–41.

104. On the possible Hindu influences on Jewish mysticism see M. Idel, *The Mystical Experience in Abraham Abulafia* (Albany, 1989), 14, 24–25, 39 and idem, *Kabbalah: New Perspectives,* 107–108.

105. My reservations concern only Scholem's extensive and recurrent recourse to gnosticism as a major component of kabbalistic mentalities. See also M. Idel, "The Problem of the Sources of the Bahir," in *The Beginnings of Jewish Mysticism in Medieval Europe,* ed., J. Dan (Jerusalem, 1987), 55–72 (Hebrew).

106. See M. Idel, "Types of Redemptive Activity in the Middle Ages," in *Messianism and Eschatology,* ed. Z. Baras (Jerusalem, 1984), 253–279 (Hebrew).

THREE

Yitzhak Baer and the Search for Authentic Judaism

ISRAEL JACOB YUVAL

Yitzhak Fritz Baer was born in 1888 in Halberstadt, Germany. Before immigrating in 1930 to what was then Palestine, he wrote in German, subsequently moving over gradually to the exclusive use of Hebrew. His only works translated into English are a small book entitled *Galut*[1] and *A History of the Jews in Christian Spain.*[2] Almost none of his many articles has been translated,[3] and as a result he has not received the worldwide recognition that he deserves as a historian. Baer remained a prophet not without honor, but only in his own country.[4]

The title "prophet" is indeed apt. Baer was the father of historical research in Israel, the founder of the first Department of Jewish History at the Hebrew University of Jerusalem and the first editor of *Zion,* the most important journal of historical research in the country. Baer and Ben-Zion Dinur (Dinaburg) are also considered the founders of the so-called "Jerusalem School" of Israeli historiography.[5]

Like S. D. Goitein, Baer, too, switched fields at the peak of his career, turning back from the Middle Ages to antiquity. And like Goitein, he made the change in the early 1950s. On the backdrop of the foundation of the modern State of Israel, Baer forsook the study of the Diaspora period and focused on another period of national independence, although his new field of interest, like his old one, concentrated on cultural rather than political history. My own focus in this essay is on the significance of Baer's decision to turn his attention to antiquity rather than to the Middle Ages.

Throughout his research career, Baer's studies revolved around the relations between the Jews and their environment.[6] In his very first speech at the Hebrew University of Jerusalem, in 1931, he declared, "Judaism is one of the forces of general history, it is influenced by them and influences them (2:12). Today there is no more room for *Wissenschaft des Judentums* without continual attention to the relations between Israel and the nations. . . ." In all his medieval work he stressed the central role of Christianity in shaping the world of Judaism. I am referring here not merely to abstract, intellectual recognition, but also to a deep realization that gripped him whenever he was dealing with the web of everyday contacts between Christians and Jews. Baer, more than East-European Jewish historians, who grew up in a rather introverted Jewish environment, sensed the Christian presence at every turn. The historian's business is comparison — and Baer was an accomplished historian. The picture as seen from his broad overview and through his penetrating eyes was one of a Jewry that, in some senses, could be considered a miniature duplication of the Christian environment. With bold brush-strokes, he painted the Jewish community in the likeness of the Christian city; he compared the piety of R. Judah he-Hasid to that of St. Francis of Assisi and Jewish martyrdom to Crusader martyrology; and he showed that kabbalistic literature had absorbed and internalized the Christian religious symbolism of the circle of Joachim da Fiore.

Naturally, Baer also took the trouble to emphasize that this Christian influence did not affect the innermost layer of what he considered the immanent qualities of Judaism. However, in an article written in 1940 on parallels between Jewish and Christian mysticism, he complained that the historical study of medieval Jewry was touched by prejudiced views of "the ghetto, the deep-seated hatred between Jews and Christians, the enormous abyss between the Torah and the Christian religion, the absolute immanence of the evolution of religious tradition in Judaism" (2:308). Baer was critical of such views. The historian, he believed, must look at the facts, and these were "the everyday contact of Jewish and Christian society and the mutual ties between them in politics and economics, their sharing of various concepts and methods in the life of the community and the individual, the common root of their religious-historical heritage. . . . the surprising affinities between the histories of their religious ideals" (2:308).

A good example of the powerful presence of Christianity in Baer's mind is his article about the beginnings of the Jewish community in the Middle Ages. Here, he describes Jewish communities in the Diaspora as "a living organism," in which each community fulfilled a specific function and all came together to form a complete, living body:

> Each community is a substantial member in the large body of the overall Community of Israel. And each community is itself a miniature organism, each person within it having his or her own place and memory, depending on his proficiency in Torah or in observance of the commandments and good deeds. . . . Only the combination of all together makes the community a single body. (2:81)

This "organism" metaphor influenced a whole generation of Israeli historians, who eagerly used it to justify such turns of speech as "the unity of Jewish history," despite the geographical, political and cultural diversity of the various Jewish communities. The same metaphor had been popular in the historiography of the 19th-century German romantic movement. I believe, however, that Baer's use of the term was based here on another association. In the same article, though in a different context, he quotes from Paul's first epistle to the Corinthians 12: "For just as the body is one and has many members, and all the members of the body, though many, are one body, so it is with Christ. . . . If one member suffers, all members suffer together; if one member is honoured, all rejoice together. Now you are the body of Christ and individually members of it" (Baer, 2:13–14). The textual similarity between Paul's description of the Church and Baer's account of the Jewish community demonstrates the extent to which Baer internalized originally Christian concepts. In his classical medieval studies, he did not hesitate to assert that this similarity was a result of Christian influence on Judaism. As the years went by, however, this evaluation was replaced by a new position, which interpreted the similarity, on the contrary, as due to Christian receptivity to Jewish ideas. I believe the turning-point in Baer's thinking occurred in the mid 1940s, perhaps on the background of the Holocaust. In the introduction to his *A History of the Jews of Spain* (1945), Baer sounds a new tune: "Our laws of charity (care for orphans, funding weddings of poor brides, hospitality, visiting the sick, burial of the dead, consolation of mourners, redemption of captives, etc.) provided the basis for the laws of Christian *caritas* and for all the charitable institutions in European urban society" (1:43).

Baer did not hesitate to postulate that the social values of the tiny Jewish minority influenced the Christian majority in medieval Europe. In his article on Rashi (1949) he states that the European bourgeoisie was first born in the Jewish community, only later establishing itself in the Christian city (2:162). In 1950 he published his article about the Jewish community in the Middle Ages, in which he argued that the Christian city learned the democratic method of majority decisions from the Jewish community. Baer was, of course, not so simple-minded as to believe that influence can be unidirectional; but the difference in tone is unmistakable. Referring to the influence of the Christian city on communal organization, he notes that "this superficial influence does not affect the foundations of Jewish self-organization" (2:87). In other words, the Jews were influenced too but only superficially, in a way that did not affect the core of Jewish life. On the other hand, he writes of the beginnings of the Christian city that "at that particular time, only the Jewish community could have influenced [it]." And he goes on to say, "This recognition may pave the way for new treatment of a historical problem that has exercised the efforts of generations of excellent historians of all European nations — when did the European city begin to take shape" (ibid.).

Baer's article on the history of the community attests to the change in his views. He began to abandon the spiritual affinity of Jews and Christians in the Middle Ages, with all its complications and disputations, focusing instead on the world of pre-Christian Judaism, the Judaism of the Land of

Israel. The personal metamorphosis of Yizhak Baer, who had left Europe for a foreign but ancient homeland, had its counterpart in his scholarly work. No longer did he place the origins of the Jewish community and its ideals in the Christian *vita communis*. The Jewish community was now for him, the manifestation of a free political ideology rooted in the conceptual world of the Greek polis. The article was published at the very time of the struggle to establish the State of Israel, so that the history of the medieval Jewish community was thrust into a modern context and thus regained some validity in the minds of the state-builders who sought to cast off the shame of exile. The medieval community was no longer an exilic institution, a product of the Dark Ages and the Christian city. Baer portrayed the Jewish community, the only Jewish polity to exist in the Middle Ages, as an institution born on the nation's native ground, before the destruction of the Temple and the Exile, even before Christianity.

The gradual ejection of Christianity from Baer's agenda, and the search for an idyllic Judaism, are clearly evident in his important study of the destruction of Jerusalem in 70 CE (1:153–217). This event left its imprint on traditional Jewish consciousness through the collection of talmudic legends known as "the legends of the destruction," a jumble of historical facts and imaginary tales.[7] Historical scholarship has made various attempts to reconstruct the realia behind the legends and to extract their historical core.[8] Baer's article criticized such efforts. He dismissed the historicity of the legends entirely, demonstrating their close similarity to 5th-century Christian legends, which proved that they had been composed long after the destruction. Baer proved his thesis most conclusively, in effect throwing open the door and revealing the ahistorical context of the legends. Surprisingly, he then stopped short and went no further in his discussion of the matter. For, even if these legends tell us little about the Great Revolt, they surely provide valuable information about Jewish-Christian polemics in the 5th century. They testify to the Jewish reaction to the most crucial event, after the Crucifixion, in the history of Christianity: its proclamation in the 4th century as the official religion of the Roman Empire. Christian legend portrays the Roman emperors Vespasian and Titus not as pagans but, anachronistically, as good Christians — just like Constantine — who had fulfilled a divine command by destroying the Temple in Jerusalem, in retribution for the crucifixion of Jesus. The talmudic legend tackles this new image of the empire by presenting reverse, mirror images of the Christian legends.[9]

In 1971, when the article was published, Baer had shown only little interest in Christianity. He had written the article to prove an entirely different thesis, namely, that the picture of late Second Temple Judea painted by both Josephus and the Talmud as a city riven by internal divisions, with a civil war raging within the besieged city of Jerusalem, was false. Indeed, Baer strove to create an idealized portrait of the Jewish state during the Second Commonwealth: "There was no difference between the defenders of Jerusalem and the Zealots of Masada, whose real character has been revealed and explained by Yigael Yadin: priests, sages and ordinary Jews . . . , just like the priests who continued to serve in the Temple from the beginning of the Revolt till its very end" (1:193–194). Baer could not accept the talmudic account of R. Yoḥanan ben Zakkai's flight from Jerusalem, to negotiate with the Romans and "rescue" Yavneh. Calling it "a terrible episode in the life and actions of R. Yoḥanan b. Zakkai" (1:206), he tried to prove that the legend was completely false, thus rehabilitating the figure of the great sage.

Baer's article "The Historical Foundations of the Halakhah" was published in two parts, the first in 1952 (1:305–359) and the second in 1962 (1:360–398). In the first he was already expressing his new view of the Second Temple period. The great religious ideas of rabbinic Judaism, he believed, had crystallized as early as the 3rd century BCE, after Alexander the Great's conquest of the country, that is, in the Hellenistic period, "in which were laid the foundations of a society . . . structured according to the ideals of the Law of Moses and the Prophets, on the one hand, and of the Greek philosophers, on the other" (1:308). The Oral Law, Baer suggests, came into being as a result of the encounter between the biblical tradition and the laws of Greece: "The comparison with the laws of Greece proves that the halakhah as taught in our Mishnah is not the creation of some sect, such as the Pharisees, but is founded on a coherent, unique outlook . . . which was absorbed by the Jewish people when they became acquainted with the framework and milieu of Hellenistic culture" (1:377–378).

Thus, whereas the accepted chronology of scholarship assigned rabbinic Judaism and the beginnings of Christianity to the first two centuries CE,

Baer pushed the foundations of rabbinic Judaism back some 400 years, thereby awarding it the status of a source far predating Christianity. Baer believed that by revealing the nature of Judaism in the Hellenistic period, "we [would be able] to understand the ways of those first pious men who laid the foundations for talmudic and rabbinic Judaism, for Christianity and European culture, and, in the final analysis, for our entire history in the Diaspora—foundations on which we might have built our lives today as well" (1:308). Here Baer the historian has almost become Baer the theologian! He had reached, he believed, the bedrock of Jewish culture, the place where it extracted the best of Greek culture in accordance with its needs. Bound together with the national myth—catapulted back several centuries—was the historian of that myth, who had fled the intensity of Europe and the Jews' struggle to assert their status and identity in the face of a victorious, violent, dominant Christianity. In the Land of Israel, in a society of pious farmers, Baer had found what he sought. And that discovery is what informs his comment on the Mishnah: "The State of Israel as described in the Mishnah was a theocratic state. . . . This state was ruled by the counsel of the Sages" . . . (1:396). The anachronistic use of the term "the State of Israel" seems to have expressed Baer's expectations of the newly founded state: it was to become a Platonic state, ruled by philosophers, like the utopian state of the Mishnah.

These views explain one of Baer's strangest articles, in which he dated one of the Dead Sea scrolls, *The Manual of Discipline,* to the 2nd century CE and ascribed it to Judaeo-Christian circles,[10] contrary to paleographic and archeological findings, which define Qumran literature as pre-Christian.[11] Baer was faced with the first discoveries from Qumran, which were gradually revealing a Judaism very different from his "mishnaic" utopia. Not only was this Judaism sectarian and distinct from that of the Mishnah, but some of the Qumran writings actually seemed to convey a message rather similar to that of early Christianity. Baer thus had to confront the threat that his one-dimensional picture of Judaism during the Second Temple period might be proven false. The conclusion he reached was that these writings must be removed from the picture of Judaism at the time. The affinities with early Christianity revealed in Qumran literature did not suggest to him that the Judaism of the Second Temple period indeed contained authentic elements from which Christianity evolved. At the end of the article Baer asserted that Jewish apocalyptic literature, which also had been assigned by scholars to Second Temple times, should properly be dated to post-Temple times. The correct identification of these literary corpora would make it possible, he thought, "to return to our central task, to understand the historical foundations of our religious tradition by the historical interpretation of the internal sources themselves" (59). For Baer, Christian-Jewish writings were not "internal sources," and so must be excluded from any discussion of "our religious tradition." And, he added, "In order to promote research, one should reinforce and stress the weight of internal criteria" (59 n. 156). Two years later he himself realized this recommendation with respect to the Gospels which, he argued, were polemical, dogmatic works of the Christian community after the destruction of the Second Temple (1:244). Thus, after Josephus and the Qumran scrolls, the Gospels too were discounted as reliable sources for a description of Judaism during the Second Temple period; the Mishnah, on the other hand, edited at the beginning of the 3rd century CE, provided reliable evidence of the ideals of the pious farmers inhabiting the Land of Israel in the 3rd century BCE.

This idyllic picture of pious farmers, taken separately, could not satisfy Baer, who was a product of western civilization, an immigrant who had not made his peace with the Orient. He sought an authentic Judaism, free of Christian influence, yet European. As we have seen, he found it in the early contacts with Greek culture. In contrast with his negative view of the role of philosophy in the world of medieval Spanish Jewry, he considered the encounter between Judea and Greece in antiquity to have produced a new, authentic Judaism. This thesis is an attempt to embrace the best of European culture and to consider "authentic" Judaism as part of the European heritage. The link with pagan Europe replaced the ties with Christian Europe. Baer may have been influenced by the predominant tendency of 19th-century German historiography to identify classical Greece as the ancient, "authentic" source of German Europeanism.[12] Indeed, he was seeking a pre-Christian Judaism just as some Germans had sought a pre-Jewish Europeanism.

The quest for roots in the Greek classics was clearly evident in two of the few articles he wrote about the Middle Ages after the metamorphosis of the

1950s (2:225–232, 233–248). Once again, he examined the moral teachings of *Sefer Ḥasidim* by comparing it to the culture of the host society. Now, however, he compared it not to St. Francis of Assisi, R. Judah he-Ḥasid's contemporary, but to Cicero and Seneca! He refers to Christian scholars only so far as they had espoused the views of the Greek and Roman thinkers. In order to explain the meaning of the similarity between Stoic doctrine and *Sefer Ḥasidim,* he writes: "I am inclined to assume that the Ashkenazi pietist found a brief summary, possibly several such works, of the Christian Stoa, that had been written in Latin" (2:236). It is hard to draw a more questionable picture than that of R. Judah he-Ḥasid reading a Latin book.

Baer's attitude to Europe and Christianity, then, was clearly rather complex. Following a time-honored Jewish tradition, he considered the Jewish people's historical encounter with Rome in conjunction with its encounter with Christianity. Rome "expelled the sages from the religious centers of Palestine and dispossessed the people from its inheritance in the Land of Judea" (1:44), while "it was Christianity which, in theory and in practice, signed the sentence of exile pronounced on the people of Israel" (1:46). That is to say, first pagan Rome laid its hands on the nation's land, and then Christian Rome created exile, humiliation, and servitude. To place Baer's views in context, perhaps one should recall that no Roman decree of expulsion was ever issued against the Jews of Palestine, other than the prohibition on entering Jerusalem; one should also note that the Diaspora was a historical reality long before the 4th century. Baer's account leaves no room for the Jewish presence in Babylon, for the ancient communities in Egypt, nor for the later encounter with Islam. His purpose was to draw the necessary conclusion: Europe had created the Jewish Diaspora and thus was expected to remedy it.

Unlike Goitein, whose change of direction was motivated by professional considerations and earned him much appreciation, Baer — who embarked on a new path for ideological reasons — did not achieve recognition in his new field. Today, his views of the Second Temple period merit little more than a polite nod. In a lecture to honor Baer's 90th birthday — in his presence — the late Professor E. E. Urbach passed severe judgment on his life-work, stating that "Baer's attitude to the sources caused whole chapters to be erased from historical reality."[13]

Baer's failure was not merely academic. He was also unsuccessful in his efforts to propose a broad historical world-view that would be meaningful to the younger generation in Israel. The new Israelis were far removed from any admiration of ancient Greece and the Stoics or from Baer's complex attitude to Christianity. At the end of his life Baer, the prophet confined to his own country, resumed his earlier role: he became a scholar walled up in his ivory tower, out of touch with the mood of his surroundings. His historiography was suited to the biography of a German immigrant who had settled in Jerusalem, but it had no bearing on the Israeli, non-European experience of pioneer-farmers who, in the meantime, had become bourgeois.

NOTES

1. *Galut* (New York, 1947).

2. Translated by Louis Schoffman (Philadelphia, 1961). The book was reviewed by Isaiah Sonne, "On Baer and His Philosophy of Jewish History," *Jewish Social Studies* 9 (1947), 61–80, and by Israel Ta-Shma, "Halakhah, Kabbalah and Philosophy in Christian Spain," *Shenaton Ha-Mishpat Ha-'Ivri* 18–19 (1992–94), 479–495.

3. His article "Rashi and the World Around Him" was translated recently and published in *Binah 3: Jewish Intellectual History in the Middle Ages,* ed. Joseph Dan (Westport, 1994), 101–118.

4. For an evaluation of his historiographical work see Shmuel Ettinger, "Yitzhak Baer (1888–1980)," *Zion* 44 (1979), 9–20; David N. Myers, *Re-Inventing the Jewish Past: European Jewish Intellectuals and the Zionist Return to History* (New York, 1995), 129–150.

5. See David N. Myers, "Was There a 'Jerusalem School'? An Inquiry into the First Generation of historical Researches at the Hebrew University," in *Reshaping the Past: Jewish History and the Historians (Studies in Contemporary Jewry* 10), ed. Jonathan Frankel (Jerusalem, 1994), 66–92.

6. His major contributions were collected and re-published in his *Studies in the History of the Jewish People* (Hebrew) vol. 1–2 (Jerusalem, 1985). All further references are to this edition.

7. Bab. Talmud, *Gittin* 55b–58a.

8. See Menahem Stein, "Yabneh and Her Scholars," *Zion* 3 (1938), 122–128; Gedalyahu Allon, "How Yabneh Became R. Johanan ben Zakkai's Residence,"

Zion 3 (1938), 183–214; and Avraham Shalit, "The Prophecies of Josephus and of Rabban Yohanan ben Zakkai on the Ascent of Vespasian to the Throne," in *Salo Wittmayer Baron. Jubilee Volume On the Occasion of His Eightieth Birthday.* Hebrew Section (Jerusalem, 1974), 425–472.

9. See Israel J. Yuval, "'The Lord Will Take Vengeance, Vengeance for His Temple'—Historia sine ira er studio," *Zion* 59 (1994), 362–373.

10. "The Manual of Discipline: A Jewish Document of the Second Century C.E. (Including a Discussion of the Damascus Document)," *Zion* 29 (1964), 1–60. This article was not included in his collected papers.

11. Geza Vermes, "The Impact of the Dead Sea Scrolls on the Study of the *New* Testament," *Journal of Jewish Studies* 27 (1976), 107–116; David Satran, "Qumran and Christian Origins," in *The Scrolls of the Judaean Desert. Forty Years of Research,* ed. Magen Broshi et al. (Jerusalem, 1992), 152–159.

12. See Eliza M. Butler, *The Tyranny of Greece over Germany Exercised by Greek Art and Poetry over the Great German Writers of the Eighteenth, Nineteenth and Twentieth Centuries* (Boston, 1958).

13. Ephraim E. Urbach, "Yemei ha-Bayit ha-Sheni u-Tequfat ha-Mishna," *Proceedings of the Israel Academy of Sciences and Humanities* 6.4 (1984), 80. See also his *The Sages: Their Concepts and Beliefs* (Jerusalem, 1979), 12–14.

FOUR

Between Diaspora and Zion: History, Memory, and the Jerusalem Scholars

DAVID N. MYERS

In introducing the monumental and justly famous historical project *Les lieux de mémoire,* Pierre Nora wrote of the "acceleration of history" that characterized the modern age, the rapid disintegration of and distantiation from the historical past.[1] Characteristic of this process was the shifting function of historical memory. Nora observed that with respect to French history, "we no longer celebrate the nation. Instead, we study its celebrations."[2] This move from commemoration of past events to study of the commemorative acts (not even the events themselves) signalled the eclipse of the active participant in collective memory by the detached recorder of history. Yosef Hayim Yerushalmi, whose seminal book *Zakhor* inaugurated a new discourse on the function of history in modern Jewish existence, formulated the problem in even more stark and poignant terms. "Memory and modern historiography," Yerushalmi wrote, "stand . . . in radically different relations to the past." The former reflects "the shared faith, cohesiveness, and will" of the Jewish community in pre-modern times. Meanwhile, historiography in its modern incarnation chronicles, or perhaps presides over the "unraveling of that common network of belief and praxis through whose mechanisms . . . the past was once made present."[3]

The nature of the relationship between history and memory has inspired a huge proliferation of scholarship for well over a decade. Scores of articles have been devoted to historical and theoretical explications of this relationship; so too is the fittingly titled journal *History and Memory*. Moreover, there is now a scholarly monograph, Patrick Hutton's *History as an Art of Memory*, that traces the historical roots and evolution of this new intellectual discourse.[4] And of course, the central theme of the present volume attests to the ongoing interest in the question of history and memory, especially among Jewish scholars.

In discussing this intense curiosity, I cannot offer an extended analysis of the complex social and historical forces that produced either the rapid "acceleration of history" of which Nora spoke or the question of history and memory as a salient topic of scholarly inquiry; that task has been performed by Hutton and others. Rather, I would like to suggest that the categories of history and memory, often cast as irreparably detached from one another, may indeed be closer to one another than we often tend to think, that they may inhabit a continuum of attitudes toward this past.[5] Further, I would suggest that the very genre of modern historiography which Prof. Yerushalmi and others have seen as the antithesis or bane of collective memory, can be and has been the bearer of group memories. Of course, this proposition is not itself novel. Pierre Nora has noted that historians writing in 19th-century Europe continued to draw inspiration from a set of collective memories which they now subjected to critical analysis.[6] More generally, historiography inspired by 19th-century nationalism became the site of a dynamic struggle between the historian's need to impart group identity, on one hand, and fealty to the newly acquired methods of the professional historical discipline, on the other. Consequently, the nationalist historian came to serve as mediator between collective memory and critical history.

A particularly illuminating and germane case in point is the assembly of scholars known as the "Jerusalem School."[7] The earliest reference I have found for this term dates from 1926 when the Galician-born scholar, L. A.

Mayer, expressed the hope that a "Jerusalem School" would arise and establish a new level of "scientific" standards for Jewish scholarship.[8] For subsequent critics, the "Jerusalem School" failed in this mission, but did succeed
in imposing upon its member-scholars a high degree of ideological conformity.[9] Even those who regard the emergence of a "Jerusalem School" in
affirmative terms herald the crystallization of a new *national* perspective on
the Jewish past.[10] What unites the assorted critics and supporters are the
shared beliefs that the "Jerusalem School" is, first, a unified entity, and
second, an extension of the much broader effort to create a new and coherent Zionist historical consciousness.

I would propose that the time is propitious to revisit this image and the
term behind it. My own deliberations on the founding generation of historical researchers at the Hebrew University, the founding generation of the
so-called "Jerusalem School," take place in an age in which the state of Israel
has achieved a degree of institutional solidity, physical security, and economic well-being unsurpassed in its history. After nearly fifty years of difficult struggle and of considerable consensus regarding external threats, Israel
is entering a new era of introspection and self-reflection regarding its origins
and purpose. This seems to be an altogether natural process in the history of
nascent states or political movements, even or especially revolutionary ones.
In the Israeli case, a half-century of bitter struggle has yielded to a new,
perhaps fleeting, moment of respite from armed conflict. This respite has
prompted some to announce the end of ideology, and particularly that
ideology, Zionism, which inspired the creation of the state. Concomitantly,
a growing number of Israeli intellectuals have begun to raise the specter of a
post-Zionist epoch, leading to an impassioned and at times vituperative
reaction.[11] Before dismissing this claim as puerile cynicism or as a sign of
slavish devotion to postmodernist fashion, it seems useful to recall that the
dominant strain of Zionist ideology, the Herzlian strain, was largely realized in 1948 with the creation of the state. To the extent that Herzl's vision
was not realized, it was because Israel had not become, at its inception, a
nation like other nations, that it remained somewhat anomalous among its
fellow states. But one must ask: are not the current conditions ripe for
consummating the process of normalization to which Herzl aspired, in
other words, for creating a bourgeois liberal state? Conversely, if normaliza-

tion is not the true aim of Zionism, what is? To serve as the catalyst for the messianic age, as some religious Zionists believe? Or perhaps as the spiritual center of Ahad Ha-'am's dreams?

Unfortunately, I have neither the space nor the prophetic capacity to answer these questions now. I have raised them in order to suggest that discussion of the end of ideology need not mean the end of ideology. In fact, the animated recent debates among Israeli academics and intellectuals indicate that ideological passions are still quite alive.[12] Moreover, these questions have served as a prod to new scrutiny of guiding assumptions, ideological sources, and foundation myths of earlier generations in the *Yishuv* and State of Israel. One sees this critical spirit in the work of the so-called "New Historians" whose research on the formative years of the State of Israel, particularly Jewish-Arab relations, has produced intense controversy within the Israeli academic establishment.[13] It does not seem far-fetched to assert that traces of this critical spirit can also be seen in the work of scholars writing on subjects far removed from contemporary political concerns. For example, the appearance of Moshe Idel's *Kabbalah: New Perspectives* — first in English in 1988 and then in Hebrew in 1993 — generated heated controversy in the pages of leading Israeli newspapers, in large measure because it challenged the near-canonical schema of Jewish mysticism set in place by a founding father of Jewish scholarship in Jerusalem, Gershom Scholem.[14] In related fashion, the historian Yisrael Yuval became the target of vehement attack after the publication of his 1993 article asserting the existence of powerful anti-Christian impulses in Jewish martyrologies following the Crusades.[15] Yuval's article made a provocative case for recontextualizing medieval Ashkenazic Jewish life by positing a subtle and unarticulated exchange of cultural and religious values between Jewish and Christian communities in the Middle Ages. Among other effects, Yuval's work dilutes the claims of his predecessors to the primacy of immanent forces in shaping Jewish history. In both cases, it was the seeming irreverence of Idel and Yuval toward conventional understandings of Jewish history, as well as toward previous generations of scholars, that transformed their rather arcane scholarship into *causes célèbres*. Undeniably, both scholars were possessed of an iconoclastic spirit that subverted accepted scholarly truths and flew in the face of the Israeli academic establishment.

The work of Idel and Yuval takes shape at a moment in Israeli history notable for its unprecedented receptivity to a critical reckoning with the past. Not coincidentally, it is at this moment that the iconoclasm of younger scholars, intent on revisiting the assumptions of their forebears, intersects with the complex relationship between history and memory; for the new critical spirit in Israeli historiography has led and will continue to lead to a refashioning of popular historical consciousness — and, by extension, collective memory.[16]

To understand fully the impact of the new historiographical directions in Israel, it is imperative to arrive at a more refined understanding of the early generations of Jewish historical researchers in Mandatory Palestine and Israel. Succeeding in this task requires resisting well-established and uninformed stereotypes about those scholars who came to be known widely and a bit deceptively as the "Jerusalem School."[17] Conversely, it is necessary to balance a number of disparate historical factors: the cultural and educational background of these scholars, their programmatic aspirations and their actual scholarly labors.

When the institutional home of these scholars opened in late December 1924, expectations for a revolutionary transformation of Jewish scholarship abounded. Surprisingly, the language used to capture the moment was permeated with religious imagery, although the new Institute for Jewish Studies was widely envisaged as a secular academy. Thus, Judah L. Magnes, a leading supporter of the Institute who would become the first chancellor of the Hebrew University, spoke of the institute as "a holy place, a sanctuary in which to learn and teach, without fear or hatred, all that Judaism has made and created from the time of the Bible."[18] This theme was echoed by Max Margolis, an American scholar serving as the first visiting professor in Bible, who declared that "this place on which we stand — Mt. Scopus, from which we can see the (remnants of the) Temple — is a sanctuary for us. This edifice and the others that will rise in the not too distant future will become for us a holy place."[19] What was at work was an intriguing conflation of traditional religious values and modern scholarly norms; *Wissenschaft,* the scientific spirit, was to become the new and sacred Torah. Hence, Judah Magnes joyously proclaimed at the opening of the Institute for Jewish Studies that "we exult in the ideal of *pure science;* and there is no place in the world with a location (*genius loci*) as suitable for *Torah* as Jerusalem." The equation, perhaps unconscious, of science and Torah reflected the dual aspirations of those gathered in Jerusalem: on one hand, to forge a new bond with an ancestral national tradition and homeland, and on the other, to assure the highest standards of objective research. The fusion of old motifs and new aspirations was reflected in the fact that speaker after speaker intoned the classic Jewish liturgical refrain to proclaim that "from Zion will go forth Torah."[20]

The resulting goal of laying the foundation for a new national scholarly edifice was seen as an antidote to the previously dominant model of modern Jewish scholarship, *Wissenschaft des Judentums*. For many critics in Jerusalem, German-Jewish scholarship provided little more than an apologia for German-Jewish assimilation. Its practitioners fundamentally distorted the Jewish past by focusing on the religious and literary evolution of Judaism rather than on the social and economic path of the Jewish nation. The new edifice of Jewish scholarship would arise then out of a paradigm shift, from faith to *Volk* as the lens through which to record Jewish history.

And yet, complicating the rise of such a new paradigm in Jerusalem was the fact that its initiators were born and trained in Europe. There were, with only a few exceptions, no Palestine-born Jewish scholars considered for an academic appointment in Jerusalem. Not only did the first generation of Jerusalem scholars emigrate (in the 1920s and 1930s) primarily from Central and Eastern Europe; most had either studied or taught in the modern rabbinical seminaries of Germany, Austria and Hungary that served as the institutional home of *Wissenschaft des Judentums*. It was there that the scholars were imbued with the spirit of *Wissenschaft* itself, of scientific rigor and objectivity. It was also there that their disciplinary priorities and expertise were acquired, a factor that inhibited the implementation of an altogether new scholarly paradigm in Jerusalem.

One instructive example should make this point clearly. In popular Zionist consciousness, the Bible was invested with great meaning, as the historical deed to the land of Israel, and more generally, as the symbol and source of national glory in that land. Conversely, the Talmud and rabbinic literature represented Jewish existence in exile, a rigid devotion to religious laws whose rationale was no longer self-evident. Given this unequivocal hierarchical ordering, it is nothing short of astonishing that no permanent professor of Bible was appointed at the Institute of Jewish Studies for some fourteen years, whereas two appointments in Talmud and rabbinic literature, Jacob Nahum Epstein and Simha Assaf, were made in the first two years of the Institute's existence. And over the next three years, the Institute attempted to lure several more European-born scholars of rabbinics to Jerusalem, among them Victor Aptowitzer and Chanoch Albeck.[21]

The reasons for this apparent inversion of priorities are complicated, at times involving very personal criteria and choices. However, to the extent that we can generalize, it seems clear that Talmud and rabbinics won quick recognition in Jerusalem precisely because these fields were well-established realms of study not only within the traditional yeshivah but also within the modern rabbinical seminary; consequently, there was a relatively large pool of qualified scholars on which to draw. By contrast, academic study of the Bible had not attracted a similarly large pool, in no small part due to the reticence of Jewish scholars in the 19th century to engage in higher biblical criticism (which Solomon Schechter equated, in a memorable turn of phrase, with "higher antisemitism"). As a result, Talmud and rabbinics fared well in the first decades of the Institute's history, while biblical studies limped along.[22]

It was not simply the quality or quantity of scholars that determined these institutional developments. Nor was it the will of scholars and administrators on the ground in Jerusalem that always carried the day. For the Institute's affairs were supervised, at times dictated, by a Governing Council comprised largely of Jewish leaders from the Diaspora, not of all of whom were Zionists. Among the most prominent figures on this Governing Council were the chief rabbis of England and France, Joseph Hertz and Israel Lévi, who, during the long search for a professor of Bible, consistently resisted attempts to hire a scholar committed to higher critical methods. Because of the chief rabbis' involvement, some feared that the Institute of Jewish Studies was destined to become a European-style rabbinical seminary, a "proper 'Golus' institution," as one critic put it, relegated to the private sphere of religion and unable to realize its potential as a Jewish *national* institution.[23]

Yet another layer of authority and complexity emanated from the World

Zionist Organization in London, whose president, Chaim Weizmann, insisted on the Organization's right to regulate the affairs of the Hebrew University, of which the Institute for Jewish Studies was part. This kind of assertion and intervention created resentment in Jerusalem, and recalls a similar pattern of quasi-colonialist relations that existed between foreign patrons and local students and faculty at the neighboring American University of Beirut.[24]

Nonetheless, with all these overlapping circles of authority—and the frustration and organizational structure that issued from them—there was a fair degree of consensus between Diaspora overseers and European-born scholars in Jerusalem on the need to create a new bastion of scientific scholarship in Palestine. Scholars and patrons alike were embarked on a veritable *mission civilisatrice* in a land at once exotic and familiar to the European—and European Jewish—mind. Here one cannot help but notice the rhetorical continuum between the Jerusalem scholars and their scorned 19th-century predecessors in Germany. Though each generation possessed its own distinct ideological orientation, both pledged unfailing allegiance to the standard of science, a commitment reflected in the nearly identical choice of terminology for Jewish studies in the respective contexts: *Wissenschaft des Judentums* in German and *mada'e ha-Yahadut* in Hebrew.[25]

To point to the rhetorical and methodological continuity between Europe and Palestine seems rather unremarkable in light of the European origins and training of the Jerusalem scholars. Still, we must bear in mind that this continuity cuts against the grain of the programmatic declarations proclaiming that a new Torah will go out from Zion. Moreover, it defies the widespread perception among contemporary scholars that a discrete "Jerusalem School" of historiography ever took rise. And yet, it is undeniable that the first generation of scholars in Jerusalem unquestionably devised conceptual models which differed from those of their German-Jewish forebears. Perhaps most importantly, the field of history—as distinct from philology, the favored discipline of 19th-century scholars—emerged as a central intellectual and institutional priority in Jerusalem.[26] It is significant not merely that history was accorded a new degree of professional respect in Jerusalem, a good deal more than it received in the rabbinical seminaries in Europe. It is also the fact that history was understood by the Jerusalem

scholars as it had been by non-Jewish researchers in 19th-century Europe —
as the story of the nation. The equation of history and nation entailed a shift
in emphasis from the literary and religious treasures of Judaism to the social
and communal existence of the Jewish people. This shift was part of a
broader process by which the Jewish past came to be understood and analyzed in material terms. Interestingly, this process, which commenced in the
last third of the 19th century, was advanced by a cadre of Jewish proto-
nationalists in Eastern Europe, who were the first agents of imagination of a
new Jewish national community. From Peretz Smolenskin's call to investigate "darkhe ha-'am" (the ways of the people) to Simon Dubnow's proposed "sociological corrective" to previous Jewish historiography, this ma-
terializing impulse emphasized the corporate and corporeal qualities of
Jewish life.[27] Scholars in Jerusalem provided new coherence and institutional weight to the "materialization" of the Jewish past. Among the salient Jerusalem variations of this theme were: first, an intense interest in the
mechanism and functioning of the pre-modern Jewish community, a tendency reflected in the work of the historians Ben-Zion Dinur and Yitzhak F. Baer (but shared by Diaspora historians such as Dubnow and Salo
Baron);[28] and second, an even more intense and distinctive interest in the
land of Israel as the primary locus of Jewish national activity, even after the
destruction of the Second Temple in 70 CE. The most obvious figure in this
regard is Ben-Zion Dinur, about whom more will be said later. For now, I'd
like to mention the Hungarian-Jewish scholar, Samuel Klein, who oversaw
the introduction of the field of Palestine studies into the curriculum at the
Institute of Jewish Studies in Jerusalem.[29] For Klein and others in Jerusalem,
Erets Yisra'el was neither an other-worldly abstraction nor merely a source
of liturgical inspiration. It was the site of this-worldly national activity
whose history modern researchers were called upon to uncover.

I must hasten to add that *Erets Yisra'el* did not only signify a geographic
or spatial realm for scholars in Jerusalem. It also represented the end of a
temporal process — the *telos* of the Jewish people's long trek through dispersion and exile. Having demarcated this terminal point, scholars now succumbed to what Isaiah Berlin once called the "retrodictive" impulse, by
which he meant the attempt to scour the past for themes or subjects that
form a coherent, linear chain of historical development.[30] A few examples

will suffice. For Yitzhak Baer, the modern return to Zion had a complex retrodictive effect. It did not only offer the prospect of ending exile, it also inspired his search for the roots of Jewish communal governance. Baer's classic 1950 article on the origins of the Jewish community, which identified an immanent, ascetic, democratic thread running from Second Temple Palestine to medieval Ashkenaz, was published two years after the creation of the state of Israel.[31] Given Baer's proclivity for identifying typological models in Jewish history, it hardly seems unreasonable to suggest that he imagined the medieval community, informed by its uniquely Jewish democratic spirit, as an idealized proto-state.[32] He himself affirmed the nexus between past and present when he declared already in 1936 that Zionism was deeply rooted in "the ancient national consciousness of the Jews."[33]

A similar tendency to project into the historical past can be noticed in the writings of Yosef Klausner, who taught modern Hebrew literature at the Hebrew University. Though Klausner's professed first love was Second Temple history, he was denied a position in this field because Diaspora patrons (and even colleagues in Jerusalem) believed him to be both a popularizer and a chauvinistic ideologue. As consolation, he was awarded a professorship in modern Hebrew literature, which tells us something about the esteem in which that field was held in 1925.[34] In any event, in the six-volume series of course lectures on modern Hebrew literature that Klausner published from 1930 to 1950, he offered a curious scheme of periodization for his field of study. Modern Hebrew literature commenced in the late 18th century with the appearance of Naphtali Herz Weisel's *Divre Shalom ve-'Emet;* meanwhile, the last author whom Klausner dealt with in his six-volume study was the late 19th-century bilingual writer, Mendele Mokher Seforim.[35] The chronological boundaries which Klausner established for modern Hebrew literature were virtually identical to those of the *Haskalah,* the Jewish Enlightenment movement. In other words, modern Hebrew literature did not commence in the late 19th century with the revival of spoken Hebrew; nor was it a product of the birth of Zionism. Rather, it emerged in the midst of a literary and historical movement which many Zionists regarded with contempt. In a surprising gesture, Klausner asserted that his own Zionism disqualified him to pass judgment on literature produced under the influence of the nationalist movement. However, he felt very much at liberty to assess the pre-Zionist period, and even to suggest an intimate connection between that period and its successor. Possessed of a certain triumphalist conviction, Klausner looked back on the literary past with magnanimity, and determined that whoever wrote in Hebrew necessarily affirmed the Jewish national will to survive.[36]

This triumphalist spirit, empowering the Zionist historian to regard the Jewish past in affirmative terms, is most pronounced in Ben-Zion Dinur. Renowned as the leading exponent of the Palestinocentric view of Jewish history — according to which all Jewish history revolves around the geographic and spiritual axis of Palestine — Dinur did indeed maintain that Jews in the Diaspora held to an undying faith in the need and benefit of the return to Zion. At the same time, Dinur identified what he called the sociopsychological factor in Diaspora Jewish history — the rituals, customs, social norms and collective memories — that preserved an ongoing sense of national coherence. Rather than discard these instruments, Dinur reclaimed them for a new Zionist version of Jewish history, much as he salvaged figures such as Baruch Spinoza and Moses Mendelssohn for his pantheon of proto-Zionist luminaries. At work was a fundamental historical principle: "Even after the [ancient Jewish] commonwealth was destroyed and the Jews dispersed and absorbed among the nations, the complete unity of the Hebrew nation did not cease."[37]

At this point, we encounter a final twist to our story. In popular Zionist political rhetoric and historical consciousness, the Diaspora past was to be excised, expunged from memory. As the old Jew yielded to the new Hebrew, so too the Diaspora past was to surrender to the glories of pre-Exilic antiquity and the promise of a post-Exilic future. The symbol, or perhaps caricature, of this perspective is Yudke, the usually taciturn hero of Haim Hazaz's short story, "Ha-Derashah," who one day blurts out to his fellow kibbutz members that he is opposed to Jewish history, a history of passive suffering and indignity.[38] And yet, it turns out that Yudke's inclination to negate Jewish history, particularly Diaspora Jewish history, was not shared unequivocally by the first generation of professional scholars at the Hebrew University in Jerusalem. While scholars such as Klausner and Dinur did in fact adhere to a "negationist" position in their politics, their scholarship reflected a more ambivalent stance. The Diaspora was presented as the repository of inspired national values; it was seen in instrumental terms, as occupying an important place in the historical current conducting the Jewish people to the land of Israel.

The effect of this observation is to complicate the very notion of a Jerusalem school of historiography by pointing to the dissonance between popular Zionist views of the Jewish past and elite scholarly attitudes. I have not even discussed the most famous Jerusalem scholar of all, Gershom Scholem; Scholem's magisterial reconstruction of the history of Jewish mysticism bears virtually no trace of the instrumental Zionist impulses found in Baer, Dinur and Klausner, though it does bear other traces of Scholem's idiosyncratic Zionism.[39] What is important to note is that Scholem and his colleagues, the first Jerusalem scholars, were a generation in transition, suspended, as it were, between Europe and Palestine, between fealty to *Wissenschaft* and loyalty to Zionism, and consequently between the instinct to uphold the standards of critical historical scholarship and the desire to forge new boundaries of collective memory.

The ceaseless mediation between critical history and collective memory, I might add, has been the lot not merely of scholars in Jerusalem; it has been the predicament of the modern Jewish scholar whether writing in 19th-century Germany, early 20th-century Russia, or even late 20th-century America. What is distinctive about the case of Jerusalem is both the critical mass — the sheer numbers of scholars and students — and the degree of institutional solidity reflected in the Hebrew University. Yet, even these qualities did not yield an historiographical monolith. Each first-generation Jerusalem scholar balanced scholarly/professional and ideological/existential impulses in his own way (gender bias intended here). The resulting range of perspectives makes it much easier to speak of a group of *Jerusalem scholars* than it does of a single *Jerusalem school*. United by certain traits, these scholars nonetheless proceeded about their work with single-minded intensity, and oftentimes in monastic solitude.

The task of refining our understanding of the idea of a Jerusalem school beyond epithet or polemical tool is worthwhile, I would hope, in its own right. But it is the connection between this task and the broader reconsideration of Zionism that moves us even further. Like the Jerusalem scholars, Zionism was a movement forever negotiating between its birthplace in

Europe and its testing ground in Palestine, between West and East. The hybrid quality that resulted from this negotiation makes the Jerusalem scholars and the entire Zionist movement more complex historical phenomena than previously imagined. Now, as Israel reaches a seminal juncture, as it redefines its relation to its surrounding environment as well as to its own past, a critical re-examination of political and intellectual origins is in order. It is in the spirit of the time that this meditation is offered. In shedding new light on the Jerusalem scholars, it seeks to serve as antidote to historical ignorance and misperception — and perhaps as stimulus to further thinking about Zionism, on the one hand, and the bond between history and memory, on the other.

NOTES

1. Pierre Nora, *Les lieux de mémoire* (Paris, 1984), 1:xvii

2. Ibid., xxv.

3. Yosef Hayim Yerushalmi, *Zakhor: Jewish History and Jewish Memory* (Seattle, 1982), 94.

4. See Patrick H. Hutton, *History as an Art of Memory* (Hanover, NH, 1993), 9.

5. See the glosses to Yerushalmi's *Zakhor* in Amos Funkenstein, "Collective Memory and Historical Consciousness," *History and Memory* 1 (Spring/Summer 1992), 123–140; and David N. Myers, "Remembering *Zakhor*: A Supercommentary," *History and Memory* 4 (Fall/Winter 1992), 129–146.

6. See Hutton, *History as an Art of Memory*, 8.

7. See David N. Myers, "Was there a Jerusalem School?: An Inquiry into the First Generation of Historical Researchers at the Hebrew University," *Studies in Contemporary Jewry* 10 (1994), 66–92. I have dealt more extensively with this group of scholars in *Re-Inventing the Jewish Past: European Jewish Intellectuals and the Zionist Return to History* (New York, 1995).

8. "Was There a Jerusalem School?" 68.

9. It has been a commonplace assumption in Jewish historiography that a cohesive "Jerusalem school" came into existence with the establishment of a new scholarly center in Jerusalem. Perhaps the most renowned opponent was the Israeli literary critic, Barukh Kurzweil. Kurzweil not only regarded the "Jerusalem School" as a monolith; he portrayed its member-scholars, particularly Gershom

Scholem, in demonic terms. See, for example, Kurzweil's essays in *Be-ma'avak 'al 'Erkhe ha-Yahadut* (Tel Aviv, 1969), 99–240.

10. See, for instance, the enthusiastic appropriation of the term "Jerusalem school" by Don Patinkin and Shmuel Ettinger in *Mehqarim be-Mada'e ha-Yahadut,* ed. M. Bar-Asher (Jerusalem, 1986).

11. A recent symposium in the Israeli newspaper *Ha-'Arets,* "On Zionism, Post-Zionism and Anti-Zionism," reveals the depth of passion and disagreement among Israeli intellectuals over the historical legacy of Zionism. See *Ha-'Arets,* October 15, 1995, 4b–5b.

12. An interesting illustration of this intense passion is the controversy generated among Israeli academics by Zev Sternhell's recent book, *Binyan 'Umah 'o Tiqun Hevrah?* (Tel Aviv, 1995). Sternhell questioned a fundamental truism of Israeli historical consciousness — namely, that the dominant Labor-Zionist movement, and particularly its "founding fathers," successfully balanced commitments to an egalitarian social order and to a Jewish national revival. On Sternhell's reading, the "founding fathers" succeeded far more in the latter than in the former commitment. Sternhell's challenge to traditional historiographical assumptions provoked heated controversy almost immediately after the appearance of his book.

13. An important starting point for the new critical orientation in Israeli historiography is Benny Morris' *The Birth of the Palestinian Refugee Problem* (Cambridge, 1988). For other expressions of this new orientation, see *New Perspectives on Israeli History: The Early Years of the State,* ed. Laurence J. Silberstein (New York, 1991). See also the recent volume of *History and Memory* 7 (Spring/Summer 1995) devoted to "Israeli Historiography Revisited."

14. The publication of Idel's book in English in 1988 provoked the eminent scholar Isaiah Tishby, among others, to respond with biting criticism in "Hafikhah be-Heqer ha-Qabalah," *Zion* 54 (1989), 209–222. Meanwhile, the Hebrew translation of Idel's book produced another storm in the pages of leading Israeli newspapers. See, for example, Michael Sassar, "Mi-'Oz — ulay — Yese' Matoq," *Davar,* November 29, 1993.

15. See Yuval's article, "Ha-Naqam veha-Qelalah, ha-Dat veha-'Alilah (mi-'Alilot Qedoshim le'Alilot Dam)," *Zion* 58 (1993), 33–90, and the responses of Ezra Fleischer and Avraham Grossman and others in the succeeding volume of *Zion.*

16. Particular attention should be paid in this regard to the interesting work of Idit Zartal and Yael Zerubavel, among others, in re-examining the legend of Tel-Hai and its function within Israeli collective memory.

17. I have expressed my reservations about the term in "Was there a Jerusalem

School," *passim,* and in *Re-Inventing the Jewish Past,* 9. For an exemplary case of a stereotypical view of the Jerusalem scholars, see Baruch Kimmerling, "Academic History Caught in the Cross-Fire: The Case of Israeli-Jewish Historiography," *History and Memory* 7 (Spring/Summer 1995), 41–65. Kimmerling's conclusions about Israeli historiography suffer from a lack of accurate biographical information, and a near total lack of engagement with actual works of historiography.

18. See Magnes' address in *Yedi'ot ha-Makhon le-Mada'e ha-Yahadut* 1 (1925), 4–5.

19. Ibid., 20.

20. This refrain is taken from Isaiah 2:3, and is chanted before the Torah is taken from the ark during the Jewish prayer service.

21. See Myers, *Re-Inventing the Jewish Past,* 83–89.

22. Ibid., 102–108.

23. The term appears in a letter from the German Zionist Robert Weltsch to Martin Buber from June 23, 1924. See Martin Buber, *Briefwechsel aus sieben Jahrzehnten* (Heidelberg, 1973), 2:195.

24. I have emphasized the parallel to the American University of Beirut, as well as the quasi-colonial nature of relations between Diaspora patrons and administrators and faculty in Jerusalem, in "A New Scholarly Colony in Jerusalem: Notes on the Early History of the Institute of Jewish Studies," *Judaism* (Spring 1996), 142–59.

25. The only difference is that the Hebrew term is literally translated as the "sciences of Judaism," whereas the German phrase connotes the "science of Judaism."

26. The roots of the transition from philology to history can be traced back to Europe, in one particularly influential instance to the German-Jewish historian Eugen Täubler, who was the revered mentor of the first two Jewish historians hired by the Hebrew University, Yitzhak Baer and Ben-Zion Dinur. See my discussion of this important figure in "Eugen Täubler: The Personification of Judaism as Tragic Existence," *Leo Baeck Institute Year Book* 39 (1994), 131–150.

27. Myers, *Re-Inventing the Jewish Past,* 31–32.

28. Ibid., 125–126, 145.

29. Along with Dinur, Klein played a key role in editing the multi-volume *Sefer ha-Yishuv,* an anthology of historical references to the Land of Israel. See Myers, *Re-Inventing the Jewish Past,* 89–93, 140–141.

30. Isaiah Berlin, "History and Theory: The Concept of Scientific History," *History and Theory* 1 (1960), 7. Berlin noted that this impulse is a defining feature of the historiographical enterprise, particularly when the historian faces a dearth of direct testimony or evidence.

31. Y. F. Baer, "Ha-Yesodot veha-Hathalot shel 'Irgun ha-Qehilah ha-Yehudit bi-Yeme ha-Benayim," *Zion* 15 (1950), 1–41.

32. Myers, *Re-Inventing the Jewish Past*, 124–128.

33. The original version of Baer's small book *Galut* was published in Berlin in 1936. I have consulted here the English *Galut*, trans. Robert Warshow (New York, 1947), 119.

34. *Re-Inventing the Jewish Past*, 94–95.

35. Ibid., 95–96.

36. Klausner, *Historyah shel ha-Sifrut ha-'Ivrit ha-Hadashah* (Jerusalem, 1949–50), 4:515. I might add that this positive evaluation of Diaspora authors stands in tension with the general thrust of Klausner's earlier history of the Second Temple period; there, it is not authors, and surely not Diaspora authors, but rather political and military leaders in Jewish Palestine who are the heros of the tale.

37. Ben-Zion Dinaburg, *Yisra'el ba-Golah*, Book 1 (Tel Aviv, 1926), 1:23–24.

38. See Haim Hazaz, "Ha-Derashah," in *Sipurim Nivharim* (Tel Aviv, 1951–52), especially 148–150.

39. For a further discussion of Scholem, see Myers, *Re-Inventing the Jewish Past*, 151–176.

FIVE

Narratives of Nation Building:
Major Themes in Zionist
Historiography

DEREK J. PENSLAR

Academic historiography on Jewish nationalism and nation-building is far younger than the Zionist movement or even the state of Israel. Beginning with classic, overarching, but impressionistic studies, Zionist historiography has, over the past twenty-five years, produced a torrent of monographic literature. Although it claims impartiality, reliance on archival sources, and positivist self-presentation, this literature is, in fact, highly politicized. Until a decade ago, certain tenets of classic Zionist ideology formed the very foundations of the scholarship on the Zionist movement and the Yishuv during its formative decades. Although some of the more recent scholarship has abandoned Zionist ideology, current writing is no less politicized — particularly the literature on the Yishuv and the early years of the State of Israel.

Whereas historiography on Jewish nationalist thought and Zionist movements in the Diaspora is written by scholars in many lands, Yishuv historiography is produced almost entirely in Israel, a crucible of fierce political and social conflicts, which in the universities take on a strong generational flavor as well. These conflicts, sustained and aggravated by Israel's unique position in the Middle East, have mobilized and factionalized many Israeli scholars. The result, unfortunately, is an atmosphere of unconventional verbal warfare, both in the universities and in the Israeli media. In so engaged an environment, it is a particular challenge to produce a satisfying historical synthesis of the Zionist project and the means by which it was realized. To be sure, Israeli writers have produced many an overview of the history of Jewish nation building. Always informative and at times brilliant, the older synthetic literature on the rise of Israel tended towards triumphalism, or at least featured an apologetic tone. The current crop, on the other hand, has a hostile edge; despite frequent claims to objectivity, it is motivated by exhaustion more than dispassion, and so tends more toward cynicism than irony.

While virtually all the monographic work on the Yishuv has been produced in Israel, much of the synthetic literature has been written in other lands, particularly the United States and Britain. An analysis of the relationship between monographic and synthetic treatments of Jewish nation building, therefore, leads of itself to a comparison between Israeli and Diaspora scholarship on the subject and between the various ideological forces behind this literature's creation.

Comprehensive histories of Zionism are almost as old as the Zionist movement itself. Shortly after World War I, Nachum Sokolow published his *History of Zionism: 1600–1918*.[1] As one can tell from the subtitle, the book is blatantly teleological and anachronistic, applying the term "Zionist" to an array of conceits, fantasies, and programs by Jew and gentile alike throughout the course of modern history. More lasting value may be found in Adolf Böhm's *Die zionistische Bewegung,* the first volume of which appeared in 1920.[2] Böhm, a veteran functionary in Austrian and international Zionism, produced a meticulous intellectual and institutional history of the Zionist movement through 1925. Böhm's narrative, biographical sketches, and statistical data remain indispensable for the scholar of early Zionist history. Unfortunately, the book's analytical framework, which depicts the relationship between political and cultural Zionism in terms of Hegelian dialectic, is both ponderous and simplistic. (For example, the conflicts within the Zionist Organization [ZO] during its first decade were multifarious, not dichotomous, as Böhm argues, and the "synthetic" Zionism preached by Chaim Weizmann at the 1907 Zionist Congress merely reconciled, and did not sublate, the opposing approaches in the ZO.)

For reflective, critical Zionist historiography with a viable analytical foundation, we cannot go back further than 1959, the year of Arthur Hertzberg's *The Zionist Idea,* an anthology of texts by Zionist ideologues preceded by a remarkable, long introduction by Hertzberg.[3] Two years later came Ben Halpern's *The Idea of the Jewish State* (1961), which, despite its title, ranged far beyond Zionist ideology and offered a general history of the international Zionist movement, the Zionist Organization's diplomatic endeavors, the Yishuv, and Israel up to the mid 1950s. Insightful and sensitively-written, the book touched on virtually every significant issue in Zionist and Israeli history. Certainly, it was limited by what we would consider today a narrow and inflexible conception of nationalism and by a bibliographic base of printed sources. Moreover, the book's organization (thematic rather than chronological) was somewhat cumbersome, and Halpern's presentation did not make the material easily accessible to the general reader. But the book remains essential, largely because Halpern— who prior to his move to academia was active as a publicist and as an administrator within the Jewish Agency—successfully placed Zionism within a broader framework of international Jewish social and political activity. Indeed, Halpern's analysis of the relationship between Zionism, international Jewish philanthropy, and the immigration crisis of the *fin de siècle* remained unsurpassed until the 1980s. Equally rich and unusual for its time is Halpern's discussion of the origins of the Jewish Agency.[4]

While scholars in America wrote the first comprehensive accounts of the Zionist experience, Israelis pioneered the monographic, archivally-based study of the Yishuv. The mid-1960s to mid-70s witnessed the beginning in Israeli universities of Zionist historiography as an academic discipline, manifested by the first doctoral dissertations in Yishuv history, learned journals such as *Tsiyonut* (1970) and *Cathedra* (1976), and research institutions such as Tel Aviv University's Weizmann Institute. For the most part, the members of this first generation (among them Israel Kolatt, Yosef Gorny, and Anita Shapira) were imbued with Labor Zionist political culture, and their books accordingly focused on the political history of the Labor sector of the Yishuv. Though sympathetic with the leaders of Labor and the ideologies they espoused, these scholars did not fail to question many of Labor Zionism's fundamental myths, such as the movement's principled commitment to democracy and probity regarding the use of violence.[5]

The scholarly revolution occurring in Israel during the 1970s had little effect on Zionist scholarship in the Diaspora. In Britain and the United States, the emphasis remained on synthesis, and the first half of the 1970s witnessed the publication of two texts still widely used to this day: Walter Laqueur's *A History of Zionism* (1972) and Howard Sachar's *A History of Israel From the Rise of Zionism to Our Time* (1976).[6] Given the massive scope of their projects, neither author was in a position to use archives, and these books were written too early to take advantage of the body of scholarly Hebrew literature on the development of the Yishuv. Instead, both books relied on the writings of Zionist leaders, ideologues, and publicists and their accounts of the development of the Yishuv drew largely from chronicles composed by Israeli labor movement activists. Laqueur, a consummate cosmopolitan intellectual with academic homes in London and Washington, D.C., as well as in Israel, produced a sophisticated analysis of Zionism's European ideological roots and its international institutional life. His analysis of the Yishuv was limited but unfailingly perceptive. Sachar's book made for a better textbook because of its smooth narrative and tight organization, but it lacked Laqueur's subtlety, and Sachar's palpable ideological biases (adoring of Labor, hostile towards the Zionist Right, and contemptuous of Palestinian nationalism) ensured that his book would become dated, whereas Laqueur's book remains fresh even today.

The best synthetic work on Zionism produced during the 1970s is also, unfortunately, the least renowned: Noah Lucas' *The Modern History of Israel* (1975). Like Laqueur and Sachar, Lucas is deeply connected to Israel but has spent most of his life and developed his academic career in the English-speaking world. Before going into academia, Lucas was a senior official of the Histadrut's Political Department, and this experience helps account for his book's masterful summaries, without parallel in non-Hebrew literature, of the Histadrut's origins and activities.[7] More important, the book as a whole is pithy, straightforward, and free of apologetics or polemics. Although Lucas is sympathetic with his subject, his book's distanced and critical approach did not endear it to Israel's champions abroad at a time when Israel, in the wake of the 1973 war, was being vilified in the international arena. But as we shall see below, many of Lucas' arguments prefigured the celebrated "new Israeli history" of the 1980s; Lucas' book was simply ahead of its time.

The mid-1970s also marked the beginning of David Vital's trilogy tracing the history of Zionism from its origins through the end of the first World War.[8] Unlike Sachar, Laqueur, or Lucas, Vital made his academic home in Israel, but in many ways he has remained an outsider to the discipline of Zionist and Yishuv history as it is practiced in Israel. The son of the Revisionist Zionist leader Meir Grossman, Vital is removed from the ideologies and sensibilities of Labor Zionism. He was educated in Britain, not Israel; his original field was Political Science, not Jewish History; and before turning to research on Zionism he wrote general analyses of state formation and international relations.[9] Not surprisingly, given this background, Vital's trilogy is primarily about Zionist politics, although the first volume (*The Origins of Zionism,* 1975) featured a pioneering analysis of the pre-Herzlian *Hibat Siyon* and a satisfying portrait of the Yishuv during the first two decades of Zionist settlement, the period of the First Aliyah.[10]

The First Aliyah was neglected by the first-generation Yishuv historians in Israel because with the exception of a small socialist contingent known as the Biluim, this pioneering wave of settlement consisted of bourgeois, observant Jews with little passion for political organization. Israeli historians preferred to focus on the Second and Third Aliyot, or more accurately, on the members of these aliyot who affected a proletarian and secular Zionist identity, indulged in ideological system-building, and devoted themselves to political organization, thereby founding the Israeli labor movement. It was only at the end of the 1970s that Israeli scholars, reflecting the decline of the Labor party throughout that decade and its electoral defeat in 1977, began to write monographic studies on the First Aliyah and on the non-Labor sectors of the Zionist polity in general. This new literature redressed a serious imbalance but at times brought with it new distortions, as previously peripheral aspects of Yishuv history were proclaimed to be central.

An example of this trend is the treatment of the Old Yishuv, the Orthodox, pre- and anti-Zionist community originating in the early 19th century, which was relegated to the trash heap of history by Labor Zionist ideologues, and only later given its due. Outstanding scholars such as Israel Bartal, Menachem Friedman, and Yehoshua Kaniel analyzed the Old Yishuv's social structure and its members' complex attitudes towards economic modernization.[11] But Arieh Morgenstern went further than the rest, arguing that the Old Yishuv was, almost from the start, charged by an active messianic fervor. Disciples of the Gaon of Vilna who emigrated to Palestine in the early 1800s believed that 1840 would mark the advent of the messianic age, which would be heralded by the expansion of Jewish settlement of the Holy Land and the construction of a viable Yishuv. After the messiah failed to arrive, this fervor died down or was suppressed, and much of the Old Yishuv's subsequent hostility to constructive settlement projects derived from this great embarrassment.[12] Morgenstern attributed settlement-oriented goals to the disciples of the Gaon of Vilna, and in so doing appeared to be claiming the likes of Rabbi Eliezer Bergmann and Rabbi Menachem Mendel of Shklov to be the true founders of Zionism.[13]

A similar situation exists in the field of historical geography, which expanded rapidly in Israeli universities in the 1980s. Scholarship on the Yishuv had always placed a heavy emphasis on geography. Zionist ideology made the associations, typical of *fin de siècle* European nationalisms, between communing with nature and collective renewal, and between the homeland's physical qualities and the *Volksgeist*. These factors, coupled with traditional Jewish veneration for the land of Israel, and the physical challenges of bringing it into Jewish hands, led from Zionism's beginning to a painstaking documentation of the acquisition, settlement, and securing of the land. Thus the Israeli historical geographers operate within an established framework; they continue to employ value-laden terminology such as "the redemption of the land" (*ge'ulat ha-'areṣ*) uncritically. At the same time, the geographers' emphasis on the Yishuv's landscape, rather than its politics, has led them to appreciate the myriad forces outside of the labor movement that assisted the construction of the Jewish state.[14] It is not coincidental, therefore, that much of the newer literature on the role of private initiative and private capital in the Yishuv has been written by geographers, not historians. The documentation of private initiative, unfortunately, can at times become a paean to the Yishuv's private sector, better reflecting contemporary Israel's rebound from decades of social-democratic hegemony than the actual experience of the Yishuv during its formative decades.[15]

The new wave of Old Yishuv and historical-geographical studies, to which should be added some pioneering work by Yishuv economic historians,[16] has not yet worked its way into the synthetic literature. During the early 1980s, the major synthetic studies took the form of biography. It is a powerful sign of the youth of Zionist historiography that until fifteen years ago there was no scholarly biography of any Zionist leader. (The exception is Theodor Herzl, a far more accessible figure to non-Israelis than the leaders of eastern European Zionism or the Yishuv, and whose Germanic orientation and myriad neuroses endear him to scholars of fin de siècle central European culture.[17]) The early 1980s, however, witnessed a flurry of biographical activity. True to form, Israelis with labor movement sympathies wrote on the leaders of Labor; in 1980, Anita Shapira, the doyenne of Yishuv historians, published a best-selling biography of Berl Katznelson, while the journalist Shabtai Teveth produced the second volume of his biography of David Ben Gurion.[18] Equally appropriately, Jehuda Reinharz — who grew up in Israel and Germany and received his higher education in the United States, where he made his academic career — took on the biography of the cosmopolitan Chaim Weizmann; the first volume was published in 1985.[19] The production of these biographies testified to the passage not only of time, but also of an era. By the 1980s, the labor movement was in eclipse, and many Israelis, feeling that the state had lost its élan, waxed nostalgic about the alleged moral values and leadership abilities once embodied by Katznelson and Ben Gurion respectively.

I would hazard an additional explanation for the popularity of biography in Israeli historiography. As I have noted above, synthetic scholarship on Zionism and the Yishuv has come from outside the Israeli historians' guild. Precisely because the Yishuv was so small an entity, and because its major historians are deeply attached to it, it is difficult for them to make the generalizations, abstractions, and deletions without which synthesis cannot be done. But scholars who would not venture to write a history of the Yishuv can satisfy the scholarly impulse to paint a broad historical canvas through biography, which, traditionally, chronicles the times as well as the life of a prominent individual. Indeed, Shapira's *Berl* offers wide-ranging narrative and analysis of the internal conflicts within the labor movement of the interwar period. Teveth's *Ben Gurion* throws new light on Yishuv political history as a whole, and Reinharz's *Chaim Weizmann* does the same for the international Zionist movement and Zionist diplomatic history.

Thus far our historiographical survey, which began in the 1960s, has taken us up to the mid-1980s. We have pointed to two waves of monographic research and synthetic scholarship on Zionism. Admittedly, the waves are separated by only a few years and they overlap considerably, but they are distinct nonetheless. Thus, we are now in position to make an informed judgment about the novelty of the so-called Israeli "new history," which began to appear in the mid-1980s. In the framework established here, the "new history" actually constitutes a third wave of Israeli historiography. And as we shall see, due to the kind of history now being written and the character of the historians themselves, the gaps between the monographic and the synthetic, between the Israeli and the foreign scholar, and between the "outsider" and the "insider," are all beginning to blur.

When it first emerged, the new history was closely identified with the 1948 Arab-Israeli war. Since 1987, Benny Morris, Avi Shlaim, and Ilan Pappé have written books that challenge fundamental assumptions in Israeli society about the origins of the Arab-Israeli conflict. Drawing on recently declassified material from Israeli archives, Morris detailed Israel's expulsion of Palestinian Arabs during the 1948 war and the prevention of their return thereafter.[20] Shlaim, focusing on Israel's relations with Transjordan, argued that the Zionist leadership reached a meeting of minds with King Abdullah to obstruct the partition of Palestine, agreeing that portions designated for an Arab state would be taken over by the Hashemite monarchy.[21] Pappé also analyzed Israeli-Jordanian relations, but he did so from the perspective of Britain's Middle-Eastern interests, which dictated the survival of Britain's Jordanian dependency. Wary that a Palestinian state led by the virulently anti-colonial Amin al-Husseini would destabilize Jordan, British policy makers supported Abdullah's expansionist plans for the West Bank, and did not oppose the establishment of Israel so long as the Negev, which Britain wanted for a military base, were in Arab hands.[22] Morris and Pappé have gone on to elaborate their views in subsequent books on the institutionalization of the Arab-Israeli conflict from 1949 to 1956.[23] Although Morris, Shlaim, and Pappé disagree on any number of issues, they concur that the Yishuv's military prowess was far greater and that of the Arab world far weaker than Zionist "official history" has it. They also concur that the Arab leadership's intentions towards the fledgling state of Israel were not uniformly malevolent.

There is a great deal more to the new history, however, than a revisionist account of the 1948 war and the events surrounding it. First, the new history is more an international than a purely Israeli undertaking. All three scholars mentioned above were educated at British universities, and until recently only Pappé held a permanent teaching position in Israel. They usually publish in English, and their works are subsequently translated into Hebrew. Second, there is no clear distinction in the new history between foreign and domestic affairs, or between politics and society. True, Morris, Shlaim, and Pappé have stuck to the diplomatic and military arenas. But Tom Segev, a journalist with an American Ph.D., argued in his first book, *1949: The First Israelis* (1986), that militarism and obsessive statism accounted for the newly-born Israel's policies as a whole — toward the Arabs, its own citizens, and the Jews of the diaspora during the era of mass immigration. Segev made his case further in *The Seventh Million: The Israelis and the Holocaust* (1993), which included a critique of the Yishuv leadership's alleged preference for state-building over rescue in the face of the Holocaust.

Segev is an investigative journalist, not an academic, and his eloquence exceeds his methodological rigor. But his holistic approach to the study of Yishuv and early Israeli society has, for some time, enjoyed currency in sociology departments in Israeli universities. In the mid-1970s, some ten years before the emergence of the Israeli new history, there occurred a sea-change in the practice of Israeli sociology. Breaking with earlier notions of sociology as a vehicle of nation-building through consensus and integration, the "new sociologists," believing Israeli society to be elitist and oppressive, developed a critical sociology intended to engender a more democratic, pluralist, and intellectually open environment.[24] Two of these sociologists, Baruch Kimmerling and Gershon Shafir, have argued for the centrality of Arab-Jewish relations and conflict to the formation of Yishuv society. According to Kimmerling, Yishuv (and then Israeli) society owed its collectivist and militaristic aspects to the Arab presence on the land the Jews coveted. The difficulties and expense associated with acquiring land necessitated concerted, public activity through national settlement institutions such as the Jewish National Fund (JNF). The impracticality of individual farming without recourse to Arab labor necessitated the development of collective agricultural settlement, which quickly assumed military functions in response to ongoing conflict with the Arabs.[25] Shafir has analyzed the effects of both the land and labor markets on Zionist colonization strategies, and in turn on Yishuv society itself, during the period of the First and Second Aliyot. Shafir argues that the important features of early Zionist settlement policy (public land-purchase and ownership by the JNF, requirements that Hebrew labor only be used on that land, and the collective, where no wages were paid) arose in response to the threat of Arab workers to integral Zionist nationalism and to the emerging Zionist national economy.[26]

Other critical sociologists have studied relations between Israelis and Palestinians, on the one hand, and between Israelis of Ashkenazic and Middle Eastern origin, on the other, within unifying frameworks such as ethnicity, class conflict, and dependency theory.[27] Although their approaches vary these sociologists, like Kimmerling and Shafir, seek to break down barriers between the study of the Yishuv and that of Palestine's Arab majority, or studies of Jews and Arabs in Israel after 1948. This agenda challenges the division in Israeli universities between Middle Eastern Studies (*mizrahanut*), on the one hand, and Zionist or Land of Israel Studies on the other. (When not taught through separate institutes or departments, Zionist and Land of Israel Studies are taught through departments of Jewish History, another product of artificial and pernicious compartmentalization.) More importantly, the new sociology features a pronounced, extra-academic, political program: the promotion of multiculturalism, Israeli-style, and the attenuation of the Arab-Israeli conflict by changing the structures and mechanisms with which Israelis view the world. It is not my intent here to ascertain the feasibility of this enterprise, or the likelihood of its reciprocation by Palestinians or other Arabs. I merely want to point out that the newest scholarship on Israeli history, like the critical sociology outlined here, is heavily engaged; its practitioners may claim to be post-Zionist, but they are not free of ideology. Academe everywhere is filled with intrigue and conflict, but in Israel academic disputes have existential ramifications, and so the line between scholarship and polemic is fine indeed.

The new historians are "outsiders" in that they normally receive their doctorates abroad, write for an international as opposed to an Israeli audience, and frequently are not integrated into the Israeli university system. But they remain "insiders" in many ways: they are Israeli by birth or have spent the bulk of their lives in Israel; they are active in Israeli public life, figuring prominently in the media; and they are engaged in a generational conflict with the somewhat older, more established academics who are first-generation Israeli historians. Their engagement in Israeli politics is visceral, not abstract. No wonder, then, that the new historians' attempts to shatter Zionist myths by refuting the narrative that nourishes them result not only in counternarratives but, at times, in countermyths as well.

The best-known feature of the new history's counternarrative is the depiction of the Yishuv leadership as militaristic and expansionist, determined to foil the creation of a Palestinian state and willing to use all means, including the mass expulsion of Palestinians, to secure the largest possible borders for the state of Israel. But counternarrative needs to be understood not merely in terms of what it says, but how and why it says it. Counternarrative is informed by a critical approach, making a clear distinction between public and private knowledge — in this case, between the information available to most of the Yishuv's population and matters known only to the political elite, such as secret negotiations or intelligence assessments. New historical counternarrative distinguishes between proclaimed and hidden intentions of Zionist and Arab political leaders and between the desired and unforseen consequences of those actions. Thus Morris shows how the implementation of the Haganah's notorious Plan D — whose goal was securing the territory and adjoining the areas allotted by the U.N. to the Jewish state — resulted only at times in outright expulsion; more often it induced panic and hence mass flight among Arab villagers. Morris' and Pappé's recreation of the events of the 1949 Lausanne conference points to a web of secret negotiations resulting in a number of possible frameworks for an Arab-Israeli peace treaty. Furthermore, a common theme running through the new history is the presence of an inverse correlation between the levels of blood-chilling rhetoric coming from the Arab world in the late 1940s and its actual military prowess.

Countermyth is distinguished from counternarrative in that in countermyth, one set of stereotypes is replaced by another, intentions determine outcomes, the categories "aggressor" and "victim" are not deconstructed, but merely reversed, and the secrecy and disinformation necessary to statecraft are equated with conspiracy. Since 1948, anti-Israel literature, in the form of crude governmental propaganda or the more refined variety found in academe throughout the western world, has featured these characteristics. Israelis themselves have written in this vein. In 1987, the late Simcha Flappan, former Arab Affairs expert for the far-left political party Mapam, published *The Birth of Israel: Myths and Realities,* a caricature of the new history, and a handy reference for individuals ill-disposed toward Israel. But do the more responsible new historians also produce countermyth?

Morris' book on the Palestinian refugee problem avoids this pitfall, although he can certainly be accused of selectivity and a failure to contextualize Jewish military policies in late 1947 and 1948. Morris does, on occasion, point to the danger facing the Yishuv during the first few months of fighting, but he underplays the connection between these early losses and the more aggressive Israeli behavior after March 1948. Morris makes much of the fact that the inhabitants of many Palestinian towns and villages wanted peace, but if Arab irregulars were indeed strangling Jewish settlements by controlling the roads, it is not clear what alternatives to conquest, if any, the Zionists faced. To provide one other example, Morris paints a grim picture of the Haganah bombardment of Safed, resulting in a mass flight of Arabs, but since Safed was in the area designated by the U.N. for the Jewish state, and the Arab Liberation Army was about to attack it, we are left unsure whether Morris' intention is to detail an act of injustice or merely an act of war.

Shlaim's work is more problematic, accusing the Zionists of chronic aggressiveness, minimizing the Jews' own suffering and sense of crisis throughout the war, and, most important, exaggerating the amorphous accords between King Abdullah and the Zionist leadership prior to the outbreak of hostilities in 1947. Although Shlaim argues explicitly that Palestinian militancy and rejectionism left the Yishuv no choice but to thwart the creation of a Palestinian state, he describes Israeli military action in the Arab areas of the UN Partition Resolution as "Jewish aggressiveness."[28] Shlaim offers a thorough narrative of Hashemite-Zionist negotiations regarding Abdullah's aspirations in Palestine, but he underplays the fact that by the time the talks broke down, Abdullah had not given his blessing to the establishment of Israel, nor was there any formal agreement to avoid hostilities. Shlaim does not have a good word to say about Haj Amin al-Husseini, but he presents the Palestinians as a whole as passive, blameless victims of foreign intrigue, in no way responsible for the tragedy that befell them.

Images of the Palestinian as weak and nonaggressive and the Jew as powerful and belligerent are clearly-drawn in Pappé's second book, *The Making of the Arab-Israeli Conflict, 1947–1951* (1992). At the time of the vote on the Partition Resolution, writes Pappé, most Palestinian Arabs were peaceful and nonaggressive; only Jewish attacks provoked them to violence, he argues, and the Jews responded viciously by means of their military underground, which was able to unite "into one mighty force at the right moment."[29] According to Pappé, Palestinian Arab military successes in the winter of 1948 were minor, limited to obstructing Jewish transportation, briefly and partially besieging Jerusalem, and attacking isolated settlements. The Haganah's Plan D amounted to an expulsion plan because it dictated that in order to avoid expulsion, Palestinians would have to surrender to the Jews and not fight against them, demands that apparently strike Pappé as unreasonable. The Arab leadership, he argues, was dragged into war in 1948 by mutual suspicion and the pressures of public opinion, not by any serious desire to annihilate the new Jewish state. There is truth in this claim, but Pappé frames it disingenuously, for his references to Arab public opinion are tangential, not direct, and he fails to confront the significance—for the future as well as the past of the Arab-Israeli conflict—of uncompromising popular hostility to Israel which Arab leaders, even in nondemocratic regimes, overlook only at their peril.

In their contributions to the Israeli press, particularly the distinguished newspaper *Ha-'Aretz,* the new historians and sociologists have been expansive about the broad ramifications of their scholarship: the rethinking of Israeli history as a whole and the transformation of Israeli collective memory. By and large, however, their scholarship has pursued more limited goals, focusing, particularly for the historians, on a well-defined theme and a fixed period of time. The most recent major work of Zionist historical synthesis was written not by a new historian of the Arab-Israeli conflict, but an established Israeli scholar of French history and of European fascism. Zev Sternhell's book *Nation-Building or a New Society? The Zionist Labor Movement (1904–1940) and the Origins of Israel*[30] returns to the subject matter dear to the first-generation Yishuv historians who are Sternhell's peers: the rise and fall of the Zionist labor movement. Sternhell employs the scholarship of Shapira, Gorny, Kolatt, and Teveth, but he does so in order to subvert them. This is an adversarial work, a harsh critique of the founders of Labor and, by extension, of the Yishuv historians who have written on them. The book has aroused considerable controversy in Israel, and it deserves careful attention.

Sternhell argues that the major forces within the Zionist labor movement, the forces that in 1930 coalesced in the political party Mapai and established the state of Israel, were never socialist but rather obsessively statist. Socialist Zionism was ideologically linked not to European social democracy, but rather to its nemesis, integral nationalism. Chauvinistic and xenophobic, integral nationalism tried to subsume class conflict through the mobilization of capital and labor alike in defense of the nation against its ostensible foes. The result was European "national socialism," which, Sternhell argues, was replicated in the Zionist labor movement. The seeds of Zionist national socialism were present from the beginning of the second Aliyah, and they germinated immediately after the first World War, with the liquidation of the formally marxist *Po'alei Ṣiyon* party and the formation of *'Aḥdut ha-'Avodah,* whose ideology was formulated by non-socialist "independents" such as Berl Katznelson. The Histadrut, founded in 1920, was designed to mobilize the worker for nation building, not for class struggle and the attainment of social equality. David Ben Gurion saw the Histadrut as a collection of disconnected, fractured, and anonymous individuals, not of autonomous, empowered groups that could challenge state authority. The Histadrut's idealization of the Hebrew laborer was merely a compensation for his objective, low social status. By venerating the worker but leaving capitalism intact, the Histadrut was a classic vehicle of Zionist national socialism. The final step, in Sternhell's view, was the creation of Mapai, which involved a union — unprecedented in the history of European social democracy — of what was technically a socialist party ('Aḥdut ha-'Avodah) with a virulently non-socialist one (Ha-Po 'el ha-Ṣa 'ir). Thus, Ben-Gurion's all-embracing statism, or *mamlakhtiyut,* which historians normally trace back to the early years of the state, was well in place by the 1920s.[31]

The book centers around unfavorable comparisons between the Zionist labor movement and "authentic," that is, western European, social democracy. Social democracy featured brilliant theoreticians, whereas their Labor Zionist equivalents, the likes of A. D. Gordon, Chaim Arlosoroff, and Katznelson, were derivative, unsystematic, and self-contradictory. Social democracy was wary of employing violence, but Ben Gurion and Katznelson chafed to force the stychic process and were willing to use any means at their disposal. (Katznelson's voluntarism and his emphases on feeling and myth, link him, by association, with Sorel's veneration of violence.[32]) Most importantly, European social democracy despised private capital, whereas Labor Zionism coveted it as a means of nation-building. The result was an unshakable alliance between Labor and bourgeois Zionists, who cynically conspired to exploit the workers for their nation-making and profit-making abilities respectively. The kibbutz and moshav, the alleged hallmarks of Labor Zionism and proofs of its socialist ethos, were, in fact, islands in a capitalist sea. Their very existence attested to Labor's acceptance of capitalism as the normative economic system. Sternhell argues that "the one serious attempt to realize socialism beyond the kibbutz fence" was made by *Gedud ha-'Avodah,* the Labor Battalion, founded by pioneers of the Third Aliyah who sincerely believed in the value of physical labor and mutual assistance, shunned political machine building, and stood for genuine democracy. But this noble experiment was crushed by Ben Gurion and his mighty political machines, 'Aḥdut ha-'Avodah and the Histadrut.[33]

Nation-Building or a New Society? exudes the impassioned anger of a long-silent victim. Sternhell tells us that Israel never was a socialist utopia, as generations were taught to believe: its urban workers labored for a pittance while Histadrut careerists lived in style, and its kibbutzniks, rather than constituting a socialist vanguard, were in fact nothing more than a warrior elite. "If the matter depended on him," suggests Sternhell, "Ben Gurion would have built the Histadrut society in the image of the class of the Guardians in Plato's *Republic:* an elite group, propertyless, living communally, and its entire existence devoted to the service of the whole."[34] Sternhell's image of a merciless Zionist statism, and of Ben Gurion as the awesome tribal father, is in keeping with much of the newer Israeli scholarship's treatment of Yishuv history during the traumatic period from the Second World War through the establishment of the state. And like other products of the new history, there is much to be said for Sternhell's book. Statism can indeed flourish without socialism; in many lands, governmental ownership of industry and control over large sectors of the economy co-exist with flagrant social inequity. But the book features a number of problems, two of which I will address here: the author's hypostatization of the concepts of social democracy and national socialism, on the one hand, and on the other, the book's tendency to "crash through open doors," that is, to present as novel arguments and evidence already made by historians, including those whom he criticizes.

Sternhell exaggerates the tangible accomplishments, morality, and ideological purity of European social democracy. During the years 1904–1940, the period covered by Sternhell's book, social democratic parties in the major European countries did not govern on the national level for protracted periods. In France, the Socialists did not enter the government as a party until 1936, and prime minister Léon Blum's celebrated Popular Front lasted less than two years. His government strove for social reform within the existing capitalist framework. True, the Popular Front's reforms were bitterly attacked by industrial interests, but so were the economic policies of the ZO and the Histadrut. (Sternhell claims that bourgeois Zionists knew that the kibbutz represented no threat to their economic interests, but in fact until the mid 1930s the kibbutz was the object of constant attack by bourgeois forces in the ZO and the Yishuv.[35]) Blum's nationalization of military industry was designed to fortify France against its enemies — a statist enterprise worthy of Ben Gurion himself. As to Germany, the notorious pact in November 1918 between SPD leader Friedrich Ebert and General Wilhelm Groener of the German military high command provides ample evidence of Social Democracy's willingness to adopt strange bedfellows when the maintenance of order was at stake. And in Austria, when the Social Democrats briefly participated in the post-war governing coalitions, they did not declare war on private capital, nor did they seek to transform the state into a dictatorship of the proletariat. As the American political theorist Mitchell Cohen noted in his 1987 book, *Zion and State* (a book whose similarities to Sternhell's I will discuss below), Otto Bauer, the leader of the Austrian Social Democrats, justified his party's actions with the claim that the Austrian republican state balanced competing class interests.[36] Thus Ben Gurion's conceptual separation of "class" from the "nation" and "state" had a European pedigree, or at least a European parallel, after all.

Even if European social democracy's record in the first half of this century were brighter, does it make sense to compare Palestine to the industrialized lands on the western half of the European continent? Labor Zionism did not function within a pre-existing nation-state; the working class did not exist but had to be created. Like Bolshevism, Labor Zionism transmuted Social Democracy into an ideological system that suited the conditions of the society and territory involved. Not surprisingly, Bolshevism — which sought to bring revolution to an economically backward land by means of the centralization of power and the collectivization of resources — was at least as important an ideological influence on the founders of Labor Zionism as was western social democracy. In Sternhell's morally-charged prose, "Bolshevik" is a term of opprobrium, and Sternhell criticizes Yishuv historians for underplaying the dictatorial qualities of the Labor Zionist founding fathers while exaggerating their humanist and social-democratic traits. Certainly, most Yishuv historians are, unlike Sternhell, sympathetic to Labor's leaders, but their analyses are more nuanced and critical than Sternhell claims them to be.

Let us start with the founding of 'Aḥdut ha-'Avodah in 1919. "[A]ll their lives," Anita Shapira has written, the leaders of 'Aḥdut ha-'Avodah "were reluctant to identify themselves and their movements with the camp of social democracy."[37] The founding of 'Aḥdut ha-'Avodah, Shapira acknowledges, represented the political suicide of the social-democratic Palestinian Po'alei Ṣiyon. Non-Po'alei Ṣiyon members dominated the party's leadership and rank-and-file alike. 'Aḥdut ha-'Avodah's platform did not include class struggle and "bore little resemblance to any of the accepted socialist theories."[38] The leaders of 'Aḥdut ha-'Avodah drew on motley intellectual influences ranging from Kropotkinesque anarchism to Bolshevism. Katznelson was "remote from dogmatic socialism," and Marxism accounted for neither his economic philosophy nor his elitist conception of the Hebrew agricultural laborer as constituting the vanguard of the Zionist homeland. Yitzhak Tabenkin, leader of the United Kibbutz movement, favored Soviet-style collectivism within the kibbutz movement but resisted *Gleichschaltung* into the Ben Gurionist state; he argued simultaneously against economic reformism abroad and in favor of Zionist constructivism in Palestine.[39] 'Aḥdut ha-'Avodah's strange brew of Bolshevik collectivism and syndicalist decentralism was not, pace Sternhell, the result of false consciousness or mendaciousness, but rather of the fact that its members were seeking to build up a country from scratch and could not, therefore, afford the luxury of ideological purity. Moreover, the non-revolutionary socialism embodied in western European social democracy did not satisfy their yearning for achievement, which made them constructivists on the ground but sincere revolutionaries in spirit.

Moving ahead in Yishuv history, Sternhell's critique of the founding of Mapai as a triumph for the non-socialist Ha-Po'el ha-Ṣa'ir was anticipated twenty years ago by Noah Lucas, who observed calmly that "[a]s Mapai became responsible for national decisions its concentration on national problems took a toll of socialist commitment, so that in practice the party was increasingly identified in the line of succession to Ha-Po'el ha-Ṣa'ir."[40] The failings of the Histadrut were acknowledged by Shabtai Teveth, whose biography of Ben Gurion describes the transformation of the Histadrut into a political machine featuring significant wage differentials between the privileged bureaucratic elite and the common worker.[41] Mapai's Bolshevik qualities were analyzed at length in the mid-1970s by the sociologist Yonatan Shapiro, and Shapira has documented Ben Gurion's scheme after 1948 to transform Mapai into a communist-style hegemonic institution, dominating the military, immigrant absorption, and education in the new state.[42]

In addition to its individual arguments, the overarching theme of *Nation Building or New Society?* was anticipated by earlier scholarship. I mentioned above Mitchell Cohen's 1987 book *Zion and State,* a stimulating and well-crafted analysis of Yishuv political history that in many ways parallels Sternhell. Cohen argues that Labor's assumption of state-building tasks after the First World War, and its struggle against Revisionism during the 1930s led to a "reification" of Zionism through a "fetishization" of the state. Whereas during Labor's infancy the interests of the working class were perceived as identical with those of the nation, during the interwar period the working class came to be seen as one group among many, with the state as the great unifying force between competing interests. Thus Ben Gurion's *mamlakhtiyut* of the 1950s was ideologically well grounded in an earlier period, as was the soulless, technocratic utopianism of Ben Gurion's protégé, Shimon Peres, who served with Ben Gurion in the splinter party Rafi during the 1960s. Both books claim that Labor deviated from an authentic socialist project and whored after the idol of statism. The main difference between Cohen and Sternhell is that the former employs a historical dialectic whose existence the latter denies. Cohen presents a historical progression in which the thesis (authentic socialism) confronts its antithesis (Revisionist integral nationalism), producing the synthesis of early Israeli *mamlakhtiyut.* This schema involves a considerable exaggeration of the Revisionist threat to the Yishuv and, even more so, of the ideological distinctions between Jabotinsky and the Mapai leadership.[43] But it is more realistic and sensitive to historical contingency than Sternhell's assumption that mainstream Labor Zionism was, from the start, a variety of national socialism.

The books by Cohen and Sternhell differ in style as well as content. There is a bitter and aggressive edge in Sternhell's writing, whereas Cohen, although clearly disappointed that Labor Zionism did not fulfill its socialist potential, maintains a civil tone throughout. Whereas Sternhell is immersed in the tense academic environment of the Hebrew University of Jerusalem, Cohen writes from the relatively tranquil perspective of the City University of New York. At the same time, Cohen is hardly a stranger to his subject; he is a longtime Zionist activist and former editor of the American Labor Zionist journal, *The Jewish Frontier.* Yet, more than the actual merits or weaknesses of the books, the fact that Sternhell resides in Israel explains why *Nation Building or a New Society?* has created a storm of controversy in Israel, and *Zion and State* did not. Sternhell may be an outsider to the guild of Yishuv historians, but he is a prominent figure in Israeli academia, and so his book demands attention, whereas critiques of Israel by foreigners are often disregarded there. Moreover, Sternhell's book is in many ways consonant with the Israeli new history which was just emerging when *Zion and State* was published, but which is now in full flower. Sternhell's book therefore provides powerful ammunition for those combatants in Israeli universities struggling to preserve, deconstruct, or reconfigure Israeli collective memory, and with it, Israeli political culture.

The Zionist historiography being written today is no less engaged than it was twenty-five years ago, although the terms of engagement have changed considerably. There has been considerable growth of interest in the field among scholars with academic specializations and academic homes outside the departments of Jewish History in Israeli universities. The scholarship continues to be dominated by Israelis: Yishuv historians and geographers, Israeli academics in other fields, scholars on the periphery of the Israeli university system, and Israeli academics abroad. But the field is developing a more international dimension. Although we have come to expect the production of Zionist intellectual history by non-Israeli scholars, two recent works by Americans — Steven Zipperstein's biography of Aḥad ha-'am and David Myers' study of the "Jerusalem school" of Jewish historiography — stand out for, among other things, their contextualization of ideas within the Zionist movement and the society of the Yishuv.[44] It is likely that the diffusion abroad of scholarship on Jewish nationalism and nation-building will attenuate the sharp tone and polarized argumentation that characterizes many works of Israeli historiography. True, most non-Israelis who write about Israel have strong feelings for or against the country; there is no simple correlation between distance and detachment. Still, an international community of Zionist and Israeli historians is sure to strengthen the comparative and analytical dimensions of the literature, and will improve the accessibility of information about Israel to a global reading public.[45] Ultimately, however, the direction taken by future Israeli historical scholarship will depend upon forces over which academics have little control. As long as Israel remains threatened from without and riven by internal strife, there will be ample grounds for partisanship among its intellectuals, mandarins and rebels alike.

NOTES

1. Nahum Sokolow, *History of Zionism 1600–1918,* (London, 1919).

2. Adolf Böhm, *Die zionistische Bewegung,* (Berlin, 1935–1937).

3. Arthur Hertzberg, *The Zionist Idea* (New York, 1959).

4. Ben Halpern, *The Idea of the Jewish State* (Cambridge, Mass., 1961), 109–30, 144–57, 179–204. For a recent analysis of the refugee crisis of the 1880s and the international Jewish philanthropic response, see Jonathan Frankel, *Prophecy and Politics: Socialism, Nationalism, and the Russian Jews, 1862–1917* (Cambridge, 1981), chapter 2 *passim.* On the origins of the Jewish Agency see Yigal Elam, *Ha-Sokhnut ha-Yehudit: Shanim Rish'onot* (Jerusalem, 1990).

5. Israel Kolatt, "'Ideologiyah u-Meṣi'ut bi-Tenu'at ha-'Avodah be-'Ereṣ Yisra'el, 1905–1919," Ph.D. diss., Hebrew University of Jerusalem, 1964; Yosef Gorny, *'Aḥdut ha-'Avodah: ha-Yesodot ha-Ra'ayoniyim veha-Shitah ha-Medinit* (Tel Aviv, 1973); Anita Shapira, *Ha-Ma'avaq ha-Nikhzav: 'Avodah 'Ivrit 1929–1939* (Tel Aviv, 1977). Other examples of this first generation include Elkana Margalit, *Ha-Shomer ha-Ṣa'ir: mi-'Adat Ne'urim le-Marksism Mahapkhani 1913–1936* (Tel Aviv, 1971); Dan Giladi, *Ha-Yishuv bi-Tequfat ha-'Aliyah ha-Revi'it (1924–1929)* (Tel Aviv, 1973); and an important work by the sociologist Yonatan Shapiro, *The Formative Years of the Israel Labour Party: The Organization of Power, 1919–1930* (London, 1976).

6. Both books remain in print.

7. Noah Lucas, *The Modern History of Israel* (New York, 1975), 82–91.

8. David Vital, *The Origins of Zionism* (Oxford, 1975); *Zionism: The Formative Years* (Oxford, 1982); *Zionism: The Crucial Phase* (Oxford, 1987).

9. David Vital, *The Inequality of States: A Study of the Small Power in International Relations* (Oxford, 1967); *The Survival of Small States: Studies in Small Power/Great Power Conflict* (London, 1971).

10. Vital, *Origins of Zionism,* 79–108. Unfortunately, the Yishuv is badly neglected in *Zionism: The Formative Years,* which covers the period from 1897 to 1911, and in *Zionism: The Crucial Phase,* which continues the narrative up through 1918.

11. On the Old Yishuv during the Ottoman period, see Yehoshua Kaniel, *Hemshekh u-Temurah: ha-Yishuv ha-Yashan veha-Yishuv he-Ḥadash bi-Tequfat ha-'Aliyah ha-Rishonah veha-Sheniyah* (Jerusalem, 1981); Israel Bartal's important collection of essays, composed between 1976 and 1989: *Galut ba'-Areṣ: Yishuv 'Ereṣ Yisra'el be-Ṭerem Ṣiyonut* (Jerusalem, 1995); and Michael Silber, "Pa 'amei lev be-'Erets ha-Ger," *Cathedra* 73 (1994), 84–105. On Orthodox Jews in Mandate Palestine, see Menachem Friedman, *Ḥevrah ve-Dat: ha-Ortodoksia halo' Ṣiyonit be-'Ereṣ Yisra'el 1918–1936* (Jerusalem 1977).

12. Arieh Morgenstern, *Meshiḥiyut ve-Yishuv 'Ereṣ-Yisra'el ba-Maḥaṣit ha-Rishonah shel ha-Me'ah ha-Yod-tet* (Jerusalem, 1985).

13. For a trenchant critique of Morgenstern's scholarship, with a rejoinder by Morgenstern, see Bartal, *Galut ba-'Areṣ*, 236–296.

14. Ran Aaronsohn has studied the influence of Baron Edmond de Rothschild's investments in the Jewish colonies in *Ha-Baron veha-Moshavot: ha-Hityashvut ha-Yehudit be-'Ereṣ Yisra'el be-Reshitah 1882–1890* (Jerusalem, 1990). On the role played by private capital during the Ottoman period, see Yossi Ben-Artsi, "Tokhnito shel M. Meirovitch u-mekomah be-Toldot ha-Hityashvut ha-Kafrit ha-Yehudit," *Ṣiyon* 53 (1988), 273–290; Ruth Kark, *Jaffa: A City in Evolution 1799–1917* (Jerusalem, 1990); and Yossi Katz, *The "Business" of Settlement: Private Entrepreneurship in the Jewish Settlement of Palestine, 1900–1914* (Jerusalem, 1994). Gideon Biger has written on the British role in the development of the Yishuv during the Mandate period in *Moshevet Keter'o-Bayit Le'umi? Hashpa'at ha-Shilṭon ha-Briti 'al 'Ereṣ Yisra'el, 1917–1930* (Jerusalem, 1983).

15. This is particularly true of Katz, *The "Business" of Settlement.*

16. For example, Nachum Gross, *Banka'i le'Umah be-Hithadshutah: Toldot Bank Le'umi le-Yisra'el* (Ramat Gan, 1977); with Yizhak Greenberg, *Bank ha-Po'alim: Ḥamishim ha-Shanim ha-Rishonot 1921–1971* (Tel Aviv, 1994); Jacob Metser, *Hon Le'umi le-Bayit Le'umi 1919–1921* (Jerusalem, 1979); idem, *Mesheq Yehudi u-Mesheq 'Aravi be-Ereṣ Yisra'el: Toṣar, Ta'asuqah, u-Ṣemiḥah bi-Tequfat ha-Mandat* (Jerusalem, 1990); Hagit Lavsky, *Yesodot ha-Taqsiv la-Mif'al ha-Ṣiyoni: Va'ad ha-Ṣirim, 1918–1921* (Jerusalem, 1980); and Giladi, *Ha-Yishuv.*

17. The first critical-biographical studies of Herzl were Carl Schorske's seminal article, "Politics in a New Key: An Austrian Tryptich," *Journal of Modern History* 34 (1967), reprinted in *Fin de Siècle Vienna: Politics and Culture* (New York, 1980), 343–386; and Amos Elon, *Herzl* (New York, 1975). See also Desmond Steward, *Theodor Herzl: Artist and Politician* (New York, 1974); Ernst Pawel, *The Labyrinth of Exile: A Life of Theodor Herzl* (New York, 1989); Steven Beller,

Herzl (London, 1991); and Jacques Kornberg, *Theodor Herzl: From Assimilation to Zionism* (Bloomington, Ind., 1993).

18. Anita Shapira, *Berl*, (Tel Aviv, 1980; abridged English edition, *Berl: The Biography of a Socialist Zionist* [Cambridge, 1984]); Shabtai Teveth, *Kinat David: Ḥaye David Ben Gurion* (Jerusalem, 1976, 1980, 1987) abridged English ed., *Ben-Gurion: The Burning Ground 1886–1948* (Boston, 1987).

19. Jehuda Reinharz, *Chaim Weizmann: The Making of a Zionist Leader* (New York, 1985).

20. Benny Morris, *The Birth of the Palestinian Refugee Problem 1947–1949* (Cambridge, 1987); idem, *1948 and After: Israel and the Palestinians* (Oxford, 1990). Morris' argument regarding the origins of the Palestinian refugee problem was prefigured by Noah Lucas; see *Modern History of Israel*, 252–253.

21. Avi Shlaim, *Collusion Across the Jordon* (New York, 1988). A significantly revised and abridged edition was published as *The Politics of Partition: King Abdullah, the Zionists, and Palestine 1921–1951* (New York, 1990).

22. Ilan Pappé, *Britain and the Arab-Israeli Conflict, 1948–51* (New York, 1988).

23. Ilan Pappé, *The Making of the Arab-Israeli Conflict 1947–51* (London, 1992); Benny Morris, *Israel's Border Wars 1949–1956* (Oxford, 1993).

24. See Uri Ram, *The Changing Agenda of Israeli Sociology* (Albany, NY, 1995).

25. Baruch Kimmerling, *Zionism and Territory: The Socio-Territorial Dimensions of Zionist Politics* (Berkeley, 1983).

26. Gershon Shafir, *Land, Labor, and the Origins of the Israeli-Palestinian Conflict 1882–1914* (Cambridge, 1989).

27. Ram, *Changing Agenda*, Chapters 6 and 7.

28. Shlaim, *Collusion Across the Jordan*, 177.

29. Pappé, *Arab-Israeli Conflict*, 65.

30. Zev Sternhell, *Binyan 'Umah 'o Tiqun Ḥevrah? Le'umiyut ve-Soṣializm bi-Tnu'at ha-'Avodah ha-Yisra'elit 1904–1940* (Tel Aviv, 1995).

31. Sternhell's argument is made forcefully, and repeatedly, throughout the long introduction and the conclusion. See especially 44, 48, and 50–54.

32. Ibid., 173.

33. Ibid., 260–273.

34. Ibid., 156.

35. Compare Sternhell, 55, with Henry Near, *The Kibbutz Movement: A History*, vol. 1, *Origins and Growth, 1909–1939* (New York, 1992), 170–71, 174; and Derek Penslar, "Technical Leadership and the Construction of the Rural Yishuv," in *Zionist Leadership*, ed. Jehuda Reinharz and Anita Shapira (forthcoming).

36. Mitchell Cohen, *Zion & State: Nation, Class, and the Shaping of Modern Israel* (New York, 1987), 129–31.

37. Anita Shapira, "Labour Zionism and the October Revolution," *Journal of Contemporary History* 24 (1989), 652.

38. Shapira, *Berl: The Biography of a Socialist Zionist,* 89.

39. Shapira, *Berl,* 72–74, 84–90; Shapira, "Labour Zionism and the October Revolution," 623–656 passim; Shapira, " 'Black Night, White Snow': Attitudes of the Palestinian Labor Movement to the Russian Revolution, 1917–1929," *Studies in Contemporary Jewry* 4 (1988), 144–171.

40. Lucas, *Modern History of Israel,* 130. The formation of Mapai, Lucas goes on to note, catalyzed the coalescence of left-socialist dissident groups within the Histadrut, so that henceforth the main source of debate within labor would no longer be Ha-Poʻel ha-Ṣaʻir's complaining about ʼAḥdut ha-ʻAvodah's "socialism," but rather a left-wing critique that Mapai is not socialist enough.

41. Teveth, *Ben-Gurion,* 242–249.

42. Shapiro, *The Formative Years of the Israel Labour Party;* Shapira, "Labour Zionism and the October Revolution," 650.

43. Cohen's discussion of Revisionism leaves the reader with the impression that the Revisionists alone mythologized the fighting Jew and esteemed Hebrew labor as a political and strategic weapon against the indigenous population (see especially *Zion & State* 143–44). But such ideas enjoyed currency among the Labor mainstream as well.

44. Steven J. Zipperstein, *Elusive Prophet: Aḥad ha-Am and the Origins of Zionism* (Berkeley, 1993); David N. Myers, *Re-inventing the Jewish Past: European Jewish Intellectuals and the Zionist Return to History* (New York, 1995). There are also a few non-Israelis who are currently working on Israeli social and political history; Noah Lucas is writing a political history of Israel, and my book *Zionism and Technocracy* deals with settlement planning in the rural Yishuv.

45. The newly-established journal *Israel Studies,* edited by Ilan Troen of Ben Gurion University and Noah Lucas at Oxford, should do much to achieve this goal.

SIX

Cecil Roth, Historian of Italian Jewry: A Reassessment

DAVID B. RUDERMAN

I have a confession to make. I have long been a fan of Cecil Roth (1899–1970) and his histories of Italian Jewry. My copy of Roth's *The Jews in the Renaissance,* published in 1959, was one of the first books in Jewish history I acquired as a youth, years before I became interested in the profession of history. This relatively worn copy still adorns my shelf and dates quite accurately my fascination with this engaging popularizer of the Jewish historical experience from my high school years.

I was drawn to the book even more when I began to study the Italian Renaissance in college. Roth was enjoyable to read because he possessed a remarkable eye for the unusual and the colorful, or as he himself notes unabashedly in his introduction: "If I have preferred the picturesque to the drab, and devoted space to the curious as well as to the important, I do not feel that an apology is needed."[1] But he also intrigued me for another reason. In my naively adolescent search for a meaningful balance between my

Jewish and American selves, I could not help but stand awestruck by Roth's incredible pronouncement about my beloved Renaissance:

> In Renaissance Italy, we have the unique phenomenon of that suc-
> cessful synthesis which is the unfulfilled hope of many today. The Jews
> who translated Averroes achieved distinction as physicians, compiled
> astronomical treatises, wrote plays, directed the theater, composed mu-
> sic and so on, were in almost every case not merely loyal Jews, but
> actively intellectual Jews, conversant with Hebrew, studying its litera-
> ture and devoted to talmudic scholarship. The papal physicians who
> dabbled in Italian letters and were engaged in scientific investigation
> acted also as rabbis of their communities; the playwright-impresario
> was at the same time a Hebrew poet who founded a synagogue; the
> same individual plays a role of major importance in the history of
> Hebrew and of Italian printing; the financiers who mingled with the
> Medicean circle in Florence were students, patrons, and sometimes
> workers in the field of Italian literature. It was perhaps the only period
> of history, with the exception of that of Arab predominance . . . when
> absorption into the civilization of the environment had no corrosive
> effect on Jewish intellectual life.[2]

Roth had no qualms about viewing the past from the perspective of the present, in searching for paradigms of cooperation and dialogue between Jews and Christians in an era still smarting from the horrific breakdown of positive interaction engendered by the Nazi Holocaust. No doubt the *Shoah* punctured the naive optimism with which he wrote about Jewish life in Italy in the pre-war years, as he readily admitted in the introduction to his collection of essays entitled *Personalities and Events in Jewish History,* published even earlier in 1953. Yet, even then he took pride in claiming to initiate "the wider reaction against what has been termed 'the lachrymose interpretation of Jewish history,'" a reaction generally associated with the historiographical position of Salo W. Baron.[3] And he was also thoroughly unrepentant in insisting that he was "still right at the time that [he] wrote" despite the fact that these essays about the past "were written in a different age from the present."[4]

At his death in 1970, Roth had left a lasting mark on Jewish scholarship with an immense literary output of some 600 works; a distinguished tenure as reader in Jewish Studies at Oxford, which he held for some 25 years; and the culminating distinction of serving as the editor-in-chief of the *Encyclopaedia Judaica,* which appeared only a year after he died. With the exception of an embarrassing episode at Bar Ilan University — where he was accused unjustly of heresy because of a statement in his popular history regarding the historicity of Moses, a statement that forced him to resign — Roth was largely acclaimed both for the prodigiousness of his scholarship and for its accessibility among a large community of readers. Roth wrote for a general reading public with a lively and elegant style in his popular surveys of Jewish history, eschewing extensive documentation. As he himself acknowledged in his presidential address before the Jewish Historical Society of England, he wrote to entertain, to discover "the historical byways hitherto unexpected or unexplored, the revealing of unknown characters and personalities — heroes, scholars, saints, charlatans, adventurers, scoundrels." In short, he wrote Jewish history because it was fun.[5]

Roth's reputation has been tarnished significantly in recent years, at least regarding his histories of Italian Jewry, by the sharp critique of the Israeli historian Robert Bonfil. While Bonfil had voiced reservations about the approach of Roth and others to the study of Italian Jewry as early as 1975, his most pointed attack appeared in an English article published in 1984.[6] In this essay, Bonfil criticized the slavish use of cultural patterns constructed for general history by Jewish historians to describe an analogous situation for the Jewish minority. He objected in particular to Roth's and others' utilization of Jacob Burckhardt's obsolete vision of the Renaissance in describing Italian Jewish history of the period. For Burckhardt and for Roth, according to Bonfil, the Renaissance for Christians and Jews represented a harmonious synthesis between contrasting elements. Captivated by Burckhardt's charming vision, Roth interpreted Jewish history exclusively in terms of participation in the general culture. Like Graetz before him, Roth considered Jewish life worthwhile only if it contributed positively to human progress, so claimed Bonfil, and given the high level of participation in the general culture by certain Jewish elites during the Renaissance, this period was especially attractive. Bonfil assumed conversely that defending one's Jewishness in this period, that is, resisting a full participation in the general cultural life, must have meant for Roth "antirationalism, fundamentalism and obscurantism."[7]

What especially incensed Bonfil about Roth's emphasis was a quotation from Roth's *The History of the Jews of Italy* (1946) about the periodic but localized persecutions of Jews in Italy. Given the importance Bonfil attaches to this statement, I shall quote it fully:

> "For it must be remembered that the Italian's temperament is no less volatile than versatile. As recent years have demonstrated, he can easily be stirred up to a frenzy by an orator who plays on his sentiment. But these moments of passion cannot last for long, and when they are passed he reverts to his easygoing, indolent, friendly self. Sometimes, a bloody riot might be caused by the inflammatory flow of rhetoric from the pulpit. But after the wave of feeling had ebbed, and the series of sermons was ended, and the friar had moved on to another city, the frenzy would die down as suddenly as it had risen. The Jew repaired his broken windows, and the needy plebeian again began to bring along his valuables in the hope of raising money, and there would be laughter and singing and perhaps drinking in the streets, and somber ecclesiastics would once again begin to mutter at the excessive cordiality, and it would again be true that in no part of the world did such a feeling of friendliness prevail as in Italy between the people and the Jews."[8]

And here is Bonfil's highly charged response to this passage:

> "One may wonder what Joseph ha-Cohen [The Jewish chronicler living in 16th-century Italy] would have said about such a picture! Persecutions, blood-libels, expulsions, the perennial precariousness of living on the terms of a *condotta* — all this was nothing more than a small cloud in a vast blue sky stretching over the heads of jolly people laughing and singing and drinking in the streets! Yet more than the scheme itself, what is particularly disturbing is the ideological bias underlying it . . . in the assumption that the maintenance of national and cultural uniqueness at all times and in all places connotes a readiness to reduce the points of contact with the surrounding culture. The assumption seems to me totally inadmissible. It leads necessarily to the

conclusion that Jewish vitality throughout twenty centuries represents no more than a cultural involution, largely inspired by the non-Jewish world's determination to impose segregation upon Jews, as well as by the supposedly obscurantist Jewish sector, finding itself sometimes unconsciously but often quite consciously on the same side as the hostile non-Jewish segregationists. This notion, whether implied or expressed, is unacceptable and urgently calls for revision."[9]

Bonfil offers one more telling example of the alleged tendentiousness of Roth's historical interpretation of Jewish life in the Renaissance. Following Burckhardt, Roth devoted several pages to examples of the emancipation of women within the Italian Jewish community. He was careful to qualify any all-too-sweeping generalization but he adds, and Bonfil underscores this remark, that "it was inevitable that this structure of society should be reflected in Jewish life as well." Among the many illustrations Roth offered, including the manuscripts written by women, their high social standing, their political influence, their poetry, and more, is the authority of some women to perform ritual slaughtering. Bonfil singles this example out for ridicule while ignoring the rest. For Bonfil, the phenomenon of women slaughterers has nothing to do with the emancipation of women but rather with economic necessity due to the geographic dispersion of Jews in the Renaissance.[10]

Bonfil once more dismisses the notion of a Jewish Italian Renaissance that reflects, as he puts it, deep intellectual and social mingling between Jews and gentiles, and minimizes their Jewishness and striving for "some kind of ecumenical cosmopolitan assimilationism." He concludes: "Expulsions were not cheerful picnics because the expelling princes were sensitive to music. . . . Jewish life was not a carousel of servile imitation; it was a perennial struggle for survival. Therefore historical presentation of that struggle means shifting our focus from stressing imitation or even adaptation to non-Jewish values and standards, whatever they may have been, to internal Jewish wrestling with the problem of maintaining the validity of Jewish cultural uniqueness while confronted with changing non-Jewish values and standards."[11]

Before addressing Bonfil's severe criticism of Roth's reconstruction of

Italian Jewish life, we might pause to consider the already noticeable impact of Bonfil's revisionism on contemporary scholarship. While Roth's position had been accepted wholeheartedly by scholars prior to Bonfil, he has been summarily dismissed by several writing afterwards, as if Bonfil's position was so self-evident and Roth's so blatantly wrong-headed to them that any further discussion of their seemingly polar positions was useless.[12] A case in point is the comprehensive historiographical overview of Italian Jewish culture in the Renaissance of Hava Tirosh-Rothschild published conveniently in 1990 in a journal edited by Robert Bonfil, which takes issue with the "harmonistic" position of Roth and clearly absorbs and approves of Bonfil's new position.[13]

This is not the place to address Bonfil's influential and important revisions of Italian Jewish history.[14] Nor is my objective a full-fledged defense or advocacy of Roth's earlier reconstruction. Cecil Roth, like all historians, viewed the past through the perspective of his own existential being and his own cultural biases. Contemporary scholarship has made major advances since his works have appeared, thanks to the writing of Robert Bonfil and others, and I am not advocating that we return uncritically to his partial and often imprecise historical reconstructions of Italian Jewish life or to the assumptions upon which these were based. But I do think that Cecil Roth has been treated unfairly in Bonfil's assault on his scholarly project, and that others have uncritically and too reflexively jumped on Bonfil's bandwagon without scrutinizing more carefully his unbalanced and selective reading of Roth. The following is not so much a critique of Bonfil's own position but rather an attempt to look again at Roth for what he actually says rather than through the partially distorted lens of Bonfil's overreading, or, shall we say, misreading of his narrative.

Let us begin by looking again at the two citations of Roth held up by Bonfil for particular scorn as exemplifying Roth's "ideological bias . . . that urgently calls for revision." What was Roth actually stating and was his meaning accurately captured in Bonfil's reaction to his words? To appreciate the context of Roth's remark regarding the temporary and sporadic nature of Italian persecutions of Jews, one must consider Roth's remarks on the preceding page. Here, Roth openly addresses the paradox in Italian society of an "undercurrent of sincere and sometimes fanatical religiosity" co-existing with "that marvelous surge of artistic and intellectual revival known as the Renaissance." Roth readily admits that accompanying the Renaissance spirit was "a no less characteristic mood of piety. . . . If one aspect constantly benefited the Jews and welcomed their participation . . . the other, which hovered in the background, was a constant menace. The balance was so delicate that their status moved between the two extremes with a rapidity which is always extraordinary and sometimes confusing . . . religious passions worked on economic greed, and smoldering prejudice burst out into violent flame."[15]

It is at this point that Roth introduces a qualifier: "This however, never blazed for long nor did it extend over a large area, Italy thus maintaining its record as the only European country which, until our own day, never knew a general persecution of the Jews."[16] Then the aforementioned quote appears with its allusion both to the more remote Renaissance and the more recent Fascist past. Orators, whether Bernardino of Siena or Benito Mussolini, had periodically incited the masses to attack Jews but the frenzy eventually died down and the cordiality between Jews and non-Jews eventually returned for, "it would again be true that in no part of the world did such a feeling of friendliness prevail as in Italy between the people and the Jews."[17]

What so irritated Bonfil about this passage and what ideological bias lurks beneath its surface? Roth makes a perfectly balanced argument that Italy was never immune from hostilities and anti-Jewish agitation; nevertheless, when they occurred, they were of limited duration and of limited geographical scope. Unlike the rest of Western Europe, there were no long-term and complete expulsions. And even where Jews had been brutalized, normal localized conditions were relatively tranquil. It is true that Roth's faith in Italian tolerance remained curiously unshaken even when writing only two years after the Nazi disaster. But was Roth's comment outrageously so off target as to elicit the sarcasm of Bonfil's biting remarks? Bonfil's rhetorical echo of Roth is a remarkable literary exercise in misrepresentation: "Immortality was not aesthetic because it was manifested during the Renaissance: expulsions were not cheerful picnics because the expelling princes were sensitive to music. . . . Jewish life was not a carousel of servile imitation, it was a perennial struggle for survival."[18] Roth's reference to music in the streets was meant to convey the sense of calm and normalcy that returned to the Jewish quarter soon after an outburst of hostility. The music did not refer to that of the expelling princes or to their aesthetic sense of art. Bonfil's language is rhetorically effective but distorts and exaggerates Roth's less extravagant claim. And what does this statement about the limited nature of Italian antisemitism have to do with the assumption "that the maintenance of national and cultural uniqueness connotes a readiness to reduce the points of contact with the surrounding culture," an assumption totally inadmissible to Bonfil but nowhere visible in the above quotation?[19]

Bonfil's discussion of Roth's reference to women slaughterers is also problematic. Roth's one brief comment on the matter is made after several pages of examples of Jewish women who enjoyed an exceptional status within Jewish society, such as Benvenida Abravanel, Gracia Nasi, various women poets, scribes, doctors, and others. Bonfil ignores all this evidence about a considerable degree of women's social mobility and focuses instead on a passing comment of no great consequence to Roth's overall argument. For Bonfil, Roth's reference to women becoming slaughterers assumes "an aspiration aimed at weakening Orthodox Jewish schemes by introducing novelty for the sake of modernity within an overall imitative mode."[20] Bonfil's explanation of the economic necessity of using these women is unrelated to their emancipation but rather focuses on the community's striving to maintain traditional orthodoxy and Jewish uniqueness against the challenge of geographic dispersion. Bonfil's interpretation of the phenomenon of female slaughterers is as hypothetical as that of Roth. The issue is neither a matter of liberality nor orthodoxy, of imitating external values or attenuating Jewish loyalties, an agenda made more pronounced in Bonfil's critique than in Roth's fleeting reference. Indeed, it is possible that neither explanation obviates the other: it may be that the economic necessity of observing kashrut went hand-in-hand with a more liberal view of the ritual role of women in Jewish life. Bonfil's elaborate critique is overdone and in no way negates Roth's overall point that some women in Italian Jewish society, primarily in elite circles, were relatively less constrained by societal norms than in other Jewish communities.

Turning from Bonfil's reading of these two specific passages to the overall assumptions informing his general critique of Roth, I would note three general misconceptions in Bonfil's reading that require modification before a fairer and more balanced picture of Roth's historiographical project can emerge. First, that Roth can legitimately be treated together with Heinrich Graetz, Moses Avigdor Shulvass, or even Isaac Barzilay, based on the assumption that all of them adopted an identical position both with respect to traditional Jewish society and to its interaction with the Renaissance. Second, that Roth arbitrarily maintained a fixed notion of the supposed openness and harmonistic creativity of the Renaissance period in contrast to the involution and sterility of the imposed ghetto period that followed. And third, that Roth distorted Jewish history by focusing exclusively on the dialogue between the Jewish minority and the Christian majority at the expense of "internal Jewish wrestling with maintaining the validity of Jewish cultural uniqueness." When this distortion is removed, so it would appear from Bonfil's remarks, Jewish life would no longer be seen as "a carousel of servile imitation" but rather "a perennial struggle for survival."

This is not the place to offer a careful and thorough explication of the differences among the scholars whom Bonfil treats as a common group in his essay: Graetz, Roth, Shulvass, and Barzilay. For Bonfil, they all identified with the Renaissance for its enlightened progress and open-mindedness and they idealized it for the opportunities it offered Jews to mingle with Christians in a new spirit of cosmopolitanism. But this is not all they believed, according to Bonfil. For Jews who wished to maintain their distinct Jewish identity, it was necessary to reduce contact with the outside world, to become segregationists and fundamentalists. To the extent that these historians painted the Renaissance in positive tones, they portrayed internal Jewish culture negatively. Sharing a perspective of traditional Judaism that was predominantly Ashkenazic, often narrow, and relatively intolerant of cultural change or pluralism, these more secularly inclined scholars overly romanticized the Renaissance while undervaluing the nature of Jewish traditional culture.

Whatever the accuracy of Bonfil's sweeping generalizations regarding this group of historians as a whole, he oversimplifies Cecil Roth's position by placing him squarely at the center of this group. Roth indeed loved Italy and the Renaissance passionately and even in its darkest moments of oppression and hostility to Jews, "Italy was still Italy, and Italians were still Italians, with all the native kindliness of their people."[21] Even in the age of Mussolini, we have already noted, Roth's faith in the ultimate goodness of the Italian people was never broken, despite his resignation during the war years from the prestigious academies of Florence and Venice of which he was a proud member.

But Roth was hardly a typical Ashkenazic Jew and certainly not one with irreverence towards rabbinic culture or Orthodox Judaism. In fact, he was a special kind of traditional Jew, "an excruciatingly English Jew," as Chaim Raphael astutely described him.[22] So quintessentially English was Roth, Raphael adds, that he carried "unmistakable overtones of the young man who would wander off to Europe in the eighteenth century on the Grand tour, returning laden with antiques and other marvels from Italy and Greece."[23] But this passion in no way diminished his loyalty to traditional Judaism. Indeed, Raphael describes him as a Dalston Orthodox Jew, a worshipper in one of the United Synagogues, the Jewish equivalent of the Church of England, "where Judaism meant a love of tradition but with an open mind to everything else."[24] While Roth lacked intense exposure to the yeshivah world, there was no antagonism in him towards Orthodoxy, no lack of appreciation of Jewish tradition, and no maskilic inferiority complex regarding Judaism in relation to other cultures. On the contrary, he was a proud Jew who could not countenance the antisemitic attacks on Jewish culture in the 1930s and took the personally heroic step of publishing his highly influential *The Jewish Contribution to Western Civilization* in the dark hour of 1938, a powerful statement of Jewish esteem and advocacy on the part of an historian who loved Italy but loved Jews more. It is true that Roth was more fascinated by Jewish dancing teachers and gamblers than rabbis and halakhic writing, but this was more a matter of personal style than ideological bias. If he was too naively enthusiastic about the magical ambiance of his beloved Italy, it did not come at the expense of a deprecatory view of Jewish tradition and rabbinic Judaism.

Bonfil was undoubtedly right in noting Roth's overemphasis on the openness and harmony of the Renaissance in contrast to the closure and cultural involution of the ghetto period. Bonfil's revisionist perspective on the cultural significance of the ghetto period represents one of his major contributions to contemporary historiography.[25] But was Roth as single-minded and inflexible about this conception as Bonfil would have us believe? If one looks carefully through Roth's writing, one discovers a more nuanced view of the supposed polarity between Jewish life in the positive Renaissance period in contrast to the negative ghetto experience.[26] In this respect, Roth's *A History of the Jews of Italy* offers a more sober and balanced portrait than Roth's less reliable and over-enthusiastic volume on Jewish life in the Renaissance, a later spin-off of his earlier writing. Of particular interest is Roth's moving and sympathetic portrayal of ghetto life, his sense that beyond the misery and squalor was the powerful sense of communal solidarity and traditional culture that the ghetto evoked. Roth could also appreciate the artistic spirit of the ghetto, the intimacy of social contacts between Jews and Christians, and the organic connection between the ghetto and the rest of Italian life: "They drank together, experimented together, gambled together, traveled together, sometimes even flirted together. . . . Christians often visited the synagogues and listened appreciatively to the sermons. . . . It could hardly be otherwise; for the ghetto was a segment no less of the Italian than the Jewish world; and no degree of regimentation could eradicate the common humanity of the two sections of the same people."

I come finally to the last of Bonfil's assumptions about Roth's work which I have labeled a misconception: his claim that Roth distorted the historical past by over-emphasizing the Jewish response to the external environment at the expense of an "internal Jewish wrestling" with the problem of cultural uniqueness. Roth's flaw was not only in anchoring his view of Jewish culture in the overly idealized positions of Jacob Burckhardt on the Renaissance; it was, rather, in interpreting Jewish history exclusively in terms of participation in the general framework of Renaissance culture. To Bonfil, this perspective was surely a product of contemporary concerns, for Roth, like Graetz before him, considered Jewish life worthwhile to the extent that it contributed "to mankind's progress," that is was organically integrated "into general non-Jewish life."[27] Bonfil argued instead that Jewish identity should not be defined merely in terms of response to an external challenge nor should any expression of openness in Jewish life be interpreted as a "total bankruptcy of Jewish ideals when confronted with positive progressive ideas diffused in general non-Jewish society."[28] Jewish life, to paraphrase

Bonfil's emphatic conclusion once more, was not a carousel of servile imitation but a perennial struggle for survival.

There is no doubt that Bonfil's observations about Roth's historical project are correct in insisting on a more balanced and nuanced view of Jewish culture in the Renaissance. His recent book bearing a title almost identical with Roth's earlier volume creatively attempts to offer such a balanced picture. By thus referring to his judgment on Roth as a misconception, I risk the error of overstatement and misrepresentation. I suspect, however, that Bonfil's corrective of Roth masks an ideological posture as evident as, and perhaps more evident than that of Roth's. In the final analysis, the historian's choice to focus more on Jewish difference or commonality with other human beings is an existential one. Is one in fundamental error by giving more weight to the influence of the general culture on Jewish thought in relation to those internal forces of communal solidarity and traditional loyalty? How should one balance the centripetal versus the centrifugal forces bearing on the formation of cultural identity in the Renaissance or in any period of history? No doubt to reduce a cultural profile of the Jewish minority to mere "servile imitation" of the majority culture is distorting and flattens Jewish culture to a mere set of responses to the Other, either positive or negative. But the opposite extreme, that of viewing a minority civilization from a purely internalist perspective, as creating its own culture in its own terms, is also distorting. It is rather the negotiation of the inside with the outside that correctly constitutes the proper focus of the historian's gaze. Bonfil's brilliant inversion of Roth's picture of Jewish life in the Renaissance — in seeing the supposedly closed ghetto rather than the previously open Renaissance as the decisive period of Jewish cultural formation — would be misleading if it assumed that the culture of the ghetto was shaped by Jewish internal forces alone. Despite the attempt to seal the borders between the Jewish and Christian communities, the ghettos were paradoxically more susceptible to Christian influence than ever before, as Bonfil's reconstruction makes patently clear.

I suspect I betray my own ideological biases as well in finding less fault in Cecil Roth's passion to study those dimensions of Jewish culture closely related to general civilization, and often positively contributing to it. On the other hand, I would never imagine the need to write a work highlighting the specific contributions of Jews to Western civilization as Roth did in 1938. But in 1938, such a book was required — both to remind the world that Jews were an integral part of the civilized culture that the Nazis were in the process of destroying, and to assure Jews of their own self worth. We share a different mind set than Roth's in being more secure about our own worth but less certain about the common decency of Western culture to tolerate and respect its minorities. One measure of the difference in perspective is to compare the tranquil and civilized Renaissance society that Jews appear to inhabit in Roth's narrative with the bloodied and tumultuous universe of Franciscan vituperations and pogroms in Bonfil's. The first extols the virtues of tolerance and benevolence of the Renaissance; the second makes a mockery of those values in claiming that they never applied to Jews. In the end, we are left to choose starkly between an overly optimistic or pessimistic view of the past, a view that informs our own preference whether to study Jewish culture from an internalist or an externalist perspective.

We now see Roth's reconstruction of Jewish-Christian synthesis in the Renaissance for what is was: partial, exceedingly naive and idyllic, incapable of capturing a much more complicated and contradictory reality. But we can also appreciate his effort for what it was: an attempt to situate the Jews within the matrix of Western civilization, to underscore their common humanity with others, and to document the lives of unremarkable Jews in such a way as to make them fascinating to historian and general reader alike. Roth was an historian lacking grand themes or a philosophical self-awareness of the implications of his intellectual project. He wrote to tell a good story because doing history was fun, and Jewish history was still suppressed and required a good telling. Our world is indeed quite different from his; our distortions of the past are of a different sort than those he imposed on the historical record. But despite our post-modern sensibilities and cynicism, and despite our fuller historical understanding, there remains in the end something honestly appealing and salutary about Roth's narratives of Jewish heroes, scholars, charlatans, adventurers, and scoundrels[29] — a love of Jews and other human beings, and a firm faith, albeit unsubstantiated, in the creative future of all humanity. Naive, perhaps, but still at the very core of values that propel historians to scour the past in search of worthwhile stories they themselves feel required to tell.

NOTES

1. Cecil Roth, *The Jews in the Renaissance* (Philadelphia, 1959), xiiii.

2. Roth, xii–xiii.

3. Cecil Roth, *Personalities and Events in Jewish History* (Philadelphia, 1953), vi. On Baron's conception, see Robert Liberles, *Salo Wittmayer Baron: Architect of Jewish History* (New York, 1995).

4. Roth, *Personalities and Events,* vi.

5. Chaim Raphael, "In Search of Cecil Roth," *Commentary* (September, 1970), 79. See also A. V. Goodman, R. Loewe, and V. D. Lipman, "Obituary Tributes at Anglo-American Jewish Historical Conference," *Transactions of the Jewish Historical Society of England* 23 (1972), 102–107; Lloyd P. Gartner, "Cecil Roth: Historian of Anglo-Jewry," *Studies in the Cultural Life of the Jews of England,* eds. Dov Noy and Issachar Ben-Ami (Jerusalem, 1975), 69–86.

6. Robert Bonfil, "Expressions of the Uniqueness of the Jewish People in Italy in the Period of the Renaissance (Hebrew)," *Sinai* 76 (1975), 36–46; idem, "The Historian's Perception of the Jews in the Italian Renaissance: Towards a Reappraisal," *Revue des études juives* 143 (1984), 59–82. See most recently where the same criticism appears, *Jewish Life in Renaissance Italy* (Berkeley, 1994), and see my review in *Renaissance Quarterly* 49 (1996), 850–853.

7. Bonfil, "Historian's Perception," 69.

8. Cecil Roth, *The History of the Jews of Italy* (Philadelphia, 1946), 156.

9. Bonfil, "Historian's Perception," 70–71. Bonfil returns to this same quote in his *Jewish Life in Renaissance Italy,* 8–9: "But was the sky of Italy so blue and so bright for the Renaissance Jew? Did he really hear in the air such joyful and seductive music, inviting him to enjoy 'laughter and singing and perhaps drinking in the streets' in an atmosphere of extreme cordiality that, according to Cecil Roth, would have shocked only the most fanatic? And what about the Jews who stayed home cultivating a tendency to cover their eyes and plug their ears so as not to see the blue sky and not to hear the marvelous music, closing themselves off in their own conservative particularism? The implications of these questions for today are immediately evident."

10. The citation is from Roth, *Renaissance,* 49, discussed by Bonfil, "The Historian's Perception," 71–74.

11. Bonfil, "Historian's Perception," 79–80. Bonfil's latest formulation of this position is in his recent book mentioned above in note 6. See also my specific reservations in my review cited there.

12. I might add that while Bonfil and others have seen my first book, *The World*

of a Renaissance Jew: The Life and Thought of Abraham ben Mordecai Farissol (Cincinnati, 1981), as written very much in the mold of Rothian assumptions, it might be more accurate to see it as a beginning of a break from Roth, explicitly expressing reservations with the notion of a harmonious Italian-Jewish synthesis in the Renaissance. See the next note below.

13. Hava Tirosh-Rothchild, "Jewish Culture in Renaissance Italy — a Methodological Survey," *Italia, Studi e ricerche sulla storia, la cultura et la letteratura degli ebre d'Italia* 9 (1990), 63–96. Compare my own historiographical essay in *Essential Papers on Jewish Culture in Renaissance and Baroque Italy,* ed. David B. Ruderman (New York, 1992), introduction.

14. In addition to my review of Bonfil's new book (above, n.6), see my earlier review of the original Hebrew edition of his seminal *The Rabbinate in Renaissance Italy* (Jerusalem, 1979), published in the *Association for Jewish Studies Newsletter,* 26 March 1980, 9–11.

15. Roth, *History of the Jews of Italy,* 155.

16. Ibid., 156.

17. Ibid.

18. Bonfil, "Historian's Perception," 80.

19. Ibid., 70.

20. Ibid., 75.

21. Roth, *History of the Jews of Italy,* 388.

22. Raphael, "In Search of Cecil Roth," 75

23. Ibid.

24. Ibid., 76.

25. See especially his aforementioned *Jewish Life in Renaissance Italy* and his earlier essay, "Change in the Cultural Patterns of a Jewish Society in Crisis: Italian Jewry at the Close of the Sixteenth Century," *Jewish History* 3 (1988), 11–30 [republished in *Essential Papers on Jewish Culture in Renaissance and Baroque Italy,* ed. David B. Ruderman (New York, 1992), 401–425].

26. Indeed, in one of his earlier essays, "European History and Jewish History: Do Their Epochs Coincide?" *Menorah Journal* 16 (1929), 293–306, Roth paints the Renaissance era as repressive and aggressively nationalistic, a dark age for Jews, hardly the harmonic paradise of his later writing.

27. Bonfil, "Historian's Perception," 66–67.

28. Ibid., 82.

29. The language is borrowed from Roth's own address cited in note 5 above.

SEVEN

Jewish Life in the Middle Ages
and the Jewish Life of Israel Abrahams

ELLIOTT HOROWITZ

I have lived, and in a sense still live, under the Pharisaic Law myself. I have felt its limitations, I have groaned under its lack of sensibility to all that we call aesthetic. I have resented its narrowness, its nationalism, on the one hand, and its claim to the Jew's undivided allegiance on the other. . . . But I have also known the law's manifold joys, its power of hallowing life, its sturdy inculcation of right, its sobriety of discipline, its laudable attempt to associate ritual with heart service, its admission that the spirit giveth life, its refusal to accept that the letter killeth. I have known men devoted to the minutest ritual details, yet simple, spiritual, saintly. Thus I have enough sympathy with the Law to do it justice, not enough sympathy to do it the injustice of unqualified flattery.

Israel Abrahams read these words in February 1899 before the Society of Historical Theology at Oxford. He was forty years old, and about to be appointed to the newly created position of Senior Tutor at London's Jews' College, where he had taught English and mathematics since 1881, and homiletics since 1894. His intimate connections with that institution, which would continue until his departure for Cambridge in 1902, went back to the time of his birth in 1858. His father Barnett—the Warsaw-born *Dayyan* and honorary *Ḥakham* of London's Spanish and Portuguese congregation (who married Jane Rodrigues Brandon)—was then serving as Headmaster of the Jews' College School. Like his father, from whom he was orphaned before entering the school, Abrahams eventually went on to study at the University of London. There, in 1881, he was the first graduate of Jews' College to proceed to the MA degree, which he took in Philosophy and Political Economy; he received prizes along the way in Logic and Philosophy of Mind, and in the University's first Hebrew and Scriptural Examination. His wide interests extended also to the subject of cricket, about which he composed a series of articles for the inaugural issues of the *Jews' College Journal* (of which, as a young student, he had been a founding editor in 1875). Shortly after joining the faculty Abrahams was instrumental in founding the Jews' College Literary Society, to whom he lectured over the years on a variety of topics, ranging in both content and chronology from "Witchcraft in the Bible," to "Sir Walter Scott."[1]

In 1885 Abrahams began to make his mark among Anglo-Jewry beyond the confines of the College, contributing the first of virtually hundreds of letters, essays, and reviews on both scholarly and political topics that were to appear over the years in London's *Jewish Chronicle*. He also occasionally published there the texts of sermons he had delivered as a lay preacher at a number of synagogues—including, from the early 1890's, London's then controversial Hampstead Synagogue, where a liberal service would be held on Sabbath afternoons at which a mixed choir of male and female voices would be accompanied by an organ. Despite his own Orthodox upbringing and traditional way of life, Abrahams supported such innovations, later becoming a founder of the Jewish Religious Union.[2] Another lay preacher at those services was Abrahams' friend, the liberal theologian Claude Goldsmid Montefiore, who in 1892—the year in which the Hampstead Synagogue was opened—delivered the prestigious Hibbert Lectures at Oxford on "The Origin and Growth of Religion as Illustrated by the Religion of the

Ancient Hebrews." In 1888, when both were some thirty years of age, the two men founded the *Jewish Quarterly Review,* for which Montefiore provided the financial support. It was in that journal, the first scholarly journal in English devoted primarily to matters Jewish, that Abrahams' Oxford lecture appeared under the title, "Professor Schürer on Life under Jewish Law."[3]

Professor Schürer needed no introduction to the members of the Society of Historical Theology, nor to most readers of the *Jewish Quarterly Review.* He was the German Protestant theologian Emil Schürer—recently elevated to the position of 'professor ordinarius' at Göttingen—who in 1876 had founded the *Theologische Literaturzeitung,* and whose best known work was his multi-volume *History of the Jewish People in the Time of Jesus Christ,* the third German edition of which had just appeared, while the second edition recently had become available in English.[4] Among its chapters was one entitled "Life under the Law"; this chapter, which gained a certain notoriety over the years,[5] is structured on a heavily Pauline argument, succinctly summarized in its final section. Schürer asserted that in Pharisaic Judaism "ethic and theology were swallowed up in jurisprudence," and spoke of the "fearful burden which a spurious legalism had laid upon the shoulders of the people," for whom, he claimed, life became "a continual torment."[6]

In his opening *apologia* Abrahams explained that the primary purpose of his request to read a paper before the Oxford Society was to protest "that what has already been said by Jewish apologists should have been wholly overlooked by Prof. Schürer in the new edition of his great book," adding that his own qualifications for criticizing the work were more existential than scholarly. "Against Prof. Schürer's judgement based on books," Abrahams asserted, "I can protest an experience based on life."[7] Yet, this experience was one that included, as he himself candidly admitted, a growing resentment of the law's lack of aesthetic sensibility, and of its narrowness, nationalism, and unrelenting demands. Abrahams' ambivalent attitude toward "life under the law" emerged again somewhat later in the lecture, when he explained that his argument with Schürer (and by implication with the apostle Paul before him) was based on empirical grounds rather than logical ones: "*A priori,* obedience to the Rabbinic Law should have been unspeakably wearisome, actually it was an ineffable joy. Against Schürer's logic," claimed Abrahams, "there is the evidence of twenty-five centuries of Jewish literature, liturgy, and life."[8]

Abrahams provided no details about how those twenty-five centuries demonstrated that obedience to the law had been far more joyous for the Jews than wearisome. It may be that he assumed his argument was familiar to considerable segments of his Oxford audience, for it had been made already by the two "Jewish apologists" Solomon Schechter and Claude Montefiore, whom Abrahams explicitly named in his lecture.[9] Schechter, in an essay entitled "The Law and Recent Criticism" and published in the *Jewish Quarterly Review,* had contrasted "the opinions of so many learned professors proclaiming *ex-cathedra* that the law was a most terrible burden," with "the testimony of a literature extending over about *twenty-five centuries*" (emphasis added).[10] These words were extensively and approvingly quoted a short time later by Montefiore in the last of his 1892 Hibbert lectures at Oxford ("From Nehemiah to the Maccabees: The Law and its Influence"), which were described by the *Jewish Chronicle* as a defense and even a "glowing glorification" of Rabbinism.[11]

In the mid-1890s both Schechter and Montefiore had again inveighed against Christian theological views of rabbinic law, the former most notably in his serialized essay "Some Aspects of Jewish Theology" (the original version of which was considerably more polemical than the one that later appeared in book form).[12] Yet, in their respective responses to the Christian critique of the law, neither admitted that he had ever experienced its observance as more of a burden than a joy—something the strictly observant Schechter apparently would not do and the minimally observant Montefiore was hardly in a position to do.[13] Israel Abrahams, by contrast, seems to have felt a need to unburden himself of such a confession. Although this may have undermined his argument somewhat, it undoubtedly strengthened his credibility.

Like Schechter and Montefiore, Abrahams cited the empirical evidence of twenty-five centuries, but characteristically referred to the evidence of Jewish life in addition to that of Jewish literature. After all, he had recently published a groundbreaking book entitled *Jewish Life in the Middle Ages.* Still, it is striking that nowhere in his response to Schürer did Abrahams single out for mention the ten centuries between the 8th and the 18th about which he had written so extensively in that 1896 work. This was perhaps because according to the model presented there the period during which "Jewish law most strongly regulated Jewish life" was that of the Ghetto,[14] a period which Abrahams, as we shall see further below, regarded as one of unmitigated decline in every imaginable respect.

Furthermore, in his criticism of Schürer's work, Abrahams asserted that "the theologian who would understand the Pharisees must cast an occasional glance into the life of Judaism to-day,"[15] yet he provided no concrete information about contemporary Jewish life that would contravene the theologian's claims, other than describing his own highly ambivalent experience of living under the Pharisaic law. Most likely, Abrahams was then no less ambivalent about modern Jewish life than he was about ancient Jewish law, as may be seen in some of the sermons that appeared in the 1895 volume, *Aspects of Judaism*. In one sermon devoted to the theme of friendship, for example, Abrahams lamented that Jewish life had lost so much of its camaraderie: "Once upon a time each Jewish congregation was one big family, the members all interested in one another." In contrast to what he unabashedly called "the good old days," when the social customs of Judaism generated "a warm atmosphere of love," Abrahams saw in the congregations of his own times only "a cold cloud of indifference, even of mutual contempt." Although he declared himself in favor of change and progress in Judaism, he saw no reason why progress should "divorce itself from poetry."[16] It was in the Middle Ages that Abrahams seems to have found, or perhaps invented, the poetry he felt was missing in modern Jewish life.

This trend in Abrahams' thought is identifiable even before the appearance of *Jewish Life in the Middle Ages*. In 1895, a year before the book's publication and the same year in which the aforementioned sermon was published, Abrahams read a short paper before the Jewish Historical Society of England entitled, "Paul of Burgos in London." It dealt with the recently published letter in rhymed Hebrew prose which, scholars believed, had been written from London on Purim day, 1389 by the Spanish Jew Solomon Levi of Burgos, who later became bishop of that town under the name Pablo de Santa Maria. Writing a century after the Jews had been expelled from England, the author of the Purim letter bemoaned his sorry fate at having to spend so festive a holiday in such inhospitable surroundings, without fellow coreligionists with whom to celebrate, and with his mind painfully clear from lack of wine. Although the great historian Heinrich Graetz — for whom Abrahams had the highest regard — had claimed that the Purim letter from London was intended to ridicule Jewish practice and had been written after Solomon's conversion to Christianity,[17] Abrahams had little doubt that it had been written while its author was still a loyal Jew. Among its other significant features, the letter displayed, in his opinion, "that combination of profound piety and playful irreverence so characteristic of the medieval Jew."[18]

But whose characterization was this of the medieval Jew? (Abrahams did not specify that the author in question was a "medieval *Spanish* Jew"). It was certainly not Graetz's view, nor was it recognizably that of any other leading 19th-century Jewish historian. The profound piety of the medieval Jew was of course commonplace, but his playful irreverence had not figured prominently in any major treatment of medieval Jewish culture, such as Moritz Güdemann's recently published three-volume survey, focusing on the Jews of Germany, France, and Italy.[19] It did manifest itself, however, in treatments of the so-called Golden Age in Muslim Spain, as in the eloquent essay on Judah Halevi by Joseph Jacobs, originally read before the Jews' College Literary Society in 1887 — an occasion at which Israel Abrahams, its longtime president,[20] was undoubtedly present. There Jacobs mentioned the story, reported by Joseph ibn Aknin, of how the young Halevi, at a gathering of friends, had wittily applied the words of the Mishna in *Ketubot* (2.1) when noting the stark contrast between the pleasing physical features of one of the women present and the unpleasant harshness of her voice.[21] "Some of the liveliness of the amusement has vanished for us with the lapse of centuries," commented Jacobs, "but the whole story gives us . . . a lively insight into the mingled pedantry, poetry, and piety that reigned in the Jewish *salons* of Granada some eight centuries ago."[22]

Both Abrahams and his older friend Jacobs looked back with a certain nostalgia from the Jewish world of late Victorian England to that of medieval Spain, from a culture in which, to paraphrase the latter, there was perhaps lively insight, to one in which there was also, even for Jewish pedants, liveliness of amusement. Yet Jacobs defined that idealized Jewish world by time and place (12th-century Andalusia), whereas Abrahams, especially in *Jewish Life in the Middle Ages,* sought, more or less, to reconstruct all medieval Jewries in that image. Here, the contrast with Güdemann is instructive as well. Although the Viennese scholar had touched on nearly every aspect of medieval Jewish life, especially its internal dimensions, the composite picture that emerged from his three volumes was less of the medieval Jew boldly balancing piety and a certain *joie de vivre* than of a Jew who was distinctly though soberly embedded in his European environment.

Whereas Güdemann had no trouble, therefore, limiting himself in his third volume to a two-page discussion of the pastimes and amusements of late medieval German Jews — which he claimed were quite limited[23] — Abrahams eight years later allowed himself the luxury, in *Jewish Life in the Middle Ages,* of devoting two entire chapters to such leisure activities, albeit over a greater period of time and a wider geographical area. In these chapters, and throughout the book, he roamed freely across East and West, between Bristol and Baghdad, drawing extensively upon the work of numerous 19th-century Jewish scholars, but also on a rich variety of primary sources, including a multitude of responsa written over more than a millennium. His range of subjects is well reflected in the index of his book, where "conversion" is followed by "cookery," "fashion" by "fasts," "games" by "Gaonim," and "Kimhi" is neatly sandwiched between "kiddush" and "kissing."

Abrahams was primarily interested in the inner life of the Jews, but he believed passionately that the vitality of Judaism was enhanced by exposure to and interaction with outside cultures. It is characteristic of his approach that the first two chapters of his book were devoted to synagogue life whereas the last two dealt with personal relations between Jews and Christians, thus creating a frame that placed equal stress on the internal and external dimensions of the medieval Jewish experience. "The Jewish nature," he wrote in his introduction, "does not produce its rarest fruits in a Jewish environment" — a statement made with reference not only to the ghetto of the past but also, quite clearly, to the aspirations of political Zionism in the present.[24]

Jewish Life in the Middle Ages appeared the same year that Theodor Herzl made his second visit to London (1896), and its preface was written in July, the same month Herzl addressed the members of the Jewish Working Men's Club and the Chovevei Zion Association, and met with Abrahams and other members of the Maccabean club in the French Room of the St. James Restaurant in Piccadilly.[25] Abrahams would later express his opposition to political Zionism more publicly and explicitly, especially after his return from a visit to Palestine in 1898 (undertaken *after* the pilgrimage, during the previous year, of some of his fellow Maccabeans);[26] but already in 1896 he felt that it was appropriate to convey his doubts about the modern movement to the readers of his book on medieval Jewish life.

Abrahams explained in his introduction that when he undertook to write about medieval Jewish life he did so under the impression that it "was everywhere more or less similar, and that it would be possible to present a generic image of it." He eventually came to the conclusion, however, that this claim was true only from the 15th century, and that during previous centuries diversity had predominated to the degree that one could speak properly not of a collective Jewish life but only of individual Jewish lives. As Abrahams saw it, Jewry returned in modern times to what he called "the old cosmopolitanism" of the middle ages; Zionism would signify the return to ghetto-like homogeneity.[27] It was therefore important for him to stress in his first chapter—despite its focus on the ostensibly parochial institution of the synagogue—that in the Middle Ages proper (by which he meant the period before the ghettoization in the 16th century), "Jewish life . . . was freshened and affected by every influence of the time."[28]

Abrahams attempted to reinforce this point throughout his book, albeit not always persuasively. "It may be asserted in general," he wrote in his chapter on costume, "that there was no distinctive Jewish dress until the law forced it upon the Jews." Similarly, he concluded his two chapters on medieval pastimes with the assertion that "as a general rule, the Jews established no independent standard of conduct with regard to their amusements. They played the same games as their Christian neighbors, and played them with the same rules and at the same tables."[29]

An issue of even greater interest to Abrahams was that of distinctions between European and Oriental Jews. He claimed that there was "less warmth in the Oriental Jewish home, less of that tenderness," which was once a common characteristic of all Jews but came eventually "to distinguish Western Jews from their gayer but more shallow brethren of the East." Similarly, Abrahams felt it possible to detect "a feebler sense of responsibility in the mental attitude of an Oriental father to his offspring, just as one detects more volubility but less intensity in the Oriental Jew's prayers."[30]

This is one of many instances where one detects clear lines of continuity between *Jewish Life of the Middle Ages* and the frequent contributions of a more popular nature made by Abrahams to the pages of London's *Jewish Chronicle,* beginning a decade or so before the book's publication. Writing just before Rosh Hashanah of 1892, for example, Abrahams contrasted the praying styles of the Portuguese and German Jews, commenting that the difference "might perhaps be summed up by saying that the former is marked by vigor, the latter by feeling." Similarly, he found more "concentrated passion" in the Ashkenazic cantorial style, whereas in the Sephardic he saw rather "a combination of gaiety and dolefulness."[31]

In his book on medieval Jewish life the dichotomy between Ashkenazic and Sephardic styles took on the broader form of European versus Oriental and was extended from the world of the synagogue to that of the home. In neither case, however, was it especially clear whether the comments were offered as ethnographic observations or historical ones, for Abrahams, like many historians of his generation (and later ones as well), would on occasion conflate the past and the present. Shortly before the publication of Abrahams' volume, there appeared a novel by Israel Zangwill titled, *Children of the Ghetto* (1892), which Abrahams viewed as something of a fictional companion volume to his own book. Set in London's East End, "the whole description" in Zangwill's novel, so Abrahams claimed, "applies in most details to the middle ages."[32] One may legitimately ask, however, why Abrahams did not feel that this was equally true of Zangwill's (non-fiction) comments in the novel's proem, where the East End's immigrants are described as having brought with them, for the most part, "nothing but their phylacteries and prayer shawls, and a good-natured contempt for Christians and Christianity."[33] Might this perspective not also reflect medieval realities?

Like Abrahams, Zangwill felt that he knew what was characteristically "Oriental" and what was not, pointing in his novel to "the Oriental instinct for gaudiness" and to "Oriental methods of insult," which survived in

London's ghetto, and referring in passing also to the "exuberance of the Oriental imagination," and the "Oriental exuberance of gesture."[34] In all these cases, however, he was speaking of Ashkenazic Jews of East European origin, whom he constructed nonetheless as "Orientals," and whose exotic otherness, he implied, was to be understood in that light. This essentializing tendency is only one of the many points of contact between Zangwill's novel and Abrahams' *Jewish Life in the Middle Ages*. Both were written in the early 1890's by members of London's Maccabean club, both combined highly imaginative and stylized writing with a deep familiarity with their material, and both were much concerned with the relationship between the Western mentality and the Oriental one, as well as between ghetto Judaism and other forms thereof.

Abrahams, in fact, wrote a highly interesting review of Zangwill's novel upon its appearance, commending its author for his "real and deep knowledge" and describing its ghetto scenes as "witty beyond praise and sympathetic beyond praise." Nonetheless, he felt that there was "too much of insistence on unsavoury details," many of which, in his opinion, were "not specifically characteristic of Jewish life at all, but will be thought so by many readers and leave an unpleasant taste in a Jewish reader's mouth." Such details were admittedly part of the novel's realistic character, but Abrahams felt that like most realistic works, Zangwill's told "too much."[35] In focusing upon the relationship between realism and truth in the novel, Abrahams anticipated some of the questions he was to confront himself when writing as a historian about medieval Jewish life. His readers were to encounter very few "unsavoury details," but any they might encounter were limited to the centuries of the ghetto.

For, no less than he stressed the differences between Oriental and European Jews, Abrahams sharply contrasted medieval Jews with those of ghetto times. The medieval Jew, he asserted, was possessed of "a strong sense of personal dignity," which manifested itself in his concern for "cleanliness in person and speech." After three centuries of ghetto life, however, Jews became "callous to the demands of fashion, indifferent to their personal appearance, [and] careless in their speech and general bearing." Consequently, Abrahams was able to assert, it was only *after* the Middle Ages had passed that "ritual hand-washing became a perfunctory rite, compatible with much personal uncleanliness."[36] He somehow knew also that "before the fifteenth century the Jews spoke the vernacular grammatically, even if they sometimes interlarded it with Hebraisms."[37] By chance, it was also after the close of the 15th century that ritual, in his view, "gained mastery" over Jewish life.[38]

Fashion, cleanliness, language, and ritual were all things about which Abrahams cared a great deal, and it was thus important for him to assert that in all these matters medieval Jews were different from those of the ghetto period, no less than it was important, in his mind, for middle-class Jews in West London to believe that in these respects they were quite different from the children of the ghetto to the East.[39] How did Abrahams know that after the Middle Ages ritual hand-washing became a "perfunctory rite, compatible with much personal uncleanliness"? More or less in the same way, it would appear, that his friend Israel Zangwill knew how to describe how a surly young man in London's East End might wash his hands before eating bread: "He put on his cap and went grudgingly to the bucket of water . . . and tipped a drop over his fingers. It is to be feared," continued Zangwill dryly, "that neither the quantity of water nor the area of hand covered reached even the minimum enjoined by Rabbinical law."[40] Abrahams evidently had similar scenes in mind, but it is not clear why he was so certain that they would not have occurred before the 15th century.

Abrahams' concerns with both fashion and cleanliness were also evident in his 1898 letters from his voyage to Palestine. In the very first of these he reported to his wife from Marseilles that he "had his hair and beard cut in proper French style," and upon arriving in the Holy City just before Passover he wrote: "Jerusalem is situated splendidly, and I am sure only needs cleaning to become one of the finest cities of the world." A few days later, after visiting Hebron and its Jewish Quarter, which he called "a ghetto in a garden," he had the following to say: "Nothing could be more disgusting. Dirty, dark, narrow covered lanes. A camel lying down in its filth in one, the children in their filth in another. Jerusalem is clean by comparison! . . . I saw the Synagogues — all dirty — I saw a dark, dirty Mikvah, the sight of which made you feel dirty for life."[41]

One understands perhaps a bit better why several months later, when speaking openly with the members of Oxford's Historical Theology Society about how he himself had felt the limitations of the Pharisaic law, Abrahams mentioned first and foremost that he had "groaned under its lack of sensibility to all that we call aesthetic." His resentment of its narrowness and nationalism can also be understood in light of his deep reservations about political Zionism, reservations which also informed his idealized reconstruction of the Jewish Middle Ages. The third kind of resentment that Abrahams mentioned on that occasion was of the law's "claim to the Jew's undivided allegiance." It is thus noteworthy that Abrahams took such efforts to construct the Medieval Jew as one who did not allow the law's claims upon his allegiance to overpower him, but rather developed a viable *modus vivendi,* viable at least through the 15th century when ritual, he claimed, "gained mastery" over Jewish life.

It is clear that Abrahams idealized the Middle Ages as a period during which "a merry spirit smiled on Jewish life."[42] His choice of the 15th century (and sometimes the 16th[43]) as the point from which decline set in must be seen against the wider background of a distinct strain in Victorian cultural and historical thought, which bemoaned the loss of a medieval utopia antedating both capitalism and the Reformation — a distinct strain of thought that looked back nostalgically to the days of "Merrie England." Representatives of this strain included such figures as William Cobbett, A. W. Pugin, Thomas Carlyle, John Ruskin, William Morris, and even so noted a historian as J. A. Froude (d. 1894), who had been much influenced by Carlyle, just as Carlyle had been deeply influenced by Cobbet.[44] Victorian nostalgia for the "lost paradise" of the Middle Ages extended not only to the lost sense of fellowship and community — believed to have characterized medieval times — but also to the genuine pleasures which had been made possible by the more robust popular culture, preceding, as some argued, the growth of puritanism and the onset of the industrial revolution.[45] Traces of this sort of nostalgia for the robust pleasures of an earlier era may be found in Abrahams' writings as well, especially in his treatment of Purim.[46]

A merry spirit smiled on Jewish life in the middle ages, joyousness forming, in the Jewish conception, the coping stone of piety. . . . There can be no greater mistake than to imagine that the Jews allowed their sufferings to blacken their life or to cramp their optimism. . . . The stern, restraining hand of religion only occasionally checked the mirth and light-heartedness with which the Jew yielded himself to all the various pleasures of which his life was capable.[47]

With these words Abrahams opened the first of his two chapters on "medieval pastimes and indoor amusements." Well before Salo Baron attacked the lachrymose conception of Jewish history[48] here was a late 19th-century Jewish historian willing to assert confidently that there was more joy in medieval Jewish life than suffering, and also, perhaps no less daringly for a Victorian, that there was more pleasure than pious restraint. Abrahams did restrain himself, however, from making the latter claim in his earlier chapter on "Social Morality," saving it for the safer terrain of games and amusements. In the earlier chapter he stressed what he called without irony the "prudery of the Jews," especially those of Europe, claiming that "prostitution was an unknown feature in Jewish life until quite recent times." Moreover, he argued that it was "certainly false to assume that Jews felt less scruple in violating the laws of chastity where women of another creed were concerned" — an assumption, incidentally, for which Abrahams himself provided ample evidence in a footnote.[49] The possibility that real life involved transgression, even in the Middle Ages, is recognized only in his discussion of dance, which he considered a "popular athletic amusement," in fact the most popular one among medieval Jews, many of whom, he claimed, "especially young men and maidens . . . disobeyed the Rabbinical rule, and not only danced together, but did so in the communal dancing hall on the Sabbath and festivals as well."[50]

Throughout *Jewish Life in the Middle Ages* one finds similar traces of a nostalgic attempt to reconstruct in medieval times an ideal balance between commitment to religion on the one hand, and enjoyment of life on the other. Just as Abrahams presented a medieval Jew in the synagogue who was "at times rigorously reverent and at others quite at his ease," so too, in his estimation, was the medieval Jew's observance of the Sabbath "strict but not sombre."[51] It was similarly important for Abrahams, himself a great fan of sports — especially cricket and rowing — [52] to find room for athletics in medieval Jewish life. Besides the "popular athletic amusement of the dance," Abrahams was willing to assert that medieval Jews "were *extremely* fond of foot-races," and that men and women *"frequently* played games in which balls were used" (emphasis added).[53] Not only did he need to present the medieval Jew as athletically inclined, but also as possessing no small degree of what he called "manliness" — a classification that had been of considerable interest to Graetz.[54] In discussing Jewish trades and occupations, and in noting that Jews "were not very prone to select those which involved mere physical exertion," Abrahams found it necessary to stress, nonetheless, that Jews were "by no means averse to dangerous occupations." Courage and manliness, he asserted, were necessary for both peddling and travel in the Middle Ages, adding that "Jewish soldiers and sailors abounded, and so did Jewish martyrs."[55] What had Jewish soldiers and sailors to do with Jewish martyrs? All evidently constituted equal proof, as far as Abrahams was concerned, that medieval Jews possessed manly courage.

Solomon Schechter, in his review of *Jewish Life in the Middle Ages,* praised Abrahams for rightly stressing the role of the synagogue as the center of medieval Jewish life. He added, however, that "the only serious fault we have to find with our learned author is that he did not more steadily cling to this center, but granted too much space for such topics as athletics, games, card-playing and similar subjects." Schechter, who was then Reader in Rabbinic Literature at Cambridge (the position which Abrahams was to assume upon Schechter's departure for New York in 1902), went on to comment disparagingly on "the thought of muscular religion which enables the young candidate for the ministry to look upon the cricket-field as a sort of consecrated ground, and upon his flannels as a kind of holy vestments." Schechter added sternly that "we are not aware that there is much room for such a deception in the Synagogue."[56]

This was a rather low blow on his part, for he must have known of the particular fondness Abrahams had long harbored for the game of cricket.[57] Even after fifteen years in England, the Rumanian-born Schechter, raised as a Ḥabad ḥasid in the Carpathians,[58] still had difficulty understanding the importance to Israel Abrahams of athletic amusement, even a certain degree of athletic worship, in his idealized view of medieval Jewish life. (An interesting parallel may be found in our own century, where some Zionist historians have needed, for their own reasons, to identify agricultural activity and military prowess among Jews in the Middle Ages.) Abrahams was capable of granting pride of place to the synagogue by devoting to it the first two chapters of his book, but he could not make it the dominant theme of the work as Schechter would have preferred. He was, after all, the sort of scholar who would later write of his brief visit to Alexandria: "I refused the Museum, because I wanted to see the streets."[59] If today *we* can see the medieval Jew in the street no less than in the synagogue, at play as well as at prayer, some of the credit must go to Israel Abrahams, whose broad view of the past and lively style of presentation left their mark upon social and cultural historians of a later generation (among them Cecil Roth, who brought out a slightly revised and amply illustrated edition of *Jewish Life in the Middle Ages* in 1932).

If his statements concerning some of the larger themes of medieval and early modern Jewish history (such as periodization or the impact of the ghetto) have faded with time, many of Abrahams' passing observations have maintained their brightness and some have been fleshed out by others (myself included) into full-fledged articles. Like Graetz's volumes, of which he was so fond, Abrahams' *Jewish Life in the Middle Ages* can still be read a century after its publication for both profit and pleasure — both by students of the distant past and by those primarily interested in 19th-century constructions of the past. I hope, in conclusion, that in these comments I have shown enough sympathy for Israel Abrahams as an historian to do him justice, if not quite enough to do him the injustice of unqualified flattery.

NOTES

1. See Isidore Harris, *History of Jews' College* (London, 1906), xviii–xix, xlviii, lxx–lxxvi, clxxxiii, cxciii; Herbert Loewe, "Israel Abrahams," *American Jewish Year Book* 28 (1926–1927), 220–222; idem, *Israel Abrahams* (Cambridge[?], 1944), 3–10.

2. See D. G. Dalin, "Israel Abrahams: Leader of Liturgical Reform in England," *Journal of Reform Judaism* 32 (1985), 69–72.

3. Israel Abrahams, "Professor Schürer on Life under Jewish Law," *JQR* o.s. 11 (1898–1899), 626–642. The lecture was cited years later for special attention in the obituary for Abrahams which appeared in the *Times* of London, October 7, 1925.

See Loewe, *Israel Abrahams,* 94. Note also the reference to it in Solomon Schechter, *Some Aspects of Rabbinic Theology* (New York, 1909), 117 n. 1.

4. *Encyclopaedia Britannica,* 11th ed., (1910–1911) s.v. "Schürer, Emil." See also the new English version, *The History of the Jewish People in the Age of Jesus Christ,* rev. and ed., Geza Vermes, Fergus Millar and Matthew Black (Edinburgh, 1973–1987).

5. See the introduction to *History of the Jewish People,* vol. 2.

6. Emil Schürer, *The History of the Jewish People in the Time of Jesus Christ,* trans. Sophia Taylor and Peter Christie (New York, 1897–1898 [?]), 2b, 120–125. The passages quoted do not appear in the revised version (referred to in note 4), in which the chapter title has been changed to "Life and the Law." See vol. 2, p. 464, and also n. 1 where the editors refer to the "questionable value judgements of the original."

7. *JQR* o.s. 11 (1898–99) 626–627.

8. Ibid., 639.

9. Ibid., 640.

10. Solomon Schechter, "The Law and Recent Criticism," *JQR* o.s. 3 (1890–91) 762. Note the reference to Schürer in that essay, 756. Schechter's essay, which purportedly was a review of Toy's *Judaism and Christianity* (Boston, 1890) but actually cast its net much wider, was republished in his *Studies in Judaism,* vol. 1 (Philadelphia, 1896), chapter 9.

11. Claude Montefiore, *Lectures on the Origin and Growth of Religion* (London, 1892), 506–508. For explicit references to Schürer, see 477, 505, 532–533, and for the claim that "to the great bulk of Jews the law was at once a privilege and a pleasure," or as Montefiore later put it, alliterating again, "a blessed and blissful privilege," see 503, 539. For its retrospective report on the Hibbert Lecture see *Jewish Chronicle,* 10 June, 1892, 11.

12. See Solomon Schechter, "Some Aspects of Rabbinic Theology: The 'Law'," and idem, "Some Aspects of Rabbinic Theology: The Torah in its Aspect of Law," *JQR* o.s. 8 (1895–1896), 1–16, 363–380 (both were later republished as chapters in Schechter's *Some Aspects*); Claude Montefiore, "On Some Misconceptions of Judaism and Christianity by Each Other," *JQR* o.s. 8 (1895–1896),193–216.

13. Contrast, for example, Schechter's scrupulous observance of the dietary laws even when travelling on the Continent (Norman Bentwich, *Solomon Schechter:* A Biography [Philadelphia, 1938], 120–21) with Montefiore's view that those laws belong "to a stage of religious custom which for all civilized persons has utterly passed away." See also Montefiore, "Dr. Wiener on the Dietary Laws," *JQR* o.s. 8

(1895–1896), 393. Montefiore reported that he had continued to abstain from such foods as pig, hare, and lobster out of respect for his mother, "but I have never found these abstentions either burdensome in themselves or preventive of my free social intercourse with Christians" (ibid., 398). For the contrast with regard to ritual observance between Schechter and Montefiore see also *Cyrus Adler: Selected Letters,* ed. I. Robinson (Philadelphia, 1985), 1: 22–23.

14. Israel Abrahams, *Jewish Life in the Middle Ages,* (London, 1896), xxvi.

15. Israel Abrahams, "Professor Schürer," 628.

16. Israel Abrahams and Claude Montefiore, *Aspects of Judaism: Being Sixteen Sermons* (London, 1895), 4–6. On "poetry" disappearing from modern Jewish life see also *ibid.,* 20, 33.

17. For Graetz's view see his *History of the Jews: From the Earliest Times to the Present Day,* ed. B. Löwy (London, 1892), 4:199. For Abrahams' admiration of Graetz see his obituary article on the latter in *Jewish Chronicle,* 11 September 1891, 13, and the more extended appreciation, "H. Graetz, The Jewish Historian," *JQR* o.s. 4 (1892), 165–93.

18. Abrahams, "Paul of Burgos in London," *Transactions of the Jewish Historical Society of England* 2 (1894–1895), 149–152. Abrahams returned to this subject a few years later, in "Paul of Burgos in London," *JQR* o.s. 12 (1900), 255–263.

19. Moritz Güdemann, *Geschichte des Erziehungs wesens und der Cultur der abendländischen Juden* (Vienna 1880–1888).

20. On Abrahams and this society see Harris, *History of Jews' College,* lxxvi, and Loewe, *Israel Abrahams,* 11–13.

21. For this anecdote from Ibn Aknin's Arabic commentary on the Song of Songs, which as Jacobs noted had been "discovered by the omniscient Steinschneider, transcribed by the obliging Neubauer, and published by the indefatigable Kaufmann," see *Divulgatio Mysteriorum Luminumque Apparentia* ed. and trans., A. S. Halkin (Jerusalem, 1964), 178–179.

22. Joseph Jacobs, "Jehuda Halevi, Poet and Pilgrim," in his *Jewish Ideals and Other Essays* (London, 1896), 111–112. For Abrahams' own idealization of Judah Halevi see his "Books and Bookmen," *Jewish Chronicle,* 23 Sept. 1892, 13–14.

23. Güdemann, *Geschichte* 3:138–140 (*Ha-Torah weha-Ḥayim* 3:112–111).

24. Abrahams, *Jewish Life,* xxii. To drive home the point further, Abrahams referred somewhat later in his introduction (xxiv) to the conception of a Jewish state as having "no roots in the past and no fruits to offer for the future."

25. S. A. Cohen, *English Zionists and British Jews: The Communal Politics of Anglo-Jewry, 1895–1920* (Princeton, 1982), 29–30.

26. On Abrahams as an opponent of political Zionism see ibid., 163–183, where his views are discussed in comparison with those of Montefiore. On the Maccabean pilgrimage see ibid., 30–31, 90.

27. Jewish Life, xxiv, xxvi.

28. Ibid., 6.

29. Ibid., 280, 398.

30. Ibid., 122. See also 24, 52, 117–118, 182.

31. Abrahams, "Books and Bookmen," 13. Compare also his article "Simchath Torah and Purim," *Jewish Chronicle,* 23 October 1891, p. 12, with his comments on the relation between these holidays in *Jewish Life,* 262.

32. *Jewish Life,* 133 n. 3.

33. Israel Zangwill, *Children of the Ghetto: Being Pictures of a Peculiar People* (Philadelphia, 1892), 1:6–7.

34. Ibid., 58, 69, 165, 350.

35. *Jewish Chronicle,* 14 October 1892, 7.

36. *Jewish Life,* 16. See also 130.

37. Ibid., 360.

38. Ibid., 155. It was for these reasons and others, argued Abrahams, that "the *Jewish* middle ages" only actually began in the 15th century, and the *Jewish* Renaissance, in which he saw his own generation still taking part, in the late 18th. See *Jewish Life,* intro., 372.

39. Note the 1897 quotation from the *Jewish World* in Israel Finestein, *Jewish Society in Victorian England: Collected Essays* (London, 1993), 184: "The life depicted in Zangwill's novels is not properly speaking Anglo-Jewish life, and the characters appear as exotic to Jews who have been here for one or two generations as to Christian Englishmen.

40. Zangwill, *Children,* 1:31.

41. Phyllis Abrahams, "The Letters of Israel Abrahams from Egypt and Palestine," *Transactions of the Jewish Historical Society of England* 24 (1973), 1–23. Some of these comments were deleted when Abrahams later published a longer account of his visit to Hebron, based on a paper read to the Jews' College Literary Society. See Harris, *History of Jews' College,* lxxiv; Abrahams, *The Book of Delight and Other Papers* (Philadelphia, 1912), 62–92.

42. *Jewish Life,* 373.

43. Note this approach already in his sermon "A New Song," published in 1895: "A certain spiritual torpor, or rather, spiritual timidity, seized us in the sixteenth century. The old beliefs of Judaism were dearly cherished, and it seemed as if the

only way to save them was by stunting them and preventing them from growing (*Aspects of Judaism,* 53).

44. On Cobbet and Carlyle see Alice Chandler, *A Dream of Order: The Medieval Ideal in Nineteenth-Century English Literature* (Lincoln, 1970), chs. 2 and 4. On Froude and the ambivalences that shaped his writing of 16th-century history, see J. W. Burrow, *A Liberal Descent: Victorian Historians and the English Past* (Cambridge, 1981), ch. 9, and note especially 240–241, 266–267.

45. Chandler, *A Dream of Order,* 3; F. S. Boos, "Alternative Victorian Futures: 'Historicism,' *Past and Present* and *A Dream of John Ball,*" in Boos, ed., *History and Community: Essays in Victorian Medievalism* (New York, 1992), 28; Chris Waters, "Marxism, Medievalism, and Popular Culture," ibid., 149–155.

46. See Elliott Horowitz, "The Rite to Be Reckless: On the Perpetration and Interpretation of Purim Violence," *Poetics Today* 15 (1994), 9–54.

47. *Jewish Life,* 373.

48. Salo W. Baron, "Ghetto and Emancipation," *The Menorah Journal* 14.6 (June 1928), 515–526. Reprint. *The Menorah Treasury* ed., L. W. Schwartz (Philadelphia, 1964), 50–63.

49. *Jewish Life,* 92–94.

50. Ibid., 380–381.

51. Ibid., 15, 374.

52. Loewe, *Israel Abrahams,* 9–10.

53. *Jewish Life,* 379.

54. See, for example, H. Graetz, *History of the Jews,* ed. B. Löwy, 3:53 on the Jews of the Arabian peninsula contrasted with those of medieval Europe: "Here they were not repulsed from the paths of honor . . . but they were allowed to openly develop their powers, and to show their manly courage," and 529, on the impact of the Jewish badge upon the Jews themselves: "So much of their manly bearing and courage left them that a child could cause them annoyance."

55. *Jewish Life,* 230–231.

56. *Critical Review of Theological and Philosophical Literature* 7 (1897), 20. Schechter's criticism of the attention given by Abrahams to such topics as athletics, games, and card-playing is reminiscent of his earlier disparagement of the work of Joseph Jacobs on the diffusion of folk-tales, a subject he rated as clearly inferior in importance to the theological teachings of the Sages. See Bentwich, *Solomon Schechter,* 68, and Jacobs, *Jewish Ideals,* 160–61, for an implicit rejoinder.

57. When as a teenager in 1875 he served as one of the founding editors of the *Jews' College Journal,* Abrahams composed for that publication a series of articles

on cricket, and when he came to Cambridge more than a quarter of a century later he took a home near the university cricket ground and quickly became a life member of "Fenners." See Harris, *History of Jews' College,* xlviii; Loewe, *Israel Abrahams,* 9.

58. See Bentwich, *Solomon Schechter,* ch. 2.

59. P. Abrahams, "Letters," *Transactions* (March 15, 1898), 5.

EIGHT

Hidden Worlds and Open Shutters:
S. D. Goitein Between Judaism and Islam

GIDEON LIBSON

Shelomo Dov Goitein was a polymath. His fields of interest and studies covered a variety of disciplines: from linguistics and literature, through Bible, ethnography, anthropology and comparative religion, to social and economic history.[1] The human drama embedded in history occupied his world and became the focus of his scholarly activity. The figure of the "Eastern Man" fascinated him; the world of the Middle East obsessed him and pervaded almost all of his publications. The tension between the East, to which he was drawn, and the West, from which he distanced himself as a youth, is clearly evident in his personal stories, which betray the dialectics of his struggle with the opposite extremes of East and West—as if his life embodied the poetic verse "From Thee shall I flee—to Thee." On the one hand, he was disenchanted with modern western culture, which he saw as mostly opposed to Jewish religious culture and which had therefore never really put down roots into the Jewish heart; he recognized the advantages offered the Jew in the world of the East.[2] On the other hand, he makes an obvious effort in his writings to narrow and even bridge the gulf between East and West. Typical in this respect is how he writes about Yemenite Jewry: "My Yemenite encounter had something precious in it: the feeling that something my forefathers, of blessed memory, had lost in their long exile in northern lands had come back to me, as if another soul had been added to my own soul."[3] And on a visit to a *ḥeder* of one of the oriental communities he comments with barely concealed irony "on some of my colleagues, who are uncultured compared with these pitiable toddlers."[4] Elsewhere, however, he writes: "Peel the shell off the Yemenite, and you will find the inside no different from that of the Jews of Eastern Europe, Hungary or southern Germany of past generations."[5]

In this article I wish to focus especially on one aspect of Goitein's scholarship, which largely derives from his unique integration of religious and humanistic values in the study of the Jewish-Muslim encounter in all its depth, diversity, and inherent complexity. This subject, one of Goitein's major interests for many years, permeates many of his studies from beginning to end. His aim was to penetrate and understand the spiritual and cultural world of the Jews of the East, their lifestyle, social order, religious world and their contacts with their host societies. My final comments in this article, which have a bearing on the Judeo-Arab encounter, concern Goitein's special attitude to Abraham Maimonides.

At times, Goitein's personal and professional biography intersects with his historical work, shaping to some extent his views and his appreciation of the phenomena and personalities he was studying. The historical events to which he was witness during his life in Germany, the United States, and Israel, are constantly present in his research. Sometimes he reveals himself explicitly, sometimes through symbols comprehensible only to the initiate,[6] and sometimes unconsciously, providing the reader with a key to an understanding of his personality, his motivation and his positions *vis-à-vis* the subjects of his research. It is thus appropriate to present here, alongside a brief personal biography, an account of Goitein's professional career.[7]

Shelomo Dov Goitein was born on April 3, 1900, in Bavaria, and died on February 6, 1985, in the United States. As a child he studied at the local

Jewish school and was a member of the Jewish youth movement Blau-Weiss, which emphasized the love of nature. After obtaining a secondary and university education at Frankfurt and Berlin during 1914–1923, he completed his studies with a doctoral dissertation on prayer in the Qur'an, under the direction of the orientalist Josef Horovitz, who later established the Hebrew University's Institute of Oriental Studies. Besides his formal education, Goitein had private teachers for his religious studies: Rabbi Jakob Posen, Rabbi Nehemiah Nobel and the well-known Jewish bibliographer Aron Freimann. In 1923 he immigrated to what was then Palestine, and taught Bible and history at the Haifa Reali School from 1923 to 1928. In 1928 he became a lecturer at the Hebrew University of Jerusalem, on the history of Islam and the Muslim peoples. Among the subjects he taught at the newly established Law School was Muslim Law. From 1938 to 1948, along with work at the university, he was employed by the Department of Education of the Mandatory Government of Palestine. During the early years of the State of Israel he was involved with the absorption of the Yemenite immigrants. He was also active in public affairs. In 1957 he was invited by the University of Pennsylvania to serve as professor of Arabic, and he taught there until 1970, when he retired. From then until his death he was a fellow at the Institute for Advanced Study in Princeton, New Jersey. His move from Israel to the United States was motivated by the more favorable conditions for his research, but the fact that later he referred to the move as a "tenfold exile" indicates that the decision must have been painful.[8] The fruits of his lifetime research comprise more than ten books and some six hundred articles, in several languages and in dozens of periodicals.

This brief biography is a mere outline of the rich and varied career in education and scholarship, of one of the greatest students of Islamic-Jewish studies to emerge in our time. During the first years of his career Goitein considered himself primarily a teacher and educator. His early publications deal with education, in particular with the teaching of Bible, but also with the teaching of Hebrew, Arabic, and related subjects. This phase of his career came to an end in the mid 1950s.

From his earliest years in Palestine, Goitein was intensely interested in the study of Yemenite Jewry, both in the Middle Ages and in the modern era. His first publication in this area was in 1931 and he subsequently continued his research in it for over fifty years. A collection of his articles on Yemenite Jewry, which appeared in 1980, even included several new studies. As he himself testifies, he viewed his acquaintance with the Yemenites as one of the greatest gifts granted him, "opening up a shutter, perhaps a large window, to the world of the East in general."[9]

His major research topics in the 1930s and 1940s, however, were Arabic historiography and the institutions of Islam and early Muslim society. Having written his doctoral dissertation (never published) on "Das Gebet im Qoran," he worked for about ten years on a critical edition of the fifth volume of al-Baladhuri's *Ansab al-Ashraf,* also writing an introduction to the entire book. Although Goitein was quite proud of this achievement, he seems later to have somewhat regretted the long time devoted to al-Baladhuri, insofar as a scholar's main preoccupation, he claimed, should be interpretation rather than publishing critical editions.[10] He indeed regarded himself as an "interpretative historical sociographer, that is, an interpreter of a culture's social history based upon its people's own texts."[11]

At an early stage of his career, in the late 1930s, Goitein was already treating the relationship between Judaism and Islam in two papers of seminal importance for his later research. The first was "The 'Arabic' Source of Israel and Its Religion," and the second, essentially a continuation, was "Some Comparative Notes on the History of Israel and the Arabs."[12] These papers provided the foundations for a series of instructive articles and studies of Islam and Judaism that he wrote (mainly in Hebrew) toward the end of the 1940s and in the early 1950s, including: "The Sanctity of Palestine in Moslem Piety";[13] "The Attitude to Authority in Judaism and Islam";[14] "The 'Stern Religion' (An Outline of the Portrayal of Judaism in Early Muslim Literature)";[15] "On Jewish-Arab Symbiosis";[16] "Who were Muhammad's Teachers?";[17] "Jerusalem in the Arab Period . . . , 638–1099";[18] *Muhammad's Islam, The Emergence of a New Religion in the Shadow of Judaism;*[19] and others.[20] Prominent in almost all these studies is Goitein's intense interest in the comparison between Judaism and Islam. This interest ultimately inspired him, in the mid 1950s, to write his *Jews and Arabs: Their Contacts Through the Ages,* a book that combined his familiarity with Islam and Yemenite Jewry with the first fruits of his genizah studies. He continued to treat Muslim subjects in the early 1960s, collecting his papers of this phase in a book, *Studies in Islamic History and Institutions,*[21] which essentially marked the end of his scholarly preoccupation with Islam. As it also contained studies based on the genizah, however, this book embodies Goitein's transition from Islamica to genizah studies. Only in 1977, upon receiving the Giorgio Levi Della Vida Award, was Goitein to return to Islam, writing what was essentially his last article in the field: "Individualism and Conformity in Classical Islam."[22]

The intertwining of Jewish and Muslim history occasionally inspired Goitein to digress from his study of the past and offer some thoughts on the future of Arab-Jewish relations. In a lecture on "The Israel-Arab Encounter,"[23] justifying such excursions into "prophecy," he defined the historian as a person who "digs deeply into the soil of the past and attempts to introduce order into what he has unearthed and explain it. But sometimes he straightens up, lays down his spade and raises his eyes in another direction . . . , the distant future."

The content and methodology of Goitein's work point to the influence of two of the greatest Islamic scholars of all times: Josef Horovitz, his dissertation supervisor at the University of Frankfurt; and Ignaz (Isaac) Goldziher, whom he knew only from his writings and letters. The regard he held for these scholars is clear from two articles he wrote about them — on Horovitz in 1932[24] and on Goldziher in 1948.[25] Horovitz influenced him mainly in three areas: (1) the study of the Qur'an and early Islamic historiography, the attitude of the Qur'an to Judaism, and the critical study of Arabic sources (as evidenced by his work on al-Baladhuri); (2) the need to investigate aspects of Islam, as represented by Goitein's studies of the Qur'an and Muslim institutions; and (3) the connection between Arabism and the culture and religion of the Hellenized East.

Goldziher's influence, which was not that of a master on his pupil, was more complex and is less easy to determine precisely. Given Goitein's appreciation of Goldziher and his devotion of a special chapter to the topic of "Goldziher between Judaism and Islam," it seems that Goldziher's deliberate decision to concentrate on Islam, ignoring Judaism, reinforced Goitein's preference for the opposite course: his studies of Islam created the basis for a study of early medieval Judaism and the links between the two cultures.[26] As Goitein wrote, Goldziher "left us no conclusive work on Judaism and

Islam, the reason being that his scholarly inclinations did not lead him in that direction."[27] Goitein's inclinations, however, were different; perhaps it was no accident that, as if a mirror reflection of the older scholar, Goitein wrote *his* comprehensive work on Jews and Arabs not long after writing his appreciation of Goldziher.[28] Goitein admired Goldziher's ability to build up a vast mosaic from minute details, drawn from the most scattered places, without allowing himself to get bogged down in them. Goldziher's methodology in comparative studies, of limiting himself to pointing out parallels rather than possible mutual influences, also left its mark on Goitein.[29] Finally, it is perhaps not insignificant that Goitein's first real acquaintance with the world of the genizah took place in the same year in which he wrote his article on Goldziher, and moreover in Budapest, where Goldziher had taught and done his research, and through the same collection on which Goldziher himself had published a series of articles in his last years.

It was in 1948 that Goitein made his first acquaintance with the genizah documents in the Kaufmann Collection at Budapest. From that time on he was entirely preoccupied with genizah studies, which were ultimately to become the crowning achievement of his scholarly activities. In the early 1950s his work with genizah materials still shared his attention with his interests in Islam and the Bible, but as that decade progressed the genizah gradually moved to the center of his scholarly world, becoming, from the mid 1960s until his death in 1985, the almost exclusive field of interest. Goitein's early genizah studies did not anticipate his later interests. His early goals were limited in scope, being mainly concerned with Jewish marine trade with India, as exemplified in his *Book of India,* which he planned and worked on from those earliest years of genizah research, but never completed. Only a few years later, toward the end of the 1950s, prodded by a commission to write a book about Jewish society, he decided — at the age of nearly 60 — to tackle the entire genizah, with the aim of describing, deciphering, and interpreting it.[30] With Goitein's genizah project, the social history of the Jewish people gained a distinguished scholar, while Islamic studies lost one of its best investigators.

The scholar hidden, as it were, behind this brief outline was a person of profound Jewish identity, whose varied scholarly interests reflected his desire to decipher the Jewish past, to locate the roots of Judaism and describe the inner and outer world of the Jews to the limits his ability and scholarly research would allow. His studies were driven by an intense desire to discover a human interior world. It was no accident that the titles of his great works focused on actual people: *Jews and Arabs, Yemenites, Letters of Medieval Jewish Traders,* rather than *Judaism and Islam, Yemenite Jewry, Medieval Jewish Trade.*[31]

Goitein's attachment to Middle Eastern culture, with its aura of mystery and romanticism, and to the people of the Middle East, whom he considered the epitome of natural perfection, is also reflected in his endeavor to uncover the Jewish religious past and the foundations of Islam, together with its links to Judaism.[32] Jews and Arabs, he believed, were the true image of the Middle Eastern world. In general, Goitein was always eager to search for the origins of things. Perhaps this was why some of his earliest work was devoted to language and Bible — language as the primordial expression of the speaking world, and Bible as a source for the beginnings of human history and monotheistic faith.[33] Small wonder, then, that some of his later Islamic studies bear titles that include words such as "source," "origin" or the like: *Muhammad's Islam, The Emergence of a New Religion in the Shadow of Judaism,* "The Birth-Hour of Muslim Law," "The Origin of the Vizierate," and so on.[34]

Goitein's constant preoccupation with manuscripts and previously unpublished documents upon which his studies of the early history of Islam, the Jews of Yemen, and the Genizah society are based also attests to his desire to explore previously uninvestigated areas. In this endeavor his early studies of Muslim historiography provided him with a methodological basis. Goitein's meticulous treatment of documents is understandable against the background of his conviction that "a detail considered unimportant from a practical standpoint will frequently prove valuable from a historical standpoint."[35] Goitein's reference to Ezekiel's vision of the dry bones in this context indicates how deeply he desires to breathe new life into the historical sources.[36]

This attention to details that come together to form a whole was a reflection of Goitein's own personality; as he once wrote, "We must strive for great things and concentrate on little ones."[37] It also reflects Goitein's understanding of human culture in general as being constituted of myriad details that form a whole. Although he never referred explicitly to these parallels, this idea surely accompanied him throughout his genizah research.

Goitein's tendency to seek out the unknown was also evident in his immediate contacts with other people, through personal interviews and long conversations; he tried, as it were, to penetrate their innermost thoughts, as he did in his studies of the Yemenites; except that here, instead of making documents speak, as in his genizah studies, he made people talk. Any discovery of unknown facts, even details, was for him an enrichment of human experience, a service to truth. Discovery of the truth, which he considered a distilled version of curiosity, is a recurrent motif in many of his works. In all areas of his research, with regard to both details and generalities, he tried to perceive the present as existing in the past, to sense the life experience of the time in human history—which, he says, the historian Ben-Zion Dinur taught him.[38]

Surely the intrusion of the present on the past influenced his understanding of the ongoing relations of Jews and Muslims. These peoples, he believed, had more in common than they had differences. They had a common language, a common culture, were neighbors and even shared a common fate. These motifs were the connecting links among Goitein's various fields of interest: linguistics, Bible, Islam and its institutions, Yemenite Jewry and Mediterranean society.[39] Goitein especially emphasized the importance of the Bible for the study of human society, as well as for the history of literature, pointing out similarities between biblical and early Arab narrative. Thus, Goitein discerned a relationship between biblical narrative and his work on Baladhuri, recognizing the prominence that biblical stories had for some important personalities of Islam's first century.[40] The Bible was for him, as he said, a gateway back "to the homeland, to the soil of Palestine, its nature and its people." There is a link between the Bible and its language on the one hand, and Arabia on the other.[41] Goitein's linguistic studies inspired him to study the culture of those who spoke the language: Hebrew, Arabic and, in particular, Judeo-Arabic, which he saw as the "merging of the two languages."

The links between Judaism on the one hand, and the Arabs and Islam on the other, also allowed Goitein to explore Jewish identity, its persistence and its uniqueness within an Islamic context. His Yemenite studies provided him with a window to a past world, as well as to the Yemenites of his own time. He saw in the Yemenites — and their women in particular — a veritable storehouse of ancient Judaism, in which Jewish religion and society were preserved in their pristine state. The Yemenite, for Goitein, was a continuation of an early reality, uninfluenced by the surroundings; an "authentic Jew," yet similar to the Arab, even though not descended from the same tribe.[42] (He once suggested that recent discoveries about monotheism in Yemen should force a reconsideration of Muhammad's Islam.)

Goitein's Yemenite interests may also be linked to the later, genizah phase of his career. Thus, while many of his 'Indian' studies contributed to his study of Yemenite Jewry, the latter in turn, as well as his introduction to Freimann's critical edition of the responsa of Abraham ben Moses Maimonides, laid the foundations (though unintentionally, as he himself pointed out), for his study of the genizah. Genizah society, with its people and institutions, preserved ancient traditions of the East and offered living evidence of Jewish life in a Muslim world.[43] Goitein's studies of Jerusalem and Palestine also demonstrate continuity, despite the change in methodology and sources. Having originally drawn on Muslim sources for these subjects, he later turned to the genizah.

One might say, therefore, that Goitein's scholarly work centered not on a variety of different subjects, but on one broad topic, with different branches being nourished by a single root: the Jewish-Arab encounter on all levels and its varying impact. Over the years, emphasis could change, attention could focus on different points in time, research tools varied; but his basic motif was always to discover the roots of human culture in the Middle East, mainly as exemplified in the meeting of Jew and Muslim. To quote from one of the letters of Halfon Abu Said (12th century) that Goitein once published, he did not see "the little in the West to be like the much of you yourselves [in the East]";[44] rather, he saw the East as "the much," the very source and cradle of Western culture and human civilization.

Despite the common thread through all Goitein's scholarly work, two main phases can be distinguished, as I have already indicated. At the start of his scientific career he focused mainly on Islam, on the background of the Jewish world from which it emerged, constantly drawing comparisons between Islam and Jewish religion and law. Take, for example, the names of some of his studies: "Zur Entstehung des Ramadans"; "*Banu Isra'il* and their Fractiousness"; "Some Comparative Notes on the History of Israel and the Arabs"; "The 'Arabic' Source of Israel and Its Religion — on the History of a Scientific Problem"; "On Jewish-Arab Symbiosis"; "The Sanctity of Palestine in Moslem Piety"; *Muhammad's Islam — the Emergence of a New Religion in the Shadow of Judaism;* "The Stern Religion — Facets of Judaism as Portrayed in Early Muslim Literature"; "Who were Muhammad's Mentors?"; "The Attitude to the Government in Islam and Judaism"; "The Origin and Nature of the Friday Worship"; and so on. Goitein was wholly familiar with the Qur'an, which provided the basis for many of his comparative essays and studies in intellectual history. His literary and linguistic talents helped him in his comparisons with the world of the Bible and Jewish law. Throughout this phase, Goitein considered himself an Islamist, as he testifies in one of his studies.

In the second phase of Goitein's scholarly career, the focus shifted to the Cairo genizah. Indeed, this later genizah research somewhat overshadowed his important Islamic studies, crowning him as *the* genizah scholar of our time and eclipsing his reputation as a scholar of early Islam.[45] Gradually, hesitantly, as a result of unplanned, even unforeseen circumstances, Jewish society came to the foreground of his scholarly activities, while Islam — its culture, religion and legal system — became a backdrop, a point of reference.[46] Goitein was fully aware — and rather apprehensive — of the transition, perhaps a little regretful, considering it a major change in his working pattern. However, his previous experience in critical editing of texts, the study of early Muslim institutions and economic fluctuations in the Arab Orient, were excellent tools for his genizah studies. The signs of his scholarly past are sometimes clearly visible, as in his article on the institution of the *nagid,* which in part recalls, methodologically speaking, his study of the Muslim Vizierate.[47] His book *Studies in Islamic History and Institutions* illustrates the transition: while the first part is based on Muslim sources, the second turns to genizah documents.

The transition affected not only the focus of attention but also the chronological framework: Goitein was now studying a somewhat later period, which moreover gave him access to an abundance of historical sources, hence the basis for a far more reliable historical evaluation. One result of these changes was that Goitein's genizah studies are rather more descriptive than analytical; they illustrate his amazing capacity to assemble details and put them together to form a vibrant picture of genizah society. His main concern in these studies was to portray economic and social institutions, not to write an intellectual history.

A scholar usually takes his or her first steps in the consideration of details, coming later to a broad, comprehensive view. With Goitein's early work in Islam the situation was, in some respects, the opposite. Here was a constant endeavor to formulate general conclusions as to the relationship between Judaism and Islam, in the context of a history of ideas; his genizah research, however, concentrates on details and documents, sometimes at the expense of the broader view. In this context it is worth quoting from one of Goitein's early works: "A book that has been born mainly not of a theory but of observations cannot pretend to provide an exhaustive, comprehensive method . . . A method worthy of the name is a world outlook translated into school life."[48] In his new guise, Goitein was to all intents and purposes a student of medieval society in general as he repeatedly insisted, no longer an Islamist, as he had first seen himself.[49]

If we do not count Goitein's early studies of Yemenite Jewry, which were concerned until the 1950s with the modern rather than the classical era, one conspicuous exception to the above division stands out, namely, Goitein's participation in 1937 in preparing a critical edition of the responsa of Abraham ben Moses Maimonides.[50] It was not his first encounter with Maimonides' family. His interest in them goes back to his youth, as he wrote of his high-school days: "The miniature edition of Maimonides' letters and responsa, published in Amsterdam (1712), was constantly in my pocket, and I would peruse it whenever I had a free moment. The wonderful combination of biographical details and ideological discourse in the letters brought me closer to the ideas themselves and helped me evaluate them."[51] It is therefore not surprising that Goitein ended his great work *A Mediterranean Society* with the personality of Maimonides' son Abraham, of which I shall have more to say later. Thus, one might say that he opened his career with Maimonides, the 'Great Eagle,' and brought it to a close with the latter's son, Abraham, the 'pietist.' But Goitein not only admired Abraham, he also seems to have identified with him, as I shall try to show below.

Another focus of Goitein's admiration was Ḥayyim Ḥabshush (d. 1899), the Yemenite guide, on whom he lavishes such accolades that one wonders whether this too might be a case of admiration turning into identification. The roots of this kinship, too, go back to Goitein's childhood memories. Goitein's brief account of Ḥabshush is similar in some respect to his description of Abraham son of Maimonides (broad interests and education, piety and observance of religious precepts combined with a critical attitude to the Jewish world, Jew in a Muslim environment);[52] and it too reveals similarities with Goitein himself.

Goitein's love and regard for the objects of his research did not affect his critical faculties. Ḥayyim Hillel Ben-Sasson, reviewing *A Mediterranean Society,* accused Goitein of allowing value judgments to distort his historical evaluations. I do not believe that this is true, although it is undeniable that Goitein does tend to utilize present events in order to throw light on the past, and his writings at times betray a degree of anachronism.[53]

I have indicated that Goitein's comments on the relationship between Judaism and Islam, and particularly between the Jewish and Muslim legal systems, occupy a prominent place in his writings.[54] In fact he tried to create a theoretical framework in which the relationship might be considered. Scholarly literature offers several alternative views in its evaluation of the mutual relationships and frequent resemblances between Jewish religion and law, on the one hand, and the Muslim faith and legal system, on the other, mainly in the context of the emergence of Islam. One approach sees the Muslim system, at least in that initial phase, as an imitation of Jewish law, borrowing from the latter both general principles and legal details — almost a "legal transplant," in the parlance of legal science.[55] Alternatively, Jewish and Islamic law may be seen as shaped by equivalent historical, economic and social circumstances, which produced similar legal rules. Parallels, therefore, between the two systems should not be attributed to mutual influence but to the similar needs of the times, to the fact that both cultures were at the same "human age."[56] Yet another approach considers the similarities as evidence of a continuation of early legal traditions shared by Jewish and Islamic law, a kind of "juristic *koiné*."[57] It is also quite legitimate to attribute parallels and similarities between the two legal systems not to a single theory, but rather to a combination of several factors that worked together to leave their imprint on both systems.

Later, in the second phase of the relationship between Judaism and Islam, approximately in the 9th and 10th centuries, after the Muslim secular power had been consolidated and the *shari'a* had reached its full development, the nature of the relationship assumed a new pattern, with the influence flowing mainly from Islamic to Jewish law in various areas. This flow has as yet not been sufficiently researched, and some of its aspects are still disputed in the scholarly world. Goitein was a social historian, not a legal scholar, and his treatments of legal matters are not independent studies but subservient to socio-historical research. Just as he believed that one cannot study a language unless one knows how its speakers lived, he was convinced that one cannot attempt an ethnological study unless one knows the laws according to which the subject society lives, or is supposed to live.[58] It was only natural, therefore, that Goitein frequently stressed the relationship between society and law.[59] At any rate, his studies have made an important, indeed unique, contribution to a correct evaluation of the encounter between the two faiths and the resulting implications, in both of its phases. Goitein loved to compare, although he was fully aware of the limitations of comparisons. His statement that "comparison is a primary tool in the study of any linguistic or historical phenomenon"[60] is equally apt in relation to law.

Goitein basically conceived of the Arab-Jewish relationship as one of symbiosis, a term he borrowed from biology and applied to the field of law. In an article written (in Hebrew) in 1949, entitled, "On Jewish-Arab Symbiosis," he defined it as follows: "the coexistence of two organs in such a way as to benefit from the proximity, in the sense that one party benefits while the other does not suffer."[61] The roots of this symbiosis, he believed, were a common origin, albeit obscure, which bequeathed to both religions a heritage of primitive democracy, similar languages, and culture, mainly rooted in religion. The symbiosis peaked, according to Goitein, in the classical period, which he defined as extending from the tenth to the thirteenth centuries. This was why he flatly rejected the view of some scholars that the origins of the Jewish religion should be sought in Arabia.[62] Goitein reiterated his own viewpoint in *Jews and Arabs* and in *A Mediterranean Society,* maintaining it throughout his life. It enabled him to combine, albeit cautiously and with considerable reservations, the three alternative approaches proposed above, each receiving a different emphasis at different phases of his scholarly career.[63]

Accordingly, Goitein preferred to speak of parallels rather than "influence," or alternative cultures, both drawing from a common "human age" or "juristic *koiné.* "[64] Nevertheless, he did not hesitate to point out certain cases of Jewish influence on Islam during the latter's formative stages.[65] It would seem that in this regard Goitein's evaluation changed with the passage of time. In his early years he explicitly spoke of "creation and continuation, source and replica," rather than of parallel development, though he recognized, of course, differences due to the discrete social and economic character of the two societies and their different historical development.[66] As late as 1956 he could still write: "It would be correct to state that Islam is nothing but Judaism in an Arabic pattern of large dimensions. . . . The entire religious typification of Islam as a faith of religious law is nothing but a reflection and an extension of Judaism."[67] Later, however, he moderated his view of the extent and intensity of the influence. In *Jews and Arabs,* though still saying that "the influence of Judaism on early Islam must have been very considerable, if not decisive," he added: "This question is extremely complicated, and an analysis of more technical details would be required to discuss it fully."[68] But in his *Studies in Islamic History and Institutions,* treating the broader question of the relationship between Judaism and Islam, he hedged his view: "However, such a great historical phenomenon as the type and essence of a religion should not be explained merely by influences. . . . We had better leave the greater question of their aboriginal affinity unanswered. It is, as a great Muslim historian would formulate it, 'a secret of the secrets of God.' "[69] In this emphasis on parallels Goitein was to some extent influenced by Goldziher, who always preferred to speak of parallels rather than influences. "Symbiosis" is a multifaceted concept. It does not necessarily imply similarity and parallels but may likewise produce substantial differences. It also implies dialogue: "The two religions define and interpret one another";[70] as Goitein himself occasionally pointed out.

Even with respect to the second phase, in which it is generally agreed that Islam had some influence on Judaism, Goitein advised caution and preferred the notion of "interplay" (with its connotation of mutuality) rather than "influence." He first introduced the term in 1958, incidentally, in an article on Maimonides as a judge,[71] and not in his book-length *Jews and Arabs,* where he dealt more specifically with the relationship between the two systems. Later, however, in *A Mediterranean Society,* he devoted a whole section to the concept,[72] and in the early 1980s in a special article.[73] At the same time, Goitein was certainly aware of the influence of Islam on Judaism at this time, and he indeed described it on various occasions, referring to it even in the aforementioned article.[74] Put briefly, his conclusion was that the "impact" (rather than "influence") of Islam affected the Jews through three channels: directly, when Judaism adopted Islamic laws; indirectly, when Jewish law adapted itself to the ruling system; and in reverse, as a negative reaction to that system. These channels, as Goitein defined them, were unidirectional from Islam to Judaism, so it is rather surprising that he chose the expression "interplay," which implies a bidirectional flow and surely does not describe the processes to which he himself was alluding. As we shall see presently, this "abuse of language" is not accidental, but derived from Goitein's far broader view of the development of Jewish law in what he calls the "classical" period, which is the crucial period, to his mind, in which *halakhah* and its institutions assumed their definitive forms. This broader view was the subject of a special article.[75] He also dealt with it in an article on women's status in the genizah documents,[76] and in another, on communal life in Maimonides' time.[77] In these and other articles he focused on methodological issues expressing some doubt as to the reality of Muslim influence on Jewish communal organization, public institutions and related areas. These include the emergence of the merchant-scholar, discussed in his first article, and public institutions and leadership, the topic of the second.

The conclusion regarding the Muslim and Jewish relationship to be drawn from the sum total of Goitein's works may be reduced to three interrelated principles:

First, the Muslim authorities were tolerant of minorities, granting them autonomy in questions of self-government and legal affairs. The Jews were thus able to maintain their judicial independence in accordance with halakhic tradition. Since religious law is personal, it also enabled the Jews to maintain their legal independence as a nation on the level of courts, institutions and leadership.[78] To use Goitein's metaphor, Jewish institutional halakhic existence was to all intents and purposes a state within a state, transcending political boundaries.[79] The Jewish people was thus able to preserve its unity and its mutual responsibility. The sense of national solidarity and responsibility was manifested in various ways during the genizah period, for example, in the ransoming of prisoners and the financial support for the leadership institutions in Baghdad.[80] Goitein stresses that the point of departure in his discussion of the Jewish community is the community as a whole, not the local communal cell.[81] The danger facing the Jewish community, in Goitein's view, was not that the Muslim authorities might intervene, but that Jews might have recourse to Muslim courts.[82] This observation was quite correct. But Goitein did not fully draw out its implications, namely, the changes that the Geonim introduced within Jewish law in order to limit such recourse.[83]

Second, earlier traditions of communal organization were more critical in maintaining the status of religious institutions than were forces in the larger environment, particularly since such political structures as the great Sanhedrin were lacking in Muslim society.[84] "Jewish society, like Christian society, assimilated to its environment in language, social and, of course, economic behavior; but in its communal organization it largely lived its own life."[85] The Muslim authorities did not create the Jewish institutions, though the latter were part of the Muslim political system; they only facilitated their regular operation.[86] Hence the diachronic aspect, that is, the heritage of the past, was decisive, and not the synchronic aspect, that is, the influence of the environment.[87] This was in keeping with Goitein's basic views as far back as the 1930s, that the development of religious organization was not an outcome of external necessity but an independent development, deeply engraved in the nature of the two religions and in the tendency of legal institutions and documents to survive from one generation to the next.[88]

In other areas, too, such as personal status or the status of the scholar turned merchant, Goitein believed that the past was more influential than present circumstances.[89] Thus, for example, *halakhah* followed past tradition in maintaining women's freedom of movement, in contrast to their social isolation in Islamic law.[90] In 1955, in *Jews and Arabs,* he expressed a similar but somewhat more complex view regarding Muslim influence on Judaism, postulating that, as Islam itself was deeply rooted in Judaism, the latter, expanding and reshaping itself, could borrow freely from Islam and from Muslim culture, at the same time preserving its independence and integrity.[91]

Third: Jewish communal organization in the Middle East was democratic in nature. Goitein considered the Jewish community to be a medieval religious democracy, that is, a body bound by divine law, with all the implications of that fact. What he described in the earliest phase of his research as the "primitive democracy" of Jewish society in the Middle East[92] was characterized by freedom of speech and respect for civil rights, although it failed to develop what one would call today democratic institutions. This society, Goitein believed, was reshaped in medieval Jewry under the influence of rabbinic tradition and became more democratic. Arab, and later Muslim, society, however, because of its different course of historical development and different socio-economic background, lagged behind and failed to develop parallel institutions of community and leadership. Goitein differed in this respect from Yitzhak Baer, who held that the prevalent principle of communal organization in the Middle East was hierarchic, dependent on the synagogue and the religious ministrants, whereas the dominant form in the West was democratic.[93] In the end Baer himself was won over by the Genizah documents and came to recognize the democratic nature of the oriental community; while, at the same time, Goitein admitted the continued importance of the hierocratic principle in the Middle East, despite the diminished role of the synagogue as a focus of social activity.[94]

In the final analysis, both Goitein and Baer sought—each in his own sphere of interest, but most probably for similar reasons—to demonstrate the continuity of Jewish communal organization from talmudic times to the Middle Ages, as it developed independently of its immediate milieu, whether in the East (Goitein) or in the West (Baer). Goitein therefore stressed, as had Baer before him, the definition of the local community in religious and national terms. Such terms as "the Holy Community" were expressive, as Baer pointed out, of "the concrete and transcendental unity of the nation," and indicative of the antiquity, originality and sanctity of the community as an integral component of Jewry, a sentiment with which Goitein would undoubtedly have agreed.

As early as the late 1940s, in his article on Jewish and Islamic attitudes to secular government, Goitein pointed out that Jewish literature in general reflected a more intensive communal life, more realistic and experienced regarding governmental matters, than the parallel Muslim literature.[95] His position as regards the autonomy of the Jewish community clashed with that of Eliahu Ashtor, who held that Jewish communal life in the East had been influenced by Muslim social organization. The Jewish community was, claimed Ashtor, a faithful reflection of the Muslim polity, and was *ipso facto* less democratic than Goitein believed.[96] This controversy had significant implications for several important aspects of the community such as the status and scope of the *taqqanah,* the authority of the *nagid,* and the emergence of that office. Goitein's position on such questions undoubtedly derived from his insistence on the uniqueness of the Jewish community and its continuous survival from talmudic times. Perhaps the differences between Goitein and Ashtor on such questions resulted from their different cultural backgrounds.[97] An echo of the argument, attesting to Goitein's sensitivity in this context, may be heard in his admonition: "In studying the Jewish community we must investigate the least detail as far as possible, while exercising caution in reaching final conclusions . . . Let us be investigative but not dogmatic."[98] A more complex and balanced tone may be discerned in an article written several years later, where he wrote: "It stands to reason that with regard to communal organization, as in other respects, the Islamic environment could not have been without influence."[99] In this article he refrained from criticizing Ashtor's views, pointing out there that the problem should be discussed in a very broad framework, taking into consideration not only Jewish history, but also Jewish tradition and the influence of the Muslim environment on Jewish organization.

Like other scholars before him, Goitein sometimes invoked a theory of "feedback" in order to explain the development of one legal institution or the other in Judaism and Islam alternately. According to this theory a Jewish legal institution or norm could have reached Islam during the first phase, been absorbed and reshaped in Islam; then, in its new guise, it could have exerted influence on Jewish law in the second phase. Of course, this theory, too, considers Jewish law, *halakhah,* as the source of Muslim law, even though the latter molded it to its own purposes.[100]

A comparison of Goitein's writings and oral communications during the long years of his scholarly life betray certain changes in his religious outlook, from what he called "medieval man" to *homo religiosus.* In addition, his Zionist convictions were perhaps somewhat shaken, as a result, among other things, of his disappointment regarding the development of Jewish-Arab relations, for which he had predicted a rosier future.[101] As we have seen, changes occurred in his field of scholarly interest, too, as indicated by the shift from Islamica to genizah studies. Nevertheless, his basic attitudes in research remained the same, barring some shifts in emphasis; but his views became more sophisticated and flexible. In many cases Goitein revised, corrected, expanded details.[102] Only seldom do we find him changing his mind; but he does so, even if unobtrusively and not always explicitly.[103]

It is evident from some of Goitein's evaluations of various personalities, whether public figures or otherwise, that he came to feel a strong and lasting affinity for them. Such were the aforementioned Yemenite Ḥayyim Ḥabshush,[104] or the Palestinian Gaon Daniel b. Azariah, of whom he wrote, "The multifaceted figure of Daniel b. Azariah appealed to my feelings or, better, my scholarly curiosity, from the very beginnings of my Genizah studies."[105] Similarly, he explained his interest in the inner life of the simple Jew, even his bedroom behavior, on the basis of personal feelings.[106] Of the 'genizah man' he writes: "This person had firm ethical views; his religiosity was simple and healthy; he was sober, pretty much free of superstition, and generally loyal to his own people. The respect for scholarship and scholars was universal and sincere."[107] But Goitein was particularly drawn to the figure of Maimonides' son Abraham, whom he frequently mentioned favorably in his articles, more often than not with laudatory adjectives, such as "his heart-warming personality" and the like.[108] Perhaps he saw in the medieval scholar's personality a reflection of his own.[109] He never said so explicitly, and of course it would be difficult to prove; but the parallels between Goitein's personality, as he saw himself — or perhaps wished to see himself — and his portrayal of Abraham Maimonides are quite obvious, suggesting that the relationship of the scholar to his subject was more than one of just scholarly interest. Many years of close attention to Abraham's personality led to a deep regard for him; the long acquaintance with all aspects and facets of Abraham's career and thought engendered, as I have already intimated, a sense of virtual identification. It was no accident that, as already mentioned, Goitein concluded his great project *A Mediterranean Society* with an account of Abraham's personality, works and leadership; after all, it was considered an honor to bring a book to a close.[110]

We, too, can do no better than end this appreciation of Goitein's personality, scholarly activities, and contributions to the history of humankind with his assessment of Abraham, son of Maimonides. Goitein, in his endeavor to revive the Jewish world of the past, seems to have found in Abraham Maimonides a source of much comfort, just as the latter's illustrious father had expressed similar sentiments.[111] Maimonides wrote of his son, "When I look at the situation of the world, I find comfort in two things alone — in philosophical introspection and in my son Abraham . . . because he is the most humble person, possessing pleasant virtues, a discriminating intelligence and much talent; he shall surely make a name for himself among the great."[112]

The father's fond prediction was certainly fulfilled in Goitein's description:

. . . His gentle nature, his penetrating reasoning and his strong will-power made him an ideal model of a moral leader and guide. . . .[113] For Abraham united in his single person three spiritual trends that were initially at odds with each other: strict legalistic orthodoxy, ascetic pietism and Greek science — sober, secular humanism. He represented all the best found in medieval Judaism, as it developed within Islamic civilization . . . he lived up to the standards that he had set in his writings. Abraham Maimonides was possessed of a most lovable personality. He combined the humanity and meekness to be expected in an ascetic with the firmness and determination required in a communal leader. His fervent religiosity and his strictness in the enforcement of the law were paired with common sense and humane consideration for special circumstances, while the lucidity and grace of his exposition revealed a disciple of the Greeks. . . . [114] The nobility of his mind and the excellence of his spiritual gifts were deserving of richer response.[115]

Perhaps the key words in this evaluation are "moral leader and guide," a person who combined the three conflicting trends of "strict legalistic orthodoxy, ascetic pietism and Greek science." Goitein particularly admired Abraham's leadership and attempts to blaze an independent trail in the orthodox Judaism of his time: to establish a pietist movement, reform religious life and institutions and offer a new interpretation of *halakhah*. This, according to Goitein, was why Abraham saw fit to follow up his father's great works — the legal code *Mishneh Torah* and the *Guide of the Perplexed* — with a work of his own; and this was why he agreed to serve the community as *nagid* instead of devoting all his time and effort to studying the Torah, a decision that Goitein considered a tragic error. Goitein highly praised Abraham's innovative biblical exegesis, which he believed so persuasive as to make even its *midrash* (homiletics) seem like *peshat* (the simple meaning of the text). He saw Abraham Maimonides' regard for the Muslim Sufi movement and his view of the Muslim pietists as the real successors of the Prophets as natural and admirable, probably because of Goitein's own "symbiotic" conception, but particularly because of Abraham's efforts to shore up these views with ancient Jewish sources and prove their continuity with early tradition. For this was exactly what Goitein himself had tried to establish in connection with Jewish communal organization and institutions. Abraham Maimonides successfully built a bridge between his personality, his life and studies, on the one hand, and the best elements of the culture of his times, on the other, so as to create what he believed to be the most perfect understanding of the Jewish ancestral faith. Goitein was also impressed by Abraham's ability to assemble a group of disciples, although they did not become a well-formed group.[116] Abraham Maimonides, for Goitein, was "a perfect man with a tragic fate," because his great work did not gain popularity and was ultimately lost, never having gained the central place in Jewish religious thought earned by his father's works; similarly, his pietist movement did not survive.[117]

Goitein's admiration for Abraham Maimonides was undoubtedly due, first and foremost, to the latter's greatness and personality, representing for Goitein the end of the humanist period of Islam and the culture of the Middle East that Goitein admired so much, in contrast to Abraham's father, who had been born in the West and generally preserved the "western"

tradition. Goitein himself hinted at this point when he explained the difference in authority between father and son. He pointed out that Maimonides
did not act as magistrate but as rabbi and *mufti,* in keeping with the western
tradition; while in the East the two offices were combined, as exemplified by
his son Abraham, who had become assimilated and taken on eastern customs.[118] Yet, ironically, their personal histories were similar. Both lost their
fathers at a young age and did not complete their major lifework.

Another point of similarity between Goitein and Abraham Maimonides
is their common concern with religion. Goitein was religiously inclined and
possessed a good Jewish education, while at the same time a scientific
scholar with extensive general knowledge, favorably disposed toward the
influence of the Muslim environment to which he had emigrated in his
youth. It is true that Goitein, somewhat dissatisfied with his ancestral religion, distanced himself from what he called "the stern religion" on account
of the spirit of enlightenment and the crises of his time (chiefly the Holocaust); having begun life as a "medieval man" whose life revolved around
religion, one who "relied on religion for his personal deportment and for his
salvation in the world to come,"[119] he became a *homo religiosus,* "fearful for
the fate of his soul and the souls of those for whom he feels himself responsible," as he hints in his life story.[120] Abraham Maimonides, however, remained wholly faithful to his ancestral religion while struggling to introduce reforms.[121]

Like Abraham Maimonides, Goitein put great value on service to the
community, particularly in the area of education and Bible teaching, in
which he engaged for a while at the expense of his scholarly career. He, too,
was solicitous for his students' welfare. He, too, tried to introduce improve-
ments and reforms in the areas under his responsibility, again, particularly in
the educational field and the teaching of Bible. His prime ideals were the
quest for truth and piety, which, however, he never carefully defined.[122] It
is no accident that Goitein's study of Abraham Maimonides and his pietist circle was dedicated to another much admired Arabic scholar, David
Baneth, "who was most pious in his behavior," and was titled—significantly—"Our Master [Heb.: *rabbenu*] Abraham Maimonides and His Pietist Circles: *New Documents from the Genizah.* "[123]

Goitein and Abraham both entertained special feelings for Yemenite

Jewry. Both first tried their hands in Bible exegesis, striving to determine the plain meaning of the text and avoid fanciful interpretations, seeking out the truth in the Scriptures as a means toward the revival of the Jewish spirit. In 1938 Goitein wrote, "The study of Bible will once again make us Jews, not only in name and in flesh but in our very bones and spirit; it will thus enable us to reunite with previous generations, that same reconciliation of parents with children and children with parents that is the unmistakable sign of real redemption."[124] Admittedly, Goitein wrote these words at an early stage of his career; nevertheless, Abraham Maimonides' exegetical activities as well as the other parallel qualities we have indicated, heightened Goitein's affinity for the medieval scholar, to the extent that his admiration bordered on identification.

Goitein once described the activities of the Maimuni family by invoking the rabbinic saying "One does not erect tombstones for the righteous; their words perpetuate their memory."[125] This judgment is no doubt apt as regards Goitein himself, whose many studies of the Jewish-Arab encounter in the Middle Ages, in general, and genizah society, in particular, are his real memorial.

One of Goitein's first publications in genizah studies, in the 1950 issue of *Tarbiz,* was entitled "Early Letters and Documents from the Collection of the Late David Kaufmann."[126] When he republished the article thirty years later, in 1980, a few years before his death, in the volume *Palestinian Jewry in Early Islamic and Crusader Times in the Light of the Geniza Documents,*[127] he altered the main title, replacing it with a quotation from one of the letters discussed in the article itself: "Once Again to Jerusalem, the City in which Your Ancestors are Buried." We shall never know what inspired him to make the change, and what went through his mind when he wrote those moving words. He opened up many a window for us, glimpses of hidden worlds; but that particular one is closed forever.

NOTES

I would like to thank Prof. M. A. Friedman for reading a draft of this paper and offering several useful comments. The final responsibility is of course my own.

1. Goitein's life and academic career have been evaluated by many authors,

some of them writing even before his death over ten years ago, others later. Among these are: D. Ayalon, "S. D. Goitein and His Academic Work" (Hebrew), in *A Bibliography of the Writings of Prof. Shelomo Dov Goitein,* ed. R. Attal (Jerusalem, 1975), 9–13; S. Shaked, "Scholar of the Historic Partnership between Judaism and Islam" (Hebrew), *Pe'amim* 22 (1985), 4–9; S. Morag, "S. D. Goitein, His Achievements in the Study of Yemenite Jewry" (Hebrew), *Pe'amim* 22 (1985), 10–15; M. A. Friedman, "Prof. S. D. Goitein, the Man and the Scholar—A Character Sketch" (Hebrew), *Yedi'on ha-Igud le-Mada'ei ha-Yahadut* 26 (1986), 51–66; A. Udovitch, Introduction to S. D. Goitein, *A Mediterranean Society,* (Berkeley, 1988), 5:9–18; J. Kraemer, "Goitein and His Mediterranean Society" (Hebrew), *Zemanim* (1990), 6; M. A. Friedman, "On S. D. Goitein's Contribution to Interdisciplinary Studies of Judeo-Arab Culture" (Hebrew), *Sefunot* 8 (n.s.) (1991), 11–20. We cannot list here the many reviews of Goitein's books.

2. S. D. Goitein, *Jews and Arabs: Their Contacts Through the Ages* (New York, 1955), 129; but compare idem, "On Jewish-Arab Symbiosis," *Molad* 2 (1949) 259–266, esp. 264–265.

3. *The Yemenites: History, Communal Organization, Spiritual Life. Selected Studies* (Hebrew), ed. M. Ben-Sasson (Jerusalem, 1983), 3.

4. *Teaching the Bible. Problems and Ways of Modern Bible Teaching* (Hebrew) (Tel Aviv, 1958), 17.

5. *The Yemenites,* 241.

6. Goitein, reminiscing on various occasions, referred to three significant "nocturnal scenes" at different stages of his life and in different parts of the world (the village of his birth, Jerusalem, and the United States), in all three of which he saw what he called his "favorite constellation on stars," Orion; the constellation presumably had some symbolic meaning for him, which I have been unable to decipher.

7. Goitein himself told the story of his life on several occasions. See mainly "The Life Story of a Scholar," in Attal, *Bibliography,* xiii–xxviii; Introduction to his *Teaching the Bible,* 7–22; "Involvement in Geniza Research," in *Religion in a Religious Age* (New York, 1974), 139–146; *A Mediterranean Society,* 5:496–502. (An interesting biography is Friedman, "Goitein, Man and Scholar"; see also the other publications listed in n. 1.)

8. He recounted his hesitation in his "Life Story," xxv. For the phrase "tenfold exile" see Goitein, *Teaching the Bible,* 7.

9. See *The Yemenites,* 3; Morag, "S. D. Goitein."

10. See his "Involvement," 146, though he adds there: "A good edition is the

highest form of interpretation." And compare with Friedman, "Man and Scholar," 60.

11. See N. Stillman, Review of *A Mediterranean Society, International Journal of Comparative Sociology* 32 (1991), 5:348–357; S. D. Goitein, *A Mediterranean Society,* vol. 5, Introduction and Epilogue; idem, *Studies in Islamic History and Institutions* (Leiden, 1966) 247.

12. *Zion* 2 (1937), 1–18; *Zion* 3 (1938), 97–117.

13. *Yedi'ot ha-Ḥevrah la-Ḥaqirat 'Erets-Yisra'el ve-'Atiqoteha* 12 (1946), 120–126.

14. *Tarbiẓ* 19 (1948), 153–159.

15. *Sefer Dinaburg,* ed. Yitzhak Baer, Joshua Gutman and Moshe Schwabe (Jerusalem, 1949), 151–164, with additional material on 423.

16. Goitein, *Jews and Arabs.*

17. *Tarbiẓ* 23 (1953), 146–159 [= *Sefer . . . Eliakim G. Weil* (Jerusalem, 1953), 10–23].

18. *Yerushalayim. Meḥqerei 'Erets Yisra'el (Sefer Press)* (Jerusalem, 1953), 82–103.

19. Jerusalem (Hebrew University, mimeographed), 1956.

20. The first article in this series, actually written in the early 1930s — "*Banu Isra'il* and their Fractiousness," *Tarbiẓ* 3 (1932), 410–422 — was essentially Goitein's first essay in the field of Islam and Judaism. See also his articles, "A Deed of Privileges in Favour of the Jews, Attributed to Muhammad, of Yemenite Origin" (Hebrew), *Kirjath Sepher* 9 (1932), 507–521; "*Isrā'Īliyāt*" (Hebrew), *Tarbiẓ* 6 (1935), 89–101, 510–522.

21. On Goitein's contribution to the study of Muslim institutions see Shaked, "Scholar," 7.

22. *Giorgio Levi Della Vida Conferences* 5 (1977), 1–17.

23. *Molad* 14 (1956), 261–266.

24. "The Academic Work of the Late Joseph Horovitz" (Hebrew), in *The Late Joseph Horovitz (1874–1931),* eds. W. J. Fischel & S. D. Goitein, 6–14.

25. "Goldziher from His Letters (Goldziher's Letters to A. S. Poznanski 1901–1922)" (Hebrew), in *Ignace Goldziher Memorial,* eds. S. Loewinger *et al.* (Budapest, 1948), 1:3–23. See also *'Atidot* 10–11 (1947), 355–358 and 363.

26. See his comment in "Goldziher's Hebrew Writings" (Hebrew), *Kirjath Sepher* 23 (1946–47), 252: "This is not the place to explain why the founder of Islamic studies did not devote a special, comprehensive study to the relations between the Jewish Oral Law and similar phenomena in the Arab religion." Com-

pare Goitein's comments on Goldziher in his review of J. Schacht's *The Origins of Muhammedan Jurisprudence,* in *Ha-Mizraḥ he-Ḥadash* 3 (1952), 412–414, esp. 413. Perhaps Goitein was influenced by the heightened interest in the relatively new discipline of Comparative Religion; see his "The 'Arabic' Source of Israel," 3.

27. "Goldziher from His Letters," 9.

28. See Friedman, "Goitein's Contribution," 19.

29. *Loc. cit.*

30. See Friedman, "Man and Scholar," 59.

31. See, for example, Goitein's comments in his *Letters of Medieval Jewish Traders* (Princeton, NJ, 1973), 11.

32. There may be some influence here, though somewhat delayed, of the romantic *Drang nach Osten* that seized Europe at the turn of the 19th century, particularly among the Jews of Germany, as represented most prominently by Martin Buber; see Paul Mendes-Flohr, "Fin de Siècle Orientalism, the *Ostjuden* and the Aesthetics of Jewish Self-Affirmation," in idem, *Divided Passions. Jewish Intellectuals and the Experience of Modernity* (Detroit, 1991), 77–132. Goitein heard Buber lecture at Frankfurt on his frequent visits to that city and may have been influenced by him; see "Life Story," xviii.

33. On the relationship between language and society see Goitein, *A Mediterranean Society,* 5:498; on the relationship between law and society see *The Yemenites,* 306.

34. See "The Origin and Historical Significance of North African Jewry," in *Proceedings of the Seminar on Muslim-Jewish Relations in North Africa,* (New York, 1975), 2–23.

35. "Jewish Community Organization in Light of the Cairo Geniza Documents" (Hebrew), *Zion* 26 (1961), 170.

36. *A Mediterranean Society,* 5:501. And see Friedman, "Goitein's Contribution," 17 n. 27a.

37. See *Teaching the Bible,* 265; Friedman, "Man and Scholar," 60 n. 41.

38. "Stern Religion," 164. See above, n. 15.

39. On Goitein's contribution to interdisciplinary studies see Friedman, "Goitein's Contribution."

40. See, for example, Goitein, *Teaching the Bible,* 22; Friedman, "Goitein's Contribution," 11–12.

41. See "The 'Arabic' Source," 2–9.

42. *The Yemenites,* 241.

43. Compare with the end of his paper, "The Twilight of the House of Maimonides: Joshua Ha-Nagid, 1310–1355" (Hebrew), *Tarbiz* 54 (1985), 104, where he

comments on his *Mediterranean Society:* ". . . explained by examining the linguistic usage of the source and interpreted *in light of Jewish tradition and the Muslim environment.*"

44. In "Early Letters and Documents from the Collection of the Late David Kaufmann" (Hebrew), *Tarbiz* 20 (1950), 203.

45. Goitein called the period in question the "genizah period"; see his *Jewish Education in Muslim Countries, Based on Records from the Cairo Geniza* (Hebrew) (Jerusalem, 1962), 17. He saw it as an *"intermediate period,* which summarized everything that went before it tidily and cleanly, and determined the patterns of thought and everyday behavior that the Jews maintained until the end of the modern era." In this respect he saw the Genizah world as a counterpart of Muslim humanism, which he called "the intermediate civilization"; see *Institutions,* 46, and *A Mediterranean Society,* 5:495. Goitein does not explain why no original Jewish culture evolved in Egypt, as it did in other major communities, such as Iraq, Spain or North Africa (see *Jewish Education,* 21).

46. See Kraemer, "Goitein and His Mediterranean Society," 11, who points out the fundamental change in Goitein during the 1960s, "in both direction and tone. It was then that the transition occurred from the Middle East to the Mediterranean Sea. Instead of the Yemenite, the Semitic man of the Orient, the 'Mediterranean Jews' ascended the stage . . ." Of course, the change was also due to the shift in his research interests, as we have already seen.

47. See "The Origin of the Vizierate and its True Character," in *Institutions,* 168–196.

48. *On the Teaching of Hebrew in Palestinian Schools* (Hebrew) (Tel Aviv, 1945), 6–7.

49. See the end of his article, "Who were Muhammad's Teachers?" 159: "I have not written this article in order to vindicate Judaism, but as an Islamist intent on solving a problem that has occupied Islamic studies from their inception." See also Goitein, *Institutions,* 59, and Friedman, "Goitein's Contribution," 15 n. 23.

50. See *Abraham Maimuni, Responsa* (Hebrew), Jerusalem 1938, xxiii–xxxvii.

51. "Chief Judge R. Hananel B. Samuel, In-law of R. Moses Maimonides" (Hebrew), *Tarbiz* 50 (1981), 372.

52. *Joseph Halévy's Journey in Yemen as Related by his Yemenite Companion Hayyim Habshush* (Hebrew) (Tel Aviv, 1939), xx–xxiii.

53. See H. H. Ben-Sasson, "A New Way to the World of the Genizah" (Hebrew), *Zion* 40 (1975), 1–46. His criticism of Goitein deserves a more detailed and exhaustive response than can be given here. In this context one might mention Goitein's story of an American rabbi who, relying on a talmudic point of law,

vetoed Goitein's uncle's levirate marriage to a deceased brother's wife, on the grounds that the uncle was in fact marrying the woman for love; the story expressed Goitein's disapproval of the rabbinate, intimating that in this respect nothing had really changed.

54. Law and *halakhah* were not Goitein's main fields of interest and he never treated them systematically; see, for example, his comment in *The Yemenites,* 306: "My interest in the question was not halakhic-legal, as I am not conversant with that field, but socio-religious." Nevertheless, some of his articles are more than relevant, and cogent observations may be found in dozens of his publications. Of the writings directly concerned with legal matters one might list the following: "Introduction to Muslim Law" (Hebrew), in *Ha-Mishpaṭ ha-Muslemi bi-Medinat Yisra'el* (Jerusalem, 1958), 1–172; *A Mediterranean Society,* 2:311–345, 395–407; and two important articles: "Human Rights in Jewish Thought and Life in the Middle Ages," in *Essays on Human Rights,* ed. D. Sidorsky (Philadelphia, 1979), 247–264; "The Interplay of Jewish and Islamic Laws," in *Jewish Law in Legal History and the Modern World,* ed. B. S. Jackson (Leiden, 1980), 61–77; *Jewish Law in Our Time,* ed. R. Link-Salinger (New York, 1982), 55–76. Other articles treat subjects of a legal nature, such as: "The Position of Women According to the Cairo Geniza Documents" (Hebrew), *Proceedings of the Fourth World Congress of Jewish Studies* (Jerusalem, 1969), 2:177–179 (English summary: 192); "Stern Religion"; "The Birth-Hour of Muslim Law? An Exercise in Exegesis," *The Muslim World* 50 (1960), 23–29. See also Goitein's introduction to the Responsa of Abraham Maimonides. In yet other articles, various methodological and legal questions involving the relationship between Jewish and Muslim law, including parallels and comparisons, are raised. Such are: "Some Comparative Notes"; "Some Basic Problems in Jewish History" (Hebrew), *Proceedings of the Fifth World Congress of Jewish Studies* (Jerusalem, 1972), 2:101–106; "Jewish Community Organization"; "Attitudes to Authority in Islam and Judaism" (Hebrew), *Tarbiz* 19 (1948), 153–159; "The Origin and Nature of the Muslim Friday Worship," in *Institutions,* 111–125; as well as isolated remarks in other papers. In some articles Goitein publishes legal deeds or judicial documents of various kinds: "Wills and Deathbed Declarations from the Cairo Geniza" (Hebrew), *Sefunot* 8 (1964), 105–126; "Court Records from the Cairo Geniza in the Jewish National and University Library" (Hebrew), *Kirjath Sepher* 41 (1966), 263–276; "Four Ancient Marriage Contracts from the Cairo Genizah" (Hebrew), *Leshonenu* 30 (1966), 197–215; and his review of Ashtor's *Toledot ha-Yehudim be-Miṣrayim uve-Suriyah . . . , Tarbiz* 41 (1972), 59–81. Long before, he had reviewed Schacht's *Origins of Muhammedan Jurisprudence.* Goitein also remarks that when teaching

Bible he also dealt with Israelite society and law in biblical times; see his *Teaching the Bible,* 18. For Goitein's contribution to this area see my "Jewish-Muslim Comparative Law: A History of Research and its Problems" (Hebrew), *Pe'amim* 62 (1995), 42–81.

55. See A. Watson, *Legal Transplants* (Charlottesville, VA, 1974).

56. Although Goitein tended to belittle the importance of external conditions in understanding legal creativity in its broad sense (see "Some Comparative Notes," 116), he considered social and economic constraints to be highly significant in the evolution of legal systems; see Libson, "Jewish-Muslim Comparative Law," 47.

57. See, for example, M. Cook, "Magian Cheese — An Arabic Problem in Islamic Law," *BSOAS* 47 (1984), 462; and compare with my "Jewish-Muslim Comparative Law," 62.

58. Goitein, *The Yemenites,* 306.

59. See, for example, Goitein, *Institutions,* 218, on the relationship between the bourgeoisie and the development of religious law.

60. Goitein, "The 'Arabic' Source," 18.

61. *Molad* 11 (1949), 259.

62. See mainly his article "The 'Arabic' Source."

63. See, for example, the following passage in "The 'Arabic' Source," 7: "It is true that, racially speaking, the Children of Israel came from Arabia, but neither race nor language are decisive in cultural creativity; the crucial factors are the land and the cultural framework. For Israel, this framework was the Ancient Near East and its culture, not some Beduin culture of an unknown nature"; and compare *ibid.,* 18. Compare also Goitein's own statement in "Some Comparative Notes," 98: "The same nature, same climatic conditions, and therefore, largely, the same economic factors influenced the history of the two peoples. There is surely some connection between these common natural conditions and the considerable similarity of social background." And *ibid.,* 115: "It was not a case of imitation, or of imitation alone, but of parallel development, perhaps based on common racial-social premisses." Compare also *ibid.,* 116, and in "The 'Arabic' Source," 9. In yet another article, "The Birth-Hour," 23, Goitein reiterates that much of the similarity may be attributed to parallel development rather than borrowing. Compare also *The Yemenites,* 147, and see the next note.

64. Concerning the idea of a common "human age," see "Jewish Community Organization"; similar remarks appear in "Human Rights," 257, in connection with traders' customs; and see "The Interplay," 61, on the "juristic *koiné.* "

65. See Goitein, "Some Comparative Notes," 116; "Stern Religion," 152; "Who were Muhammad's Teachers?" 149; "The Birth-Hour," 126; "Introduction to Mus-

lim Law," *passim*; *Jews and Arabs, passim*; and compare my "Jewish-Muslim Comparative Law," 47 n. 19.

66. See "Some Comparative Notes," 114.

67. "On the Israel-Arab Encounter" (Hebrew), *Molad* 95 (1956), 265.

68. *Jews and Arabs,* 60.

69. *Institutions,* 22.

70. "Attitudes to Authority," 153.

71. "Maimonides as Chief Justice: the Newly Edited Arabic Originals of Maimonides' Responsa," *JQR* 49 (1959), 201.

72. *A Mediterranean Society,* 2:395–402.

73. "Interplay."

74. See, for example, "Interplay," 69, where he points out Muslim influence on Jewish practices in connection with partnership. At times he speaks of social rather than legal influence, as in *ibid.*, 74. Needless to say, Goitein was well acquainted with Islamic law and made frequent use of it in order to explain Jewish sources; see, for example, his introduction to the Responsa of Abraham Maimonides, xxxvii, in connection with guardianship; and his discussion of the prohibition on Jewish residence in Jerusalem, in *Palestinian Jewry in Early Islamic and Crusader Times in the Light of the Geniza Documents,* ed. J. Hacker (Jerusalem, 1980), 41, where he cites the work of the Muslim jurist Khassaf and draws historical conclusions. See also *Yemenites,* 211, where, in connection with the communal organization of the Jews in Yemen, he discusses the role of the *'āqil* (president) relying on elements of the Muslim system. On the use of the Muslim term *'arūbā* in Shafi'i's *Kitāb al-Umm* see *Institutions,* 117; such examples could be multiplied. Sometimes Goitein refers to a Muslim law without citing the source; see, for example, "Comparative Notes," 105, where he asserts that, as defined by Islamic jurists, marriage signifies the husband's acquisition of the wife's sexual organs. In this connection, M. A. Friedman had called my attention to the work of S. Haeri, *Law of Desire: Temporary Marriage in Shi'i Law* (Syracuse, 1989), 41–43, and to the sources cited there. See also Abu Bakr al-Kasāni, *Kitāb Badā'i 'al-Sanā'i' fī Tartīb al-Sharā'i'* (Cairo, 1909), 4:200; Muhammad Shams al-Dīn al-Sarakhsī, *Kitāb al-Mabsūt,* (Cairo, 1906), 5:184.

75. "Some Basic Problems."

76. "Position of Women."

77. "Jewish Community Organization."

78. Goitein frequently stresses the personal, rather than territorial, nature of religious law. See, for example, *Letters of Medieval Jewish Traders,* 11.

79. See Goitein, "Jewish Society and Institutions under Islam," *Journal of World*

History 11 (1968), 181; "Interplay," 59; and see H. H. Ben-Sasson's comment that in this context "political boundaries" meant "the limits of Muslim rule in a given region"; see Ben-Sasson, "A New Way," 2.

80. There may be some reflection here of Goitein's Zionism.

81. "Jewish Community Organization," 177. Throughout his writings Goitein frequently stressed the organizational and institutional aspects of Jewish community life and their vital importance for Jewish life in general; see, for example, *Jewish Education*, 14.

82. See "Minority Selfrule and Government Control in Islam," *Islamica* 31 (1970), 101–116.

83. Goitein did recognize that appeals to gentile courts were dangerous in themselves; see, for example, his "Wills and Deathbed Declarations," 108; *A Mediterranean Society*, 2:401–402; and see my "Jewish-Muslim Comparative Law," 70. On Muslim government intervention in cases involving the violation of public regulations see Goitein, "Minority Selfrule," 106–107.

84. Of course, Islam possesses its own religious courts; Goitein was probably alluding to some such institution as the Sanhedrin or Great Court (*Bet Din Gadol*) as conceived by the Geonim.

85. "Some Basic Problems," 106; and compare *Jewish Education*, Introduction, 15: "Our historians seem to be inclined to ascribe to these developments [the Arab conquests and the establishment of the Islamic empire] more decisive influence than they actually had. The new order that emerged with the rise of the Islamic empire shattered the heavy chains that had shackled the Jewish people and opened up previously inconceivable prospects for them. But most of their spiritual assets . . . as well as their communal institutions — yeshivot, the exilarchs and the local communities — had existed before the advent of Islam."

86. See "Basic Problems," 106. Thus, for example, Goitein believes that the office of the nagid developed under special circumstances and was not created by the Muslim authorities; see *A Mediterranean Society*, 2:27; "The Title and Office of the Nagid — A Re-examination," *JQR* 53 (1962), 98–99; "The Principal of the Palestine Yeshivah as Leader of the Jews in the Fatimid State" (Hebrew), in J. Hacker, ed., *Palestinian Jewry*, 58; "Political Conflict and the Use of Power in the World of the Geniza," in *Kinship and Consent: The Jewish Political Tradition and its Contemporary Uses*, ed. D. J. Elazar (Ramat Gan, 1981), 176–177; "The Yemenite Negidim" (Hebrew), in *The Yemenites*, 75.

87. See "Jewish Community Organization," 179.

88. "Introduction to Islamic Law," 8; "The Sexual Mores of the Common People," in *Society and the Sexes in Medieval Islam* (Malibu, CA, 1979), 48, in connec-

tion with marriage contracts. See also "The Jewish Family of the High Middle Ages as Revealed by the Documents of the Cairo Geniza," in *Settimane di studio del Centro italiano di studi sull' alto medioevo, vol. 26, Gli Ebrei nell'Alto Medioevo, Spoleto, . . . 1978* (Spoleto, 1980), 718, 733; "Jewish Houses and Neighborhoods in the City of San'a," in *The Yemenites,* 147; *Institutions,* 246.

89. On the status of the scholar as trader see his discussion in "Basic Problems," 102. On the status of women see "Position of Women."

90. "Sexual Mores," 48.

91. *Jews and Arabs,* 129; compare also "Jewish-Arab Encounter," 265.

92. See "Jewish-Arab Symbiosis," 285; *Jews and Arabs,* 27; "Political Conflict," 171.

93. See Y. Baer, "The Foundations and Beginnings of Jewish Community Organization in the Middle Ages" (Hebrew), *Zion* 15 (1950), 1–41.

94. See Goitein, "The Struggle between the Synagogue and the Community" (Hebrew), in *Sefer Ḥayyim Schirmann* (Jerusalem, 1970), 70. For an account of the Jewish community in Egypt see his "The Local Community in the Light of the Cairo Geniza Records," *JJS* 12 (1961), 133–158; *A Mediterranean Society,* 2:40–90.

95. See "Attitudes to Authority," 153; and "Jewish Community Organization," 178.

96. See E. Ashtor, "Some Typical Features of the Jewish Community in Egypt in the Middle Ages" (Hebrew), *Zion* 30 (1955), 61–78; *Zion* 31 (1956), 128–157.

97. Ashtor's academic activities and research, unlike those of Goitein, have almost never been discussed and evaluated in print. One of the few appreciations is a short note in *The Medieval Levant. Studies in Memory of Eliyahu Ashtor (1914–1984),* eds. A. L. Udovitch and B. Z. Kedar (= *Asian and African Studies* 22 [1988]), 7–10.

98. "Jewish Community Organization," 177.

99. "Jewish Society," 181.

100. See *Jews and Arabs,* 178–189; "Comparative Notes," 116 and n. 140; compare my "Jewish-Muslim Comparative Law," 59 n. 62.

101. "Israel-Arab Encounter," 262; and compare Kraemer, "Goitein and his *A Mediterranean Society,* " 10. These aspects of Goitein's career need further study, mainly through his letters, which are beyond the scope of this article.

102. See, for example, "Who were Muhammad's Teachers?" 148.

103. See, for example, J. Kraemer, "Six Letters from the Cairo Geniza," *Maimonidean Studies* 2 (1991), 77 n. 77; and cf. Goitein, "Comparative Notes," 117 n. 43.

104. *Joseph Halévy's Journey,* 20–22.

105. "Daniel b. Azariah, Prince and Gaon" (Hebrew), in J. Hacker, ed., *Palestinian Jewry*, 132. But compare the identical remarks about R. Joshua Nagid in Goitein, "The Twilight of the House of Maimonides: Joshua Ha-Nagid, 1310–1355" (Hebrew), *Tarbiz* 54 (1985), 67. Goitein's admiration of Habshush is evident from his own account (see previous note).

106. "Sexual Mores," 45: "I venture to do so because I feel myself almost one of them."

107. *Jewish Education*, 19.

108. See, for example, his article "The Muslim Government as Seen by its Non-Muslim Subjects," *Journal of the Pakistan Historical Society* 12 (1964), 7. And compare "Documents on Abraham Maimonides and His Pietist Circle" (Hebrew), *Tarbiz* 33 (1964), 181–197, esp. 181: "For the master was a pietist not only in his views, as we learn from his works, but also in his behavior, as attested by his letters and responsa." At the very outset of his academic career Goitein considered Abraham Maimonides an intriguing figure; see, for example, his comment in a review (in Hebrew) of S. Rosenblatt's *The Highways to Perfection of Abraham Maimonides, Kirjath Sepher* 15 (1938–39), 442–444, where he wrote: "Somebody should now undertake to attempt a new portrayal of this interesting religious figure. . . ." Goitein's regard for Abraham Maimonides seems to have evolved gradually. Papers published in the 1950s betray no particular admiration or praise; see, for example, "A Jewish Addict to Sufism in the Time of the Nagid David II Maimonides," *JQR* 44 (1953–54), 37; "The Renewal of the Controversy over the Prayer for the Head of the Community at Abraham Maimuni's Time" (Hebrew), *Goldziher Memorial Volume*, (Jerusalem, 1958), 2:51; "Who were Muhammad's Teachers?" 157; *Jews and Arabs*, 183.

109. See Friedman, "Goitein's Contribution," 20.

110. See "Attitudes to Authority," 154.

111. The parallels between Goitein and Abraham Maimonides were already noted by Udovitch in his introduction to *A Mediterranean Society*, 5:ix–xviii.

112. See D. Z. Baneth, *Igerot ha-Rambam* (Jerusalem, 1946), 96; cited in Goitein, "Twilight," 104; compare also *A Mediterranean Society*, 5:475.

113. *A Mediterranean Society*, 5:475.

114. *Ibid.*, 481–482.

115. *Ibid.*, 492.

116. Compare Friedman, "Man and Scholar," 66.

117. Why this should be the case is an intriguing question, which was never discussed by Goitein but deserves further examination.

118. See "Maimonides' Life in the Light of New Discoveries from the Cairo

Genizah" (Hebrew), *Perakim* 4 (1966), 34. Long before, in his introduction to Abraham Maimonides' Responsa (xxiv), he had compared Maimonides with his son, writing, "In the father one could still discern traces of the Arabic dialect spoken in the Maghreb, but he [Abraham] showed signs of the Egyptian dialect."

119. "Muslim Government," 12.

120. "Life Story," xiv; for the definition of the term see *Yemenites,* 141.

121. It is striking that Goitein also applied the term *homo religiosus* to the Yemenite traveler Hayyim Habshush whom, as already pointed out (*see n. 106*), he greatly admired.

122. See Goitein, "My Methodology in Researching the Yemenite Jews," in *The Yemenites,* 6.

123. See above, n. 109.

124. *Teaching the Bible,* 300.

125. "Chief Judge R. Hananel B. Samuel, In-law of R. Moses Maimonides" (Hebrew), *Tarbiz* 50 (1981), 372.

126. See above, n. 45.

127. *Palestine Jewry,* 205.

WORKS CITED

Attal, R., ed. *A Bibliography of the Writings of Prof. Shelomo Dov Goitein* (Jerusalem, 1975).

Ben-Sasson, H. H. "A New Way to the World of the Genizah" (Hebrew), *Zion* 40 (1975), 1–46.

Friedman, M. A. "On S. D. Goitein's Contribution to Interdisciplinary Studies of Judeo-Arab Culture" (Hebrew), *Sefunot* 8 (n.s.) (1991), 11–20.

———. "Prof S. D. Goitein, the Man and the Scholar — a Character Sketch" (Hebrew), *Yedi'on ha-Igud le-Mada'ei ha-Yahadut* 26 (1986), 51–66.

Goitein, S. D. "The 'Arabic' Source of Israel and its Religion," *Zion* 2 (1937), 1–18.

———. "Attitudes to Authority in Judaism and Islam," *Tarbiz* 19 (1948), 153–159.

———. "The Birth-Hour of Muslim Law? An Exercise in Exegesis," *The Muslim World* 50 (1960), 23–29.

———. "Human Rights in Jewish Thought and Life in the Middle Ages," in *Essays on Human Rights,* ed. D. Sidorsky (Philadelphia, 1979), 247–264.

———. "The Interplay of Jewish and Islamic Laws," in *Jewish Law in Legal History and the Modern World,* ed. B. S. Jackson (Leiden, 1980), 61–77. Reprint. *Jewish Law in Our Time,* ed. R. Link-Salinger (New York, 1982), 55–76.

——. "Introduction to Muslim Law" (Hebrew), in *Ha-Mishpaṭ ha-Muslemi bi-Medinat Yisra'el* (Jerusalem, 1958), 1–172.

——. "The Israel-Arab Encounter," *Molad* 14 (1956), 261–266.

——. "Jewish-Arab Symbiosis," *Molad* 2 (1949), 259–266.

——. "Jewish Community Organization in Light of the Cairo Geniza Documents" (Hebrew), *Zion* 26 (1961), 170.

——. *Jewish Education in Muslim Countries, Based on Records from the Cairo Geniza* (Hebrew) (Jerusalem, 1962).

——. "Jewish Society and Institutions under Islam," *Journal of World History* 11 (1968), 170–84.

——. *Jews and Arabs: Their Contacts Through the Ages* (New York, 1955).

——. *Joseph Halévy's Journey in Yemen as Related by his Yemenite Companion Hayyim Habshush* (Hebrew) (Tel Aviv, 1939).

——. *Letters of Medieval Jewish Traders* (Princeton, NJ, 1973).

——. "The Life Story of a Scholar," in *Bibliography,* ed. Attal.

——. *A Mediterranean Society* (Berkeley, 1988).

——. "The Muslim Government as Seen by its Non-Muslim Subjects," *Journal of the Pakistan Historical Society* 12 (1964), 1–13.

——. "The Position of Women According to the Cairo Geniza Documents" (Hebrew), *Proceedings of the Fourth World Congress of Jewish Studies* (Jerusalem, 1969), 2:177–179.

——. Review of J. Schacht, *The Origins of Muhammedan Jurisprudence, Ha-Mizraḥ he-Ḥadash* 3 (1952), 412–414.

——. "The Sexual Mores of the Common People," *in Society and the Sexes in Medieval Islam* (Malibu, CA, 1979).

——. "Some Basic Problems in Jewish History" (Hebrew), *Proceedings of the Fifth World Congress of Jewish Studies* (Jerusalem, 1972), 2: 101–106.

——. "Some Comparative Notes on the History of Israel and the Arabs," *Zion* 3 (1938), 97–117.

——. "The 'Stern Religion' (An Outline of the Portrayal of Judaism in Early Muslim Literature)" (Hebrew), in *Sefer Dinaburg,* ed. Yitzhak Baer, Joshua Gutman and Moshe Schwabe (Jerusalem, 1949), 151–164.

——. *Studies in Islamic History and Institutions* (Leiden, 1966).

——. *Teaching the Bible: Problems and Ways of Modern Bible Teaching* (Hebrew) (Tel Aviv, 1958).

——. "The Twilight of the House of Maimonides: Joshua Ha-Nagid, 1310–1355" (Hebrew), *Tarbiz* 54 (1985), 67–104.

——. "Who Were Muhammad's Teachers?" *Tarbiz* 23 (1953), 146–159.

——. *The Yemenites: History, Communal Organization, Spiritual Life. Selected Studies* (Hebrew), ed. M. Ben-Sasson (Jerusalem, 1983).

Hacker, J., ed. *Palestinian Jewry in Early Islamic and Crusader Times in the Light of the Geniza Documents* (Jerusalem, 1980).

Kraemer, J. "Goitein and His Mediterranean Society" (Hebrew), *Zemanim*, 34–35. (1990), 4–16.

Morag, S. "S. D. Goitein, His Achievements in the Study of Yemenite Jewry" (Hebrew), *Peʿamim* 22 (1985), 10–15.

Shaked, S. "Scholar of the Historic Partnership between Judaism and Islam" (Hebrew), *Peʿamim* 22 (1985), 4–9.

Elias Bickerman on Judaism and Hellenism

M A R T H A   H I M M E L F A R B

Alexander the Great could not have realized that from the point of view of later generations the most momentous result of his campaign of world conquest was neither the unification of all Greece nor the fall of the Persian empire, but rather the exposure of the Jews — a small and unimportant people — to the culture of their new rulers. The Jews, for their part, seem to have recognized Greek culture as qualitatively different from the cultures of earlier conquerors. No prophet had ever stopped to consider that there might exist an Assyrian or a Babylonian culture apart from idolatry. But the author of 2 Maccabees, even as he excoriates the Jews who succumbed to the attractions of Greek culture, characterizes that culture not by reference to its (false) gods, but by the gymnasium (2 Macc. 4:7–17). He treats Judaism and Hellenism, *Ioudaïsmos* and *Hellenismos,* as utterly opposed, indeed as locked in mortal combat, but also as comparable; thus the pair of abstract nouns. *Ioudaïsmos* appears to have been his coinage, intended to serve as a counterpart for the already existing term *Hellenismos,* whose meaning, however, he transformed; the term usually referred to language rather than way of life.[1] For more than two thousand years since, the pairing of Judaism and Hellenism has been of profound significance for the self-understanding of the West, as indicated by repeated struggles over the nature of the relationship and indeed over the meaning of the terms themselves.

The hero of my essay is Elias Bickerman, whose contribution to our understanding of the relationship between Judaism and Hellenism in antiquity seems to me unsurpassed. Bickerman saw the hellenization of the Jews as involving what I am going to call the restructuring of ancient Judaism. (I borrow the term from the title of a book by my colleague Robert Wuthnow, *The Restructuring of American Religion.*)[2] By restructuring, I mean the adaptation of Greek institutions and practices to Judaism and the consequent changes in Judaism. Where other scholars attempt to measure how much is Jewish and how much Greek in a particular text, Bickerman concerned himself with the *dynamics* of the reception of Greek culture by the Jews: he questions how the Jews transformed Hellenism and how, in turn, Judaism was transformed.

Most of Bickerman's writing on the Jews reflects on the problem of the relationship between Judaism and Hellenism — either implicitly or explicitly — but as far as I know Bickerman never set out a formal theory on the subject. The only methods he would have acknowledged were the tools of the ancient historian's craft as traditionally understood: philology and careful reading, which he used to remarkable effect. The closest he came to a general statement of his approach is that wonderful semi-popular juxtaposition of two previously published essays, *From Ezra to the Last of the Maccabees,*[3] and it is to this work more than anything else he wrote that I found myself turning in an effort to trace the outlines of his views.

Until the middle of this century, the dominant context for the discussion of Judaism and Hellenism was New Testament scholarship, in which the two categories are treated as the background for Christianity.[4] The existence of a more hellenized Judaism in the diaspora is noted,[5] but the term "Judaism" is used to refer primarily to Palestinian Judaism, the religion of the Jews in the Land of Israel, Jews who spoke and wrote in Hebrew or Aramaic and who are assumed to have remained free of the influence of Hellenism.

In this picture Christianity provides the solution to the failings of its predecessors, legalism and exclusivism in Judaism,[6] the lack of personal relationship to God or the problem of dualism in Hellenism.[7]

But even this sketch, with its clearly theological coloring, provides a starting point for a more complex and historically accurate picture in its recognition of the existence of communities of Jews who spoke and wrote Greek. Indeed, the corpus of Jewish literature in Greek is considerably larger than that of any other subject people of the hellenistic empires. The last half century has seen a significant body of research that develops the picture further by showing the deep penetration of Greek language and Greek ideas among the Jews of Palestine. In addition to Bickerman's work, I think here particularly of the groundbreaking work of Victor Tcherikover,[8] who treated not only Egypt but Palestine; of Martin Hengel's monumental contribution;[9] of Morton Smith's work[10]; and, for the rabbinic period, of the pioneering studies of Saul Lieberman[11] and Henry Fischel.[12]

But even as scholars have discovered the richness and variety of Jewish responses to Greek culture, they have had trouble describing the interaction between Judaism and Hellenism. The dominant model—which goes all the way back to Droysen and the invention of the idea of hellenization—has been influence, that is, the influence of Hellenism on Judaism. Hengel writes about the limited influence of Stoic philosophy and Greek customs on Joshua Ben Sira, the early 2nd-century BCE teacher and author of the Wisdom of Ben Sira (Ecclesiasticus), whom he sees as a conservative hostile to Greek culture.[13] On the other hand, Tcherikover denies that Ben Sira was influenced by Hellenism at all because he returned from his travels abroad an "orthodox" Jew.[14] Implicit in both of these views is an understanding of Judaism as the passive recipient of Greek influence. Further, inasmuch as Judaism becomes hellenized, it also becomes less Jewish.

As the tone of these scholars' formulations suggests, there is more at stake here than the best possible understanding of an ancient text. Hengel is alone among the scholars I have mentioned, in approaching ancient Judaism as a student of the New Testament; it is not hard to detect the influence of Christian theology on his work.[15] Tcherikover, on the other hand, was an ancient historian who came to his work on Jewish history only after writing a book on the foundation of cities in the hellenistic empires.[16] He was also a

Zionist. For Hengel, resistance to Hellenism is a sign of Jewish exclusivism, while for Tcherikover accepting Greek ideas implies assimilation. Of course the positions of both scholars are more nuanced than my very brief discussion indicates, but I do not believe that my characterizations are unfair.

Between the New Testament scholar's preference for hellenic universalism, and the Zionist or simply Jewish disapproval of hellenization as assimilation, Bickerman took not a middle path but an altogether different one, emphasizing the character of the interaction between Judaism and Hellenism rather than charting the presence and degree of Greek influence on Jews. Like Tcherikover, Bickerman was an ancient historian by training; both men, as refugees from the Russian Revolution, found themselves studying ancient history at the University of Berlin in the early 1920s.[17] Bickerman's first book on a Jewish subject was *Der Gott der Makkabäer* in 1937;[18] it reflects his profound knowledge of Seleucid imperial practice, the subject of his *Institutions des Séleucides,* which appeared the next year.[19] He was already the author of a considerable body of work on other aspects of ancient legal and institutional history.

Bickerman's work as a general hellenistic historian gave him a broad perspective on the problem of Judaism and Hellenism. The Jews were certainly not the only people of the Near East with a well-developed sense of identity and an ancient literary tradition to fall under the sway of the Greeks, and Bickerman, more than most who wrote about these questions, kept this point firmly in view. In his pithy formulation, "Whether or not to accept [Greek] culture was . . . a question of life and death for every people. . . . [T]he problem was actually solved by only two peoples, the Romans and the Jews."[20] The Roman solution, of course, was conquest, a solution unavailable to the Jews. Since Bickerman wrote, some historians of the hellenistic empires have been arguing for greater dynamism in the native responses to hellenistic rule than earlier scholars had assumed.[21] But in the long term, from the perspective of the end of the second Christian millennium, Bickerman was surely correct. His attention to the comparative dimension of the question has the advantage of placing in relief certain crucial aspects of Judaism such as the centrality of the Torah.

Bickerman's approach to the relationship between Judaism and Hellenism can be seen in his treatment of Ben Sira, which stands in contrast to that of Hengel and Tcherikover. Like them, Bickerman takes Ben Sira as a conservative; he contrasts his attitude toward Hellenism with those of the accommodationists on the one hand and the radical traditionalists on the other. (I shall turn to this paradoxical formulation in a moment). Yet, he sets himself apart when he writes:

> Historians classify, but life's strands are inextricably interwoven. The traditionalist Ben Sira is at the same time the first Jewish author to put his own name to his work and to emphasize his literary personality and individuality.... He is bringing doctrine "for all those who seek instruction" and, like a Greek wandering philosopher of his time, proclaims: "Hear me, you great ones of the people and give ear to me, you, rulers of the congregation." He not only accepts the figure of personified wisdom . . . , which appears in Proverbs, but puts this profane knowledge on a level with "the book of the Covenant of the Most High, the law which Moses commanded"—a rather bold effort to reconcile the synagogue with the Greek Academy, Jerusalem with Athens.[22]

Thus, Bickerman suggests that traditionalists such as Ben Sira were also trying to come to terms with Greek culture. To me, this is a more persuasive reading of Ben Sira's book than the alternatives of Hengel or Tcherikover.

Bickerman's understanding of radical traditionalism, of which his favorite example is the Book of Jubilees, rests on a similar basis.

> As it often happens, in order to uphold traditional values, their apologists themselves propose the most radical innovations. The author of the Book of Jubilees outdoes the later talmudic teaching in his severity as to the observance of ritual prescriptions. But to assert the everlasting validity of the Torah, this traditionalist places his own composition beside and even above Scripture. . . . In his paraphrase the author of Jubilees attacks the lunisolar calendar and strongly urges the adoption of his own system of a year of 364 days in which each holiday always falls on the same day of the week as ordained by God. . . . The reason for his revolutionary idea is significant: the irregularity of the moon confuses the times. Thus, without realizing it, this traditionalist succumbs to the seduction of the Greek penchant for rationalization.[23]

The discovery of the Dead Sea Scrolls came too late to have much of an impact on Bickerman's already well-developed views about ancient Judaism,[24] but they do confirm this observation about radical innovation in defense of traditional values.

Bickerman's account of Ben Sira hints at what he clearly identified as the most important aspect of the restructuring of Judaism in the hellenistic period, "the formation of a Jewish intelligentsia, different from the clergy and not dependent on the sanctuary," that is, the scribes. Earlier, the scribe had been a civil servant, an advisor to kings, and thus a purveyor of wisdom. But for the Jews, from the Persian period, the scribe as civil servant became the interpreter of the Torah, the law of the Jewish people. Originally, among the Jews as among the other peoples of the ancient Near East, the functions of teaching and interpreting religious lore belonged to the priests. Only among the Jews do scribes emerge as a group distinct from the priests. As Bickerman sees it, it is this democratizing separation between heredity and authority that will make possible the more thoroughgoing democratization of the Pharisees a few generations later.[25] (The language of "democracy" here is mine, not Bickerman's, but I believe it captures his meaning.)

In another context Bickerman might have offered some refinements to this bold schema. The relationship between scribe and priest in ancient Judaism remained extremely close, if sometimes tense. Many of the scribes known to us by name, including Ezra and Ben Sira, were in fact priests by heredity.[26] Yet Bickerman is right to insist that the existence of the role of scribe apart from the priesthood is an essential feature of ancient Judaism, one that sets it apart from other hellenistic cultures.

The great innovation of the Pharisees, according to Bickerman, is their claim that Wisdom, that is, the Torah, should be available to all Jewish men. Ben Sira still assumed that only the wealthy could become wise. Not so the Pharisees. While their goal was the biblical goal of making Israel a holy nation, the belief in the power of education to achieve such a goal is Greek, indeed Platonic; it was the Greeks who introduced to the world the idea that membership in a civilization could be achieved by education rather than birth, an idea that had a profound influence on Judaism, though the hereditary aspect of Jewish identity certainly remained central. Nor is this the only idea the traditionalist Pharisees learned from the Greeks. Bickerman notes also the importance of the afterlife.[27]

Bickerman argues in *From Ezra to the Last of the Maccabees* that it was the success of the Maccabean revolt that led to this type of hellenization among the Jews: "The reform party wished to assimilate the Torah to Hellenism; the Maccabees wished to incorporate Hellenic culture in the Torah."[28] He provides the following example: Barbarians throughout the hellenistic world claimed kinship with the Greeks; but the letter in 1 Maccabees (Chapter 12) from the Spartans to Jonathan — which is, of course, a Jewish fabrication — has the Spartans embrace the Jews as brothers, claiming descent from Abraham.

This is a powerful example, but Bickerman himself has shown beyond any doubt that the same sort of incorporation took place in the Wisdom of Ben Sira and many other works before the revolt. Bickerman's periodization reflects his view of the Maccabean revolt as a turning point of crucial significance to the course of Jewish history. But it is by no means obvious that the pace of such incorporation intensified after the Maccabean revolt. Indeed, the success of the Maccabees and their emergence as a dynasty in the hellenistic style provokes a traditionalizing reaction — of which the Qumran community is the most striking example — that complicates the picture. Of course, as Bickerman pointed out, traditionalizing need not mean the absence of hellenization.

There are other points at which Bickerman is less than entirely satisfactory, for instance in his treatment of pseudepigrapha such as the Enochic corpus, the Testaments of the Twelve Patriarchs, and Jubilees. What little Bickerman says about 1 Enoch seems to me misguided; I take the Book of the Watchers to be less sectarian and more influential than Bickerman does, and not merely the reading matter for "zany zealots."[29] Bickerman pays a great deal of attention to the Testaments of the Twelve Patriarchs, which he explicates in terms of the recasting of biblical stories in light of concerns introduced by contact with Greek culture.[30] The comments are typical Bickerman, perceptive and suggestive. But Bickerman shows no signs of anxiety about the Jewish character of the composition, whether in his revision during the 1970s of his 1950 article on the date of the Testaments[31] or in *The*

Jews in the Greek Age;[32] in the revised version of the article he notes the work of Marinus de Jonge, who has offered powerful arguments for the Testaments as a Christian product, only to dismiss it.[33] In relation to Jubilees, I can only lament the unfootnoted character of *The Jews in the Greek Age*, which makes it possible for Bickerman to claim that the written text of Jubilees was accompanied by a "secret oral teaching" that revealed the eschatological significance of the dates for past events, without offering any defense of this position.[34] (My inclination is to attribute this deviation from his usual moderation to the influence of his good friend on Morningside Heights, that well-known proponent of secret oral teachings, Morton Smith.)

But all these objections are quibbles. Nonetheless, there is one more profound problem in Bickerman's work as I see it. Bickerman's treatment of the hellenistic reform and the Maccabean Revolt, surely his most famous contribution to the discussion of ancient Jewish history, offers an understanding of Judaism and Hellenism that contrasts with the dialectical understanding I have just discussed. Bickerman first put forward his reading of the hellenistic reform in *Der Gott der Makkabäer* in 1937; he offered it again in the second essay in *From Ezra to the Last of the Maccabees*. Its outlines are well known: the reform was the effort of a Jewish elite to revise Judaism in keeping with the critique of the Greek intellectuals who admired its monotheism — which made the Jews "a race of philosophers" — while they viewed most of its customs as misanthropic superstition. The persecution was the result of the attempts of the reformers to force their reform upon an unwilling people.[35]

Bickerman claims, uncharacteristically, it seems to me, that the reformers had utterly abandoned Judaism. The introduction of the gymnasium, he insists, must have involved participation in idolatrous worship; there could be no games without libations to the gods.[36] This view has been rejected by several recent scholars.[37] Why not a Jewish gymnasium without idolatry, a gymnasium that some Jews could see as not in violation of the laws of the Torah, a document which, after all, has nothing to say about gymnasia? We learn in 2 Maccabees of the ambassadors sent from Jerusalem to Tyre who could not find it in their hearts to use the 300 silver drachmas they carried as a contribution for sacrifices to Herakles as per the instructions of the high priest Jason, the arch-reformer; instead they used the money to have triremes built for Tyre (2 Macc. 18–20). We see that although Jason had no problem with sacrifices to other gods, some of his supporters clearly did.[38] Would these ambassadors have been willing to participate in a gymnasium that included the cult of foreign gods?

For Bickerman, monotheism itself was at stake in the reform. If the Maccabees had not resisted, there would be no Judaism today — nor would there be Christianity or Islam.[39] True, the Jews of the diaspora would have remained — it is important for Bickerman's view that they were untouched by the persecution[40] — but with the Temple itself a temple of idols, the traditions of Judaism could not have been preserved for long.[41]

In *From Ezra to the Last of the Maccabees,* though not in *The God of the Maccabees,* Bickerman quickly returns to form, noting that the Maccabees' establishment of a festival to mark the occasion of their liberation and purification of the temple reflected the Greek practice of marking important events, and that aspects of the observance of the festival parallel features of Greek festivals.[42] Still, the stark picture of the meaning of the persecution and revolt remains, even in *From Ezra to the Last of the Maccabees.*

The explanation for Bickerman's treatment of the Maccabees lies outside scholarship. We learn from the introduction to the English translation of *The God of the Maccabees* that for Bickerman the resistance of the Maccabees was associated with the fate of the Jews under the Nazis. "The final draft of my book was written three years later [1936] and its style naturally reflected the new political situation. (For instance, I wrote that the Maccabees identified their own party with the Jewish people.) Nevertheless I was surprised that my academic and even pedantic book (published by Schocken, Jüdischer Buchverlag) could offer consolation to the persecuted Jews in Germany, as several letters I received from my readers told me."[43] With such a terrible lense through which to read these ancient events, it is hardly surprising that Bickerman ends the introduction by reasserting a position that in other circumstances a historian as careful as he might well find problematic: "There can be no doubt that Menelaos' Reformation would have succeeded in Jerusalem and become a new orthodoxy, and the remaining Old Believers would [have] be[en] only a small heretic minority among the paganized Jews — if the Maccabees had lost. 'Except the Lord keeps [a] city, the watchman waketh but in vain'" (Ps. 127:1).⁴⁴ The second essay in *From Ezra to the Last of the Maccabees,* the one on the Maccabees, is dedicated "To T. B., Deported by the Germans, Ps. 35:17."⁴⁵

One can only sympathize with Bickerman's response to the horror of the events he lived through. And *The God of the Maccabees* remains a seminal contribution to the study of the Maccabean revolt and the sources that describe it; no one can write about the revolt without reference to it. But despite the importance of *The God of the Maccabees,* I believe that Bickerman's greatest scholarly legacy is the picture of the restructuring of Judaism in *From Ezra to the Last of the Maccabees.* It is his signal contribution to have looked beyond the fact of the influence of Hellenism on Judaism to show us the many ways in which Jews actively drew from Greek culture and reshaped Judaism in the process.

NOTES

1. On the terms, see Martin Hengel, *Judaism and Hellenism: Studies in Their Encounter in Palestine during the Early Hellenistic Period,* trans. John Bowden (Philadelphia, 1974) 1:1–2.

2. Robert Wuthnow, *The Restructuring of American Religion: Society and Faith Since World War II* (Princeton, 1988).

3. Elias Bickerman, *From Ezra to the Last of the Maccabees: Foundations of Post-Biblical Judaism* (New York, 1962). This volume consists of two essays, the first originally published as "The Historical Foundations of Postbiblical Judaism," in *The Jews: Their History, Culture, and Religion,* ed. Louis Finkelstein (New York, 1949), and the second as *The Maccabees: An Account of Their History from the Beginnings to the Fall of the House of the Hasmoneans* (New York, 1947). Chapter 7 of "The Historical Foundations" is omitted in *From Ezra to the Last of the Maccabees.*

4. For a fine example of this genre, see Rudolf Bultmann, *Primitive Christianity in Its Contemporary Setting,* trans. R. H. Fuller (London, 1956).

5. Bultmann, *Primitive Christianity,* devotes a chapter (94–100) to this issue at the end of his section on Judaism.

6. Bultmann, *Primitive Christianity,* 59–79. "Legalism" in this negative sense

has been a favorite category for describing the Judaism of Jesus' time in New Testament scholarship until very recently.

7. The problem of dualism is Bultmann's choice. See *Primitive Christianity,* especially 162–71. Bultmann also comments on the problem of (lack of) freedom, as understood by the philosophical elite in Stoicism and the masses in astrology (135–55).

8. Victor Tcherikover, *Hellenistic Civilization and the Jews* (1959; Reprint. New York, 1974).

9. In addition to *Judaism and Hellenism,* see *Jews, Greeks, and Barbarians: Aspects of the Hellenization of Judaism in the pre-Christian Period,* trans. John Bowden (Philadelphia, 1980).

10. His programmatic statement is the semi-popular "Palestinian Judaism in the First Century," in *Israel: Its Role in Civilization,* ed. Moshe Davis (New York, 1956). Many of his essays are also relevant. See the bibliography through 1973 in *Christianity, Judaism and Other Greco-Roman Cults: Studies for Morton Smith at Sixty,* ed. Jacob Neusner (Leiden, 1975), 4:190–200.

11. Saul Lieberman, *Greek in Jewish Palestine* (New York, 1942); *Hellenism in Jewish Palestine* (New York, 1950).

12. Henry A. Fischel, *Rabbinic Literature and Greco-Roman Philosophy* (Leiden, 1973).

13. Hengel, *Judaism and Hellenism,* 1:131–53.

14. Tcherikover, *Hellenistic Civilization,* 142–51; travels and return as "orthodox Jew," 143–44.

15. See especially Hengel, *Judaism and Hellenism,* 1:306–314.

16. Tcherikover, *Die hellenistischen Städtbegründungen von Alexander dem Grossen bis auf die Römerzeit, Philologus,* Supplementband 19.1 (Leipzig, 1927. Reprint. New York, 1973). Note the spelling of Tcherikover's name, which, like Bickerman's, was spelled differently in different linguistic settings.

17. For Tcherikover's biography, I rely on the article by Alexander Fuks, *Encyclopedia Judaica* 15:875–876. For Bickerman's, I am dependent on the biographical note by Morton Smith at the beginning of the third volume of the collection of (many of) Bickerman's essays, *Studies in Jewish and Christian History* (Leiden, 1976–86), 3:xi–xiii. I have not been able to see the autobiographies of Bickerman's father, Joseph, and brother, Jacob, which Jacob published under the title, *Two Bikermans* (New York, 1975). (The family name was spelled variously after the family left Russia.) Arnoldo Momigliano's essay, "The Absence of the Third Bickerman," in *Essays on Ancient and Modern Judaism,* ed. Silvia Berti, trans. Maura

Masella-Gayley (Chicago, 1994), 217–221, discusses some of the information about Elias Bickerman to be gleaned from this work.

18. Bickerman, *Der Gott der Makkabäer: Untersuchungen über Sinn und Ursprung der makkabäischen Erhebung* (Berlin, 1937). In what follows I will refer to the English translation, *The God of the Maccabees: Studies on the Meaning and Origin of the Maccabean Revolt,* trans. Horst R. Moehring (Leiden, 1979).

19. Bikerman, *Institutions des Séleucides* (Paris, 1938). Note the spelling of Bickerman's name.

20. Bickerman, *From Ezra,* 104; see also the remarks in his conclusion to the essay on the Maccabees in *From Ezra,* 178–180. Arnaldo Momigliano, the third great Jewish ancient historian of that generation, makes a similar observation in *Alien Wisdom: The Limits of Hellenization* (Cambridge, 1975), 10–11.

21. See, for example, the essays in *Hellenism in the East: Interaction of Greek and non-Greek Civilizations from Syria to Central Asia After Alexander,* ed. Amelie Kuhrt and Susan Sherwin-White (London, 1987), which tend to emphasize the persistence of native culture alongside Greek.

22. Bickerman, *From Ezra,* 63–65; quotation, 64–65.

23. Ibid., 59–63; quotation 62–63.

24. The Scrolls receive some attention in Bickerman's posthumously published *The Jews in the Greek Age* (Cambridge, MA, 1988).

25. Bickerman, *From Ezra,* 67–71; quotation, 67.

26. On this subject, see Martha Himmelfarb, *Ascent to Heaven in Jewish and Christian Apocalypses* (New York, 1993), 23–25, and references there.

27. Bickerman, *From Ezra,* 160–65.

28. Ibid., 156.

29. Bickerman, *Greek Age,* 210–211.

30. Ibid., 205–211.

31. Bickerman, "The Date of the Testaments of the Twelve Patriarchs," *Studies in Jewish and Christian History* 2:1–23; first published in *Journal of Biblical Literature* 69 (1950), 245–60.

32. Bickerman, *Greek Age,* 204–210, 268–274, 302–304, and passim.

33. Bickerman, "Date," 2–3, especially n. 5. Bickerman refers there to de Jonge's essays in *Studies on the Testaments of the Twelve Patriarchs: Text and Interpretation,* ed. Marinus de Jonge (Leiden, 1975). De Jonge has not abandoned the position that the Testaments is a Christian work, although he has refined it considerably over the years. See his essays on the Testaments included in *Jewish Eschatology, Early Christian Christology and the Testaments of the Twelve Patriarchs: Collected Essays of Marinus de Jonge* (Leiden, 1991).

34. Bickerman, *Greek Age*, 215.

35. Bickerman, *God of the Maccabees*, 76–92; *From Ezra*, 93–111.

36. Bickerman, *God of the Maccabees*, 41. Compare his comments about the gymnasium and post-Maccabean Jews, *From Ezra*, 181.

37. See, for example, Klaus Bringmann, *Hellenistische Reform und Religionsverfolgung in Judäa: Eine Untersuchung zur jüdisch-hellenistischen Geschichte (175–163 v. Chr.)* (Gottingen, 1983), 83; Victor Tcherikover, *Hellenistic Civilization*, 166; Edouard Will and Claude Orrieux, *Ioudaïsmos-hellenismos: Essai sur le judaïsme judéen à l'époque hellenistique* (Nancy, 1986), 119.

38. Bringmann, *Hellenistische Reform*, 83; Tcherikover, *Hellenistic Civilization*, 166–167; Will and Orrieux, *Ioudaïsmos-hellenismos*, 136.

39. Bickerman, *God of the Maccabees*, 62.

40. Ibid., 79–80.

41. Ibid., 91.

42. Bickerman, *From Ezra*, 120–121.

43. Bickerman, *God of the Maccabees*, xii.

44. Ibid., xiii.

45. Bickerman, *From Ezra*, 92.

TEN

In Search of Ancient Israel:
Revisionism at All Costs

SARA JAPHET

In Search of Ancient Israel is the title of a book by Philip Davies, professor of Bible at the University of Sheffield, and one of the editors of the *Journal for the Study of the Old Testament* and its monograph series (JSOTS). The book was published in 1992, as JSOTS volume 148. Davies describes his task as methodological: to scrutinize modern historical research of Israel in antiquity, taking into account the new movements in the discipline of biblical criticism, and in particular the impact of literary and sociological studies (11).

The book, however, goes far beyond this methodological framework, and proposes a very general review of the history of Israel and its social development up to the Hasmonean period, the origin and composition of the biblical books, and the emergence of Scripture, i.e. the Bible, as a definite canon. Without going into systematic detail, but touching on a multitude of topics and disciplines (history, archeology, epigraphy, social order and institutions, religion, literature, language, and more), Davies proposes answers to pertinent questions of origin, identity and continuity: Who is Israel? How and when did Israel come into being? What is its history? What is the Bible? How and when did the Bible come into being?

In Search of Ancient Israel assumes a semi-popular form. Although the author is a learned university lecturer, he defines his views as "sketchy ideas" and declares that "I have written this book for students rather more than for my colleagues, for scholars of the future rather than for those of the past or present. . . . Hence a certain amount of repetition. . . . There is also a conscious frugality in the citation of secondary scholarship" (7). To his own words I would add: Hence a tone of authority, sweeping generalizations on numerous subjects, a self-centered professorial stance, and rhetorical expression that tends to be assertive, even provocative.

I chose this book as the focal point of my presentation neither for its merit nor in order to recommend it, but because — far from being "the product of one fevered brain" (7) — it aims to serve as a mouthpiece for a contemporary vocal current in biblical scholarship, steadily gaining in popularity.[1] The book's semi-popular character, and its extreme, sometimes unrestrained phrasing give clear expression to views that might be less assertively argued in more cautious and understated scholarly discourse.

Davies' opens with a seemingly innocent methodological demand for a distinction between three terms: "biblical Israel," "historical Israel," and "ancient Israel." Since these definitions form the axis of the book's terminology, and the major instrument of its analysis and synthesis, they need to be clarified.

The easiest term to explain is "biblical Israel," which derives from the general premise that the Bible is literature and must be studied from an exclusively literary perspective: "Any character or event in the Bible is in the first instance (and possibly the last) a literary character or event. . . . The deity who destroys Sodom and Gomorrah and the fish that swallows Jonah are each characters in a narrative constructed by an author and, as the phrase goes, any resemblance to real or actual persons or events may be purely coincidental" (12). Therefore, no credence should be given to any of the characters: "There are no literary criteria for believing David to be more historical than Joshua, Joshua more historical than Abraham, and Abraham more historical than Adam" (12).

The major "character" of the Bible is, of course, Israel, to which the same rules apply: it is a "literary character" in a "narrative constructed by an author," and "is no more no less than what the writers have made it" (12). Therefore, Davies states, "there is no basis for claiming that the biblical Israel has any particular relationship to history" (60). At the conclusion of a long discussion, Davies takes the definition of this term one step further: "Biblical Israel is an idea, a concept, a construct, and not a historical society" (74).

"Ancient Israel," the subject of all "histories of ancient Israel" is, according to Davies, a scholarly construct. Modern biblical historians mistakenly and blindly regarded the story of the Bible, of the "biblical Israel," as historical fact and proceeded to describe its history and life accordingly. These scholars, however, were not, as Davies notes, true historians but theologians who "pretend to do some history. But this is, of course, not history at all. . . . Biblical historians assume an 'ancient Israel' after the manner of the biblical story, and then seek rationalistic explanations for it" (29).

Furthermore, "histories of ancient Israel" are not the only misguided enterprises that hinder scholarship rather than promote it; equally futile in Davies' mind are monographs on "the faith (or religion) of ancient Israel" for, something that did not exist cannot have a "faith" or a "religion." While a "religion of the Bible" clearly does exist, it is tied to an ideological construct — "biblical Israel" — conceptualized by those who composed the Bible, and reflects neither a real society nor the society that lived in the land at the time assumed in the Bible (38). Similarly, there is no point in looking for the "historical background" of biblical figures such as Isaiah, Ezekiel or others, since they are merely literary characters who belong in the realm of the literary "biblical Israel." "Ancient Israel" is, thus, a "theological construct" (44) that serves the theological needs of its practitioners, but has nothing to do with history.

If "biblical Israel" is a literary concept, created by those who wrote the Bible, and "ancient Israel" is a scholarly construct, a theological endeavor to find history in the Bible, one must then ask whether there was an "Israel" at all? Davies answers in the affirmative and in so doing, establishes the meaning of his third term, "historical Israel," as the Israel that did exist. Davies provides the geographical and chronological parameters and the sources for this "Israel": a society that lived in Palestine[2] for some time during the Iron Age,[3] and for which the sources are nonbiblical: archeology, epigraphy, extra-biblical literature, and so on.

The argument goes as follows: since, according to archeological surveys, the territory under consideration had indeed been inhabited during this period, and since the name "Israel" appears in nonbiblical inscriptions, albeit scarcely, the existence of some entity called "Israel" cannot be denied.[4] As for its nature, "[I]t can be defined as a society or as a state but hardly both. It may be that the name 'Israel' originated as a name of a society.[5] However, the history of a state is much more tangible. . . . So, historical Israel is probably best defined by the historian as a state, i.e., a kingdom" (66). Israel was established as a state sometime in the 9th century and existed, rather precariously, for almost 150 years (until 722 BCE). During this period it "became vassal to Assyria . . . shortly afterwards it became an Assyrian province. By the time that Samaria fell its territory had already nearly vanished and what there was of it was incorporated into the Assyrian provincial system. Although Samaria was rebuilt, there was to be no more state called 'Israel' in the strict sense" (67), that is, no more "historical Israel."

As for its neighboring state, the kingdom of Judah, Davies describes it as follows: "It is quite likely that Judah was formed as a secondary state perhaps in the 9th century, and possibly by the Assyrians. Some suggest that Judah became a state, and Jerusalem a major administrative center, only in the 8th century BCE at the earliest" (69). Judah survived the kingdom of Israel by about 140 years. It was conquered by the Babylonians in 587 BCE, and its king and population were deported to Babylon.

Both kingdoms, according to Davies, were ethnically mixed societies, with religions that amounted to a cult of a high god called by various names — Yah, Yahu and Yahweh — who also had a consort. The cult of this high god was in no way exclusive, as there were other cults in existence at the time, and he was in no way regarded as the one, universal god, so there is no reason to speak about 'monotheism'. Neither was his cult restricted to these two kingdoms, as the god was "a well-known deity also outside Israel and Judah" . . . (72). Therefore, we must be wary of making an equation between the cult of YHWH and the territory or populations of these two kingdoms (72).

In order to appreciate fully the meaning and consequences of this construction of "historical Israel," mention should be made of the components that were excluded from it — a matter the author repeatedly stresses. Most important is the claim that there never existed a "united Israel," that is, any kind of social or political reality in which the people who later comprised the two kingdoms formed one whole. Even the idea of a comprehensive "Israel" never existed at this time. The term "Israel," in fact, refers only to those individuals and groups belonging to the kingdom that existed for less than 150 years in the hills of Samaria.

Thus, as Davies argues, "the 'patriarchal age' is an epoch in the literary, biblical story but not in the history of the ancient world" (27). The Exodus, the wilderness period and the conquest were recognized long ago for their fictitious character. The period of the judges is certainly ahistorical and "the fact that the biblical literature offers a chronology of this last period is beside the point. . . . Indeed chronology is almost an indication of non-historicity!" (27). Davies further suggests that "[t]he biblical 'empire' of David and Solomon has not the faintest echo in the archeological finds . . . the formation of an empire of any size looks out of the question. . . . This kingdom, which exists at present exclusively in the biblical literature . . . remains theoretical" (67–69).

The argument thus comes full circle: If this is "historical Israel," it has no connection with the Bible. If the concept of the twelve tribes, the period of the judges, the united kingdom of David and Solomon, the division of the monarchy into two kingdoms (which had common roots and a shared heritage) is all pure fiction; if the people of this "Israel" is a mixed population of unknown origin; if their religion is the non-exclusive "cult of a high god"; and if the narratives, the legal instructions, the prophecies, or the psalms are unrelated to them, then this "historical Israel" indeed did not write the Bible. And if all this is fiction — why should "historical Israel" need it? (70).

What great mind, then, invented the concept of "biblical Israel"? Where did it come from? Certainly not from the exilic period, since for Davies, the "exile" is a theological construct — "a so-called exile" (41), in which nothing was preserved or written (42); "exile" is "the central myth of the biblical account of the past" (87). The Dead Sea scrolls set a terminus ad quem for the existence of "the bulk of this literature," and these scrolls "range from the end of the third century BCE to the end of the first century" (75). The only period when biblical literature might have been produced is therefore the short intervening Persian period. Davies concludes therefore that Judah of the Persian period — the province known as Yehudah in Hebrew and Yehud in Aramaic — is the origin of almost all the biblical literature (some of it is later still), and first and foremost, of the concept of "biblical Israel."

In order to sustain this proposition, Davies has to prove a correlation between the social, political and cultural circumstances of this political entity, and the form, contents, concepts and ideology of the biblical literature. Had he followed his own principles, laid down so assertively in the first part of his book, he would have portrayed the Persian period on the exclusive basis of nonbiblical, archeological and epigraphic material. Yet he does not do so. Since, as he admits, "our archeological sources for Palestine in this period, alas, are even more meagre than for the Iron Age . . . it is more difficult relying on archeological evidence to write even an outline of the society" of this period, and a different approach "becomes necessary" (75–76). The approach he now takes up as the proper method for the history of the Persian period is the same one he condemned so vehemently in the first chapters of the book: the depiction of a historical reality on the basis of the biblical evidence. Davies is aware of his problem: "The danger here, perhaps, is the falling into the methodological trap that I so strenuously criticized earlier, namely of using the biblical story as a framework for reconstructing history" (86). Elsewhere he notes that "[i]t is often protested that since we know so little of the Persian–early Hellenistic period, we cannot confidently commit ourselves to assigning the biblical literature to that time" (76). But he dismisses this objection in his usual assertive style: "This is nonsense" (76).[6] Taking the biblical date as his source, he then proceeds to rationalize and rephrase, to add and omit at will, until the data serve his own purposes. The argument that emerges, in very broad lines, is as follows:

The restoration of the province of Yehud was the result of a deliberate Persian policy, namely a strategy to reorganize the empire (85). . . .

The "returnees" to Yehud were not necessarily Judaean exiles coming home . . . but subjects of transportation, moved to under-developed or sensitive regions for reasons of imperial economic and political policy. . . . Whether originally from Judah or not, these people or their descendants would be likely to believe, or to claim that they were, indigenous. Indeed, the Persians may well have tried, in order to facilitate compliance with the process, to persuade these transportees that they were being resettled in their "homeland," and examples of this ploy in the imperial history of humankind could be cited (82). . . . The creation of what was in truth a new society, marking a definitive break with what had preceded, was accompanied by — or at least generated — an ideological superstructure which denied its more recent origins, its imperial basis, and instead indigenised itself. (87)

In this "earliest plausible context for the creation of the biblical Israel" (85), the emergence of the biblical literature should be seen as "an adventure of creativity" (113), "an exercise" (113), for whose reconstruction one is called "to deploy some imagination" (93). According to this reconstruction, the "ruling caste" of Yehud, or "the government," hired a host of scribes and commissioned them to write: "The literature was commissioned and then written to order" (120). The task was to invent a "myth of origin," "the establishment of a national identity in which the status of the existing rulers, of recent immigration, as the indigenous elite, was secured" (114). The scribes, themselves part of this "ruling caste," but nevertheless hired and kept by "the government," promptly set to work, and in a very short time — "two or three generations" (120) — with exceptional industry and diligence, executed what they were told to do. They produced the names, events, characters, myths, and speeches. Indeed, as Davies puts it, "the new society generated its own identity, via literature, through the production of history" (117–118).

Therefore, past approaches to biblical literature, including scholarship's numerous methods and terminologies, were all based on misconceptions and misunderstandings. Terms like "traditions," "schools," "circles," "authors," "reductions" and many more are all to be put in quotes (101) and new definitions are to be supplied; "prophecy" — which cannot have been written before the 5th century — is termed "political poetry" (125), akin to "street theater" (123); the law is "quasi-legal" literature (114) and what scholars have defined as "biblical religion" is, in fact, "an act of ideological imperialism [of a] ruling caste" (115), to name a few examples.

This is how biblical literature was written. The creation of "Scripture," however, of the Bible as a canon, is the work of a later generation, that of the Hasmoneans. This aggressive, politically ambitious regime of doubtful origin and with pretensions to the priesthood, is responsible for the establishment of the canon, that is, the limited library of authoritative books that forms the basis, from that period on, for all religious behavior (134–154). Davies' treatment of this issue is of a different nature, and I will reserve my remarks on the matter for another opportunity.

Although my reaction to Davies' book upon its publication was a shrug of the shoulders, I now feel that the phenomenon it represents does deserve more serious consideration. The book has joined the growing library of similar works, and although Davies himself described his views as "sketchy ideas" (7), his text has been cited already as a reliable basis for further research.[7] I will focus my examination on matters of method, and deal with them under two headings: the book's methodology, as professed and practiced, and the proposed "Persian period" origin for the emergence of the "concept of biblical Israel" and the creation of the biblical literature.

The book's starting point and major methodological claim — the distinction between "ancient Israel" and historical Israel — is no more than a play in terminology, a pretense of methodological distinction. What Davies is actually saying is this: What I describe as history is indeed history, and therefore mine is "historical Israel"; what you describe as history is your own "theological construct" and therefore "ancient Israel."[8] In fact, historical Israel and ancient Israel are two definitions for the same thing. Critical scholars of the past and present, who have written "histories of ancient Israel," have been looking for the same "historical Israel" as Davies does — the Israel that existed historically at a given place and time. The history of this Israel was to be reconstructed and described in valid modern and rational terminology applicable in the historical discipline, within the conceptual framework and working presuppositions of the field. Since the success of such enterprises varies from one scholar to another, and since each scholar is a child of his time, both the presuppositions and final achievements have reflected a constant movement of revision and change, remaining nevertheless within the general definition of historical research. The difference between earlier historians of ancient Israel, whom Davies attacks so severely, and Davies himself lies in their respective positions regarding a crucial methodological issue that pertains to any writing of history — that is, the question of sources. What are the legitimate sources for the reconstruction of ancient history? Or, phrased more specifically, should the Bible be regarded as one of these sources for the writing of history — of Israel, Palestine, the Ancient Near East in general, and so forth — or should it not? Davies categorically denies any use of the Bible as a historical source,[9] whereas the scholars he criticizes have decided to make use of the Bible in their own reconstructions, applying judicious consideration to the validity of the data and to its value. Davies' theoretical denial of the biblical source does not make his "Israel" more "historical" than that of the other scholars, only different to a certain degree.

This quasi-methodological distinction becomes even more evident in the face of Davies' own practice in the reconstruction of history. In spite of his categorical rejection of the approach, he does use the biblical material for reconstructing history, and is thus no different even in method from those he criticizes so harshly. This fact comes across in various aspects of the book, but primarily in the portrait of Judah in the Persian period. Here, his historical reconstruction is based exclusively on the biblical material, not because of a different definition or appraisal of the biblical sources, but because his theory demands that some portrait of the "society" of Judah be provided and it cannot be drawn without the biblical sources.[10] The basic assumption of a "return" from Babylon to Judah (or "transportation," as he chooses to term it), the existence of a temple, not to say its rebuilding, the introduction of a lawcode, a social structure of "Burger-Temple-Gemeinde,"[11] a self-definition of ethnic exclusivity, the very names of the political figures of the time, and more — all these have no support from either archeological or nonbiblical material, and all are learned from the Bible, specifically from the problematic book of Ezra-Nehemiah. The most Davies succeeds in doing is to suggest some "general Achaemenid policy" (81), offer "parallels" (85), or mention "a distinct social model" (83), that is, various analogies that should serve for the reconstruction of the history of Judah, but he cannot offer any direct archeological and epigraphic sources.[12] His historical source remains the biblical story alone. Again regarding the postbiblical period, Davies invests a great amount of credence in certain books of the Apocrypha, but the treatment of this period is outside our present scope.

The book is thus inconsistent in its treatment of the various historical periods, the marking line being the end of political independence and the destruction of the Judaean monarchy. For the earlier period, his methodology comprises a certain view and judgment of the biblical literature, which may be described as an ascending line of premises and deductions; all the rest are corollaries:

1. The Bible is literature, a "literary artifact." The exclusive approach to the Bible should therefore be from a literary perspective.

2. This literature is complex, and the picture that emerges from it is inconsistent and sometimes contradictory. It is not the kind of material the historian can use or count on.

3. No distinction should be made between the various parts of the Bible. They may represent various genres — narrative, poetry, proverbs, instructions, and more — but they all fall into the same category of "literature," for which the same considerations apply.

4. Biblical literature, like any other literature, is a creation of its authors, that is, a product of "creative imagination." The persons mentioned therein are "literary characters," the events are "the literary plot," and so on. Biblical literature — including each and every genre and piece — is thus fiction. Even if occasionally a name may have had its origin in some kind of historical memory, it is of the same category as the appearance of Julius Caesar in a Shakespearian play. The great majority of names, the time-setting in which they are placed, and all the events, are purely fictitious, fruits of invention.

5. Consequently, no historical value whatsoever, from whatever perspective, should be attached to any part of this literature.

6. Moreover, "fiction" means "ideology." Biblical literature was not written innocently, out of a neutral creative impulse, but was motivated all along by a conscious, programmatic ideology.

7. Biblical literature is, therefore, the outcome of a plotted scheme, a

conspiracy; it is a deliberate falsification and fabrication, initiated and carried out by a certain political group of official authority, for the attainment of political goals.

Over against this dismissal of the Bible lies a whole-hearted acceptance of archeology as the major, almost exclusive source for the writing of history. Davies' book displays an unqualified and naive trust in archeology and its possibilities, and an obliviousness to the distinction between the "mute" stones themselves and their historical interpretation. It also displays an absolute faith in sociological considerations and theories, notwithstanding their own rapid change. The methodological question should thus be doubled-edged: Is a total rejection of the Bible on the one hand, and an unqualified adoption of archeological interpretations on the other hand, methodologically sound?

Some of Davies' assertions are certainly true. No hypercriticism is needed to realize that some of the biblical narrative is fiction, and no critical scholar would regard the story of Eden, the serpent's talk to Eve or the delivery of Jonah from the belly of the big fish as historical facts. There is also a general consensus that biblical narrative is informed by ideology—or better, ideologies—of various shapes and colors: Pro-monarchical and anti-monarchical, pro-Judah and anti-Judah, pro-priestly and anti-priestly, and many many more. This is, in fact, self-evident. Is it at all possible to write anything without a "point of view"? Moreover, no consecutive historical course can be conceived without an underlying concept of cause and effect. In the context of biblical history-writing, and of ancient Near Eastern history in general, this would inevitably be presented in terms of religious ideology. It is also true that archeology may be used as a significant tool in the hands of the historian, and extrabiblical epigraphic evidence has become an indispensable instrument in enriching, correcting and solidifying the ancient history of Israel.

What Davies does, however, is to take each of these truisms to its utmost extreme and suggest the simplest, most fundamental answers for matters of the greatest variety and complexity. And this course may produce a stronger rhetorical effect than the detailed, multifaceted and complex considerations of "conventional" biblical criticism. The Bible is indeed "literature" in the broadest possible sense of the term, that is a work written by humans. But this literature comprises many genres and a variety of individual pieces, which should be studied each in its own category and by the criteria applicable to it. Certainly, not all "literature" is "fiction." It seems obvious that the Song of Songs cannot be compared with the Book of the Covenant, but even within the more limited category of "narrative" one cannot compare the story of the flood with the lists of unconquered territories in the first chapter of Judges, or the administrative structure of Judah (Joshua 15) with the story of the conquest of Jericho.

Moreover, while one may not agree with the religious causality and ideology as presented in biblical historiography, its literary genre as historiography is not thereby refuted. Similar to the study of any other historiography, here too the modern scholar is called to distinguish between facts and interpretations. Additionally, the widespread definition of biblical historiography as "narrative" — a term now commonly used for many historical works — which calls for additional considerations in the study of this literature, does not abolish its literary essence as historiography.

The definition "literature" for the biblical corpus should not imply that only "literary" criteria, in the strictest sense of the term, are applicable to its study. The disciplines of philology, comparative linguistics, literary-historical criticism and historical criticism in general, are all applicable to the study of the Bible. Ignoring these disciplines, and the rich results of scholarly work along many generations, is akin to someone covering his eyes with his own hands, and then complaining that he cannot see.

Seen from the opposite, positive, direction, scholars have proven again and again that the Bible can and should be used as a source for reconstructing the history of Israel. In the continuing complaint that not enough extrabiblical material has been discovered to support the biblical story,[13] an amazing fact has been overlooked: all epigraphic material related to Israel and Judah discovered until now, in all the lands of the ancient Near East — including Mesopotamia, Egypt and Israel itself — has systematically supported the biblical evidence! We would have been happier, of course, if more epigraphic material had been in our possession, and if more direct documents from Palestine itself were found, but this should not blind our view of what does exist — a continuous confirmation of the biblical facts.

There is no need to mention all the details, since they are incorporated into all responsible histories of Israel, but a few remarks may be in order.[14]

The stele of Marnephtah places Israel in Canaan at precisely the same time when scholarship, on the basis of the biblical story, has suggested placing pre-monarchical Israel there, that is, the late Bronze and Early Iron age. The inscription of the Egyptian Shoshenk (or biblical Shushak) in Karnak places this king precisely where the biblical story has put him and, moreover, it ascribes to him a military campaign in Canaan at exactly the same time that the Bible does. The names of the Assyrian kings Tiglath-Pilesser, Sargon, Shalmanesser and Sennacherib all appear in the Assyrian records where they were expected to be found according to the biblical evidence. Even the same expeditions are ascribed to them, with similar results. Various kings of Judah and Israel are mentioned in Assyrian and Babylonian documents, correctly juxtaposed with the appropriate Assyrian and Babylonian emperors, and even the details—the conquest of the fortified cities of Judah and the siege of Jerusalem in the time of Hezekiah (and Sennacherib), the exile of Jehoiachin to Babylon and his survival there, and many more—are attested by these sources. In the same way, the Mesha inscription places this king precisely at the same place and in the same context as does the Book of Kings, and so is the existence of Ahab attested from both Moabite and Assyrian sources. Similarly the inscription found recently at Tel Dan, attesting to the relationship between Israel and Aram, is placed precisely in the place and time where the Bible has identified the Israel-Aram conflicts.[15] Even the figure of the non-Israelite prophet, Balaam the son of Be'or, who appears already in the Pentateuch as a rather mythological figure, has now turned up in archeological excavations.[16] The Tel Dan inscription is justly famous for its mention of the "House of David," a title certain scholars have invested much effort in denying. It is interesting, nevertheless, that this title too appears at the right time, and makes one wonder how the "inventors" of the Persian period knew to place the empire of David and Solomon precisely in the intermediate period, when both Assyria and Egypt were busy in their own internal affairs.

It is this overwhelming harmony between the facts of the biblical story and extra-biblical written material that must form the basis for assessing the reliability of biblical historiography. This kind of information must have been drawn, in the last instance, from official and reliable sources, and their accuracy points poignantly to the form of their employment by the biblical historians. There is no need to repeat that the modern historian should deal with all these from a critical point of view, since criticism, in its various aspects, is the most basic tool of any discipline, but the attitude to it from the outset should be positive rather than negative.

This same correlation between the biblical facts and extrabiblical evidence is displayed in other areas as well. Not only the geographical, but also the historical-geographical aspect of the biblical stories is confirmed by archeological surveys and excavations. Sites are found where they are expected to be, and information is confirmed about the various peoples and states that surrounded Israel throughout the Bronze and Iron Ages. Moab, Ammon, Edom, Tyre, the various Aramean states, Arabs, Philistines and more all appear at exactly the places and times where the Bible places them. This coincidence is somehow taken for granted by skeptical historians, while the discrepancies in presentation, and particularly in interpretation, are exaggerated beyond proportion. The same is true of the archeological finds on the one hand and the linguistic facts on the other. Surveys of the central highlands of the Land of Israel have revealed an unprecedented expansion of settlement during the last two (or three) centuries of the second millennium,[17] combined with a change in the methods of agricultural cultivation, which implies a substantial increase of population. Again, all these events coincide perfectly with the emergence of the people of Israel where and when we would expect them to be found. The causes of this development — whether internal socioeconomic processes or invasion from the outside (or possibly both) — need to be discussed and clarified, and various considerations should be brought from the sociological, historical and other disciplines, but the archeological facts themselves confirm and support the biblical story. Additional examples may be offered,[18] but on the basis of these details, it is the underlying characteristic of the biblical evidence that should be emphasized.

The linguistic evidence is taken very lightly in Davies' treatment and is actually brushed aside (102–105), but here again the extrabiblical world of Semitic and non-Semitic languages joins the biblical evidence to form a coherent picture. The position of Hebrew in the general constellation of ancient Semitic languages, the numerous borrowed vocables from the languages of the surrounding peoples, near and more remote, the reflections of various dialects, the inner development of phonetics, morphology and semantics — all point to an extended, living, process, the various aspects and complexity of which are gradually unfolding.

The modern historian is not called on to repeat the theological interpretation of history as presented in biblical historiography. Nor is he or she asked to accept at face value the tendentious portraits of the historical figures, positive or negative. But historians should not forego the distinction between history and literature, between fact and interpretation, for the sake of simplicity and unequivocality, which do not and cannot exist in the face of this kind of evidence. It remains for the archeologist to uncover the sites of the past, for the linguist to decipher the secrets of language, for the literary historian to analyze the biblical literature, and for the historian to interpret the facts with the help of relevant disciplines; still, their inter-dependence and elucidation are indispensable in the study of ancient history.

Is the author's view of the Persian-period origin of all biblical literature, and in particular the "concept" of biblical Israel valid and sustainable? The answer should depend upon two issues: the correlation between the "society" that is supposed to be the origin of "biblical Israel" and of this concept, and the feasibility of the literary process that is thereby assumed.

The examination of these issues can be performed only in the context of Davies' own terms, since both his picture of Judah/Yehud of the Persian period and his "concept of biblical Israel" are idiosyncratic. Davies bases his picture of the province of Judah in the Persian period on a single biblical source, the book of Ezra-Nehemiah, from which he then selects what he deems right, which he then presents in his own rational terms. Not only does he ignore what he defines as the late, "political poetry" of 2 Isaiah and Ezekiel, but he also omits from consideration the most important prophetic books of Haggai, Zechariah and Malachi (which he never mentions), the story of Ruth, which surely sheds light on ethnic and sociological concepts of the time, and the institutional and theological testimony of Chronicles. He also overlooks some of the archeological and epigraphic material for the period. The picture of Yehud in this period of over 200 years, and certainly the social and ideological currents prevailing in it, are much more complicated than Davies assumes.[19] His pictures of the "ruling caste," its privileged position, political power and aspirations, and extended literary activity, deviate greatly from that suggested by his own source, the book of Ezra-Nehemiah.

Davies' "concept of biblical Israel" is also problematic, as it presents an ideal uniformity which the texts do not confirm. Davies himself states that "Israel" is a multivalent term, but in presenting his "biblical Israel" he speaks of "a concept" or "a story" in the singular, ignoring the multiplicity he himself has indicated. In fact, there are many concepts and different stories: Israel of Kings is different from Israel of Chronicles; Israel of the book of Judges is different from that of Samuel; origin from Mesopotamia competes with origin from Egypt; the patriarchs Abraham and Jacob are both successive and competitive in the biblical stories, and more. We will therefore limit our examination to Davies' own presuppositions and terminology.

To briefly recapitulate his view, the inventors of biblical literature were the "foreign transportees" of unknown origin and background, brought to Judah under coercion by the Persians for the purpose of agrarian development. They soon became the "ruling elite" or the "ruling caste" and very quickly generated a distinguished "literate class," which produced hosts of scribes. These were commissioned to invent "from scratch," with no precedent or tradition, a history and a literature. Under the order of their masters, they wrote some of the world's greatest literature in narrative, poetry and prophecy, all in the shortest time possible, "for their own satisfaction as much as anyone else's" (114). It is hard to see how Davies' proposed concept of "biblical Israel" indeed provides the answers for the proposed needs of this society, and a few examples may illustrate the problem.

If, as claimed, the main goal of the "foreign transportees" was to "indigenise themselves," why did they do precisely the opposite? The most salient feature of the biblical concept of "Israel" is its nonautochthonic emphasis. The dominant biblical view, expressed in various forms and from different perspectives, presents Israel as having come to the land from the outside and being, then and forever, "sojourners" in the land, dependent on the grace of their God.[20] Why would anyone interested in "indigenization" invent a concept that counters his own claim and undermines his ideology? Why not invent, as other peoples did, a truly autochthonic myth, connecting the people to the very soil they were tilling or, alternatively, ignore the issue altogether? Moreover, since the territory to which these people were transported was Judah, and since they had no original ties with "Israel" — which was just a name among others with no symbolic connotations — why choose Israel and not Judah for the assumed identity? The latter at least would correctly define a territorial continuity, which the name Israel did not.

If, as Davies claims, these people invented the figures of David and Solomon, as well as the united monarchy, for the promotion of their "imperialistic ideology," why did they attribute to Solomon the severe flaws that represented the diametrical opposite of their own ideals: idolatry, marriage with foreign wives, constant political unrest and eventual decline? What kind of idealistic "golden age" is this? Furthermore, why did they invent the territorial expanse of the Davidic-Solomonic empire in the way they did, including inside it the Transjordanian provinces of Edom, Moab and Ammon and the remote Aramean states, but omitting the nearer, more vital territory of the coastal plains, leaving it for the autonomous Philistines (1 Kings 2:39ff, 5:1)?

This issue of territory presents another problem. As is well known, "the promised land" is defined in the biblical literature both in general terms and in more specific delineations of boundaries: "From the river of Egypt to the great river, the river Euphrates" (Genesis 15:18), from "the Sea of Reeds to the Sea of Philistia" (Exodus 23:30), "from the wilderness to the Lebanon and from the River, the Euphrates, to the Western Sea" (Deuteronomy 11:24), etc. Different territorial concepts are expressed in Numbers 34, Deuteronomy 34, Joshua 13:1, Kings 5, and more. If the origin of this "imaginative invention" is an official view during a very limited period, why are the territorial concepts so diverse and even contradictory? Why describe a certain territorial idea and then proceed to explain how it was not realized (Joshua 13:1–5; Judges 1)? Furthermore, how would these territorial and political aspirations be explained to the actual rulers of the province, the Persian emperors and their bureaucracy? Wouldn't it be interpreted as a call for independence, that is, a revolt?

According to Davies, the concept of the "twelve tribes" was a late attempt at a genealogical unification and ethnicization of a mixed society, with no earlier roots in reality or tradition. If that were the case, for what purpose did the "elite caste" of Yehud invent this useless social and ethnic structure? The society of Yehud, however its social structure may be conceived, was not structured along the lines of the "twelve tribes," and its kinship system is presented differently. The most one may find is occasional vague affiliation to three of the tribes, Judah, Benjamin and Levi. If the biblical picture of the tribes is an invented concept, why then is it so varied in detail, comprising different internal constellations (including or excluding Levi, counting Joseph as one or two tribes, and more)? As for the details, why, for example, was Reuben chosen to be the first born — this element is consistent in all the forms of this tradition — and Judah relegated to the fourth place? What is the meaning of the division between the Cisjordanian tribes and the Trans-jordanian ones of Reuben, Gad and Manasseh, in the political reality of Yehud? Going beyond the tribal structure to broader concepts of kinship and ethnicity, why, on the background of the Persian period animosity, did this "elite caste" of Yehud invent a structure that granted Edom, Moab, Ammon, Ishmael and others the position of blood-related brothers?

Similar questions apply to Davies' view regarding the emergence and composition of the biblical works. If written in "two or three generations" in an "artificial scribal language" (104), how can one explain the enormous diversity and variety on every level — language, style, literary form, contents, views — which point to a process of development and change? How would one explain the relationships between various works, of "sources" and "re-daction," of text and interpretation? The literary relationship between the Book of the Covenant and Deuteronomy, or between Samuel-Kings and Chronicles, may serve as examples. And why is the composition of the Pentateuch such a complex issue, if everything was done and finished so quickly?

Even more difficult is Davies' explanation for the existence and nature of the nonhistorical genres, of which prophecy may serve as an example. Defin-ing prophecy as "political poetry" and placing its origins in the 5th century BCE at the earliest (124), prophecy is left with no relation to reality and without any reason for existing. Is it conceivable that such literature was composed by commissioned scribes as "an effort to master a genre (and improve one's scribal classical Hebrew at the same time)" (124)? Ignoring completely the social and spiritual phenomenon of prophecy, what remains of it in Davies' reconstruction is a "scribal school exercise" (123).

Questions of this sort might be multiplied seven score, and some of them are sometimes brought up but then washed away. In the mode of sweeping generalizations that the book adopts, why should such "trifles" cast shadows on the brightening horizon?

It seems, rather, that the choice of the Persian period as the origin of the biblical literature in its entirety is for Davies (and others) a choice of default rather than of conscious decision. The true issue at stake is the denial of authenticity to any biblical evidence related to the history of Israel in the monarchical period or earlier, and this includes historiography in the first place but also prophecy, law, poetry, etc. When the time frame for the composition of all this literature is pushed ahead to a postexilic period, with the Qumran scrolls determining the latest date, the Persian period is all that remains as a possibility; it is, for Davies, the period when "the biblical literature ought to have been composed" (75). Davies indeed made a great effort to justify this default, recruiting for the project not merely his scholarship, but also his unsupported judgments (stating continuously what is "logical," "possible," and more often, what is "senseless"), his imagination and obvious rhetorical talents. How much this effort was successful is for the reader to judge.

Davies describes his own critique of biblical scholarship as "savage" and "over general" (47),[21] while Halpern describes it as "venom."[22] Indeed, the book's consistent tone is that of fervent rhetoric and an all-embracing iconoclastic crusade; it is actually spitting fire in every direction and on every issue. All these indicate that deeper issues are at stake than scholarly methodologies. What the book presents in fact is another theology. We may call it, following the author's own remark, a "theology of disbelief" (47 note 22), or even better, "a theology of condemnation." But this urgent request for the "truth," the undertaking to "unmask" the biblical "falsification," to reveal the "scheme," and to bring light to a world cast in darkness, is in fact theology, and nothing else.

NOTES

1. The most prolific and characteristic of this group are John Van Seters, Thomas L. Thompson, and Niels-Peter Lemche, while G. Garbini is probably the most extreme. See J. Van Seters, *In Search of History: Historiography in the Ancient World and the Origins of Biblical History* (New Haven, 1983); T. L. Thompson, *The Early History of the Israelite People: The Literary and Archeological Evidence* (Leiden, 1992); N. P. Lemche, *Early Israel* (Leiden, 1985); idem, *The Canaanites and their Land: The Tradition of the Canaanites,* JSOTS 110 (Sheffield, 1990); G. Garbini, *History and Ideology in Ancient Israel* (New York, 1988). A useful survey article is E. Yamauchi, "The Current State of Old Testament Historiography," in *Faith, Tradition and History,* ed. A. R. Millard, J. Hoffmeier, and D. W. Baker (Winona Lake, 1994), 1–36.

2. The manner in which Davies uses this term is problematic, but the matter as a whole deserves a special study. The author justifies his choice of this term on 23 n. 2.

3. Defined as between around 1250 and 600 BCE (23).

4. "Israel" had appeared three times when Davies' book was written: in the Mernephtah inscription of the 13th century; in a reference to "Ahab the Israelite" in the inscription of Shalmanesser the 3rd, dated to 854 BCE; and in the references in the Mesha inscription close to it (around 840 BCE). Since then, the title "king of Israel" and the name "Israel" appeared in an Aramaic inscription from Tel Dan, published in 1993 and dated to the 9th century BCE. A. Biran and J. Naveh, "An Aramaic Stele Fragment from Tel Dan," *IEJ* 43 (1993), 81–98. For the heated debate around this inscription, see N. P. Lemche and T. L. Thompson, "Did Biran Kill David? The Bible in the Light of Archeology," *JSOT* 64 (1994), 3–22.

5. "Society" is a common term in Davies' book, though its meaning, as he uses it, is obscure and therefore it falls outside common sociological categories.

6. His argument, "this . . . had not prevented the 'exilic period' from being overloaded with literary works" (76), sounds strange. Its logic is that there is nothing wrong in the method itself, and in the same way that others used it for the exilic period, so can he employ it for the Persian period. What, then, was the purpose of the earlier severe criticism?

7. See, for instance, Lemche and Thompson, "Did Biran Kill David?" 18 n. 38.

8. See also B. Halpern, review of *In Search of Ancient Israel, Ioudaios Review* 3.021 (August 1993), § 3.1 (I wish to thank Dr. D. J. Reimer for kindly providing me with this review).

9. Although he does not deal with this question in the manner it deserves, see Davies, 31–36. See also Lemche: "We know that the OT scarcely contains historical sources about Israel's past" (*Early Israel,* 414, and throughout the book). For a more moderate discussion of the matter, with similar results, see Gösta W. Ahlström, *The History of Ancient Palestine* (Minneapolis, 1993), 19–53.

10. His view of Ezra-Nehemiah is not made very clear. He certainly regards it as removed from the events themselves, and does not regard it as historically reliable (80, 85), but does not state its time of authorship. He doubts the authenticity of the documents (89) and the full historicity of Nehemiah and Ezra, "the latter perhaps not historical at all" (86; 80 n. 6). Since Ezra is not mentioned by Ben Sira (141) and presumably was not known to him, one may conclude that Davies attributes at least the "story of Ezra" and the final form of the book to the 2nd century BCE at the earliest.

11. This term was introduced to biblical scholarship by Joel P. Weinberg. See, e.g., inter al. "Die Agrarverhältnisse in der Bürger-Temple-Gemeinde der Achämenidenzeit," *Acta Antiqua* 22 (1974), 473–486, and other essays. For a partial criticism of the applicability of this concept to Judah of the Persian period, see J. Blenkinsopp, "Temple and Society in Achaemenid Judah," *Studies in the Second Temple,* ed. P. R. Davies (Sheffield, 1991), 22–53.

12. The only archeological point that he makes is the claim that according to archeological surveys, in the Persian period the population of Judah increased by 25%, whereas the population of the surrounding territories declined (80–81). This, of course, may make a "return" possible, but is certainly no proof of it. The other issues do not even have this little support. It is certainly interesting that Davies does not avail himself of all the extant archeological evidence of the period. See L. L. Grabbe, *Judaism from Cyrus to Hadrian* (Minneapolis, 1992) 1:67–73.

13. See, for example, G. Garbini (above, note 1), 16–20.

14. See also Halpern (above, note 8), §§ 4.1–4.4

15. See note 4.

16. See M. Dijkstra, "Is Balaam among the Prophets," *Journal of Biblical Literature* 114 (1995), 43–64, for the earlier bibliography as well.

17. See I. Finkelstein, *The Archeology of the Israelite Settlement* (Jerusalem: Israel Exploration Society, 1988); idem, "The Iron I in the Land of Ephraim — A Second Thought," in *From Nomadism to Monarchy: Archeological and Historical Aspects of Early Israel* (in Hebrew), ed. N. Na'aman and I. Finkelstein (Jerusalem, 1990), 101–130; idem, "The Emergence of Israel: A Phase in the Cyclic History of Canaan in the Third and Second Milenia BCE," in *From Nomadism to Monarchy,* 150–178.

18. See also Halpern, § 4.1

19. See, among others, S. Japhet, "People and Land in the Restoration Period," in *Das Land Israel in biblischer Zeit,* ed. G. Strecker (Göttingen, 1983); eadem, "Post Exilic Historiography" (forthcoming).

20. See M. Buber, *Israel and Palestine: The History of an Idea* (New York, 1952), 3–30 (Published also as *On Zion: The History of an Idea* [New York, 1973]). The alternative, "autochthonic" concept of the origins of Israel is reflected in Chronicles, among others; see S. Japhet, *The Ideology of the Book of Chronicles and its Place in Biblical Thought* (Frankfurt am Main, 1989), 116–124, 362–393. The existence of these alternative concepts puts in relief both the plurality of "the concepts of Israel" and the prevalent non-autochtonic view. An autochthonic view was possible and actually in existence, but not where Davies has been looking for it.

21. Referred to also by Halpern, § 2.0

22. Ibid, § 3.3

Index

DATE DUE